# RACE DEFACED

# RACE DEFACED

*Paradigms of Pessimism, Politics of Possibility*

Christopher Kyriakides and
Rodolfo D. Torres

Stanford University Press
Stanford, California

Stanford University Press
Stanford, California



Library of Congress Cataloging-in-Publication Data

Kyriakides, Christopher, author.

Race defaced : paradigms of pessimism, politics of possibility / Christopher Kyriakides and Rodolfo D. Torres.

pages cm

Includes bibliographical references and index.

ISBN 978-0-8047-6334-9 (cloth : alk. paper)—ISBN 978-0-8047-6335-6 (pbk. : alk. paper)

1. United States—Race relations—Political aspects—History. 2. Great Britain—Race relations—Political aspects—History. 3. Racism—United States—History. 4. Racism—Great Britain—History. 5. Anti-racism—United States—History. 6. Anti-racism—Great Britain—History. 7. Capitalism—Social aspects—United States—History. 8. Capitalism—Social aspects—Great Britain—History. I. Torres, Rodolfo D., 1949– author. II. Title.

E184.A1K97 2012

305.800973—dc23

2012009551

Typeset by Newgen in 10.5/15 Adobe Garamond

# CONTENTS

# PREFACE

We, the authors, met in the summer of 2006 while attending a Marxism and Racism workshop at the University of Glasgow. One of us (CK) was just completing a two-year research fellowship with the Departments of Sociology at Glasgow and Bristol, an England-Scotland comparative study of the relationship between racism, nationalism, and Muslim inclusion/exclusion. The fellowship had followed from doctoral work at Glasgow on the antiracist state. The other (RDT) was at Glasgow as an Adam Smith Foundation visiting fellow with the Department of Sociology and had just published *Savage State* and *After Race*. Despite having lived our lives on different continents—CK born and raised in Glasgow and RDT in East Los Angeles—we connected intellectually and on the basis of our shared antiracist activism and internationalist perspective.

Theory-wise we were both tired of irresolvable debates around race versus class, not that we didn't hold strong and strident positions. Rather, there was a sense in which moving forward had become almost impossible both theoretically and politically. We were both equally exasperated with post-Marxism, postmodernism, and the cultural turn, in that although each ism brought insight, we felt stuck in a critical impasse, a present without release. This was the negative that connected us. The positive was our mutual respect for Left radical theory. At the time we were reading Ernst Bloch and Cornelius Castoriadis—writers who were in many ways on the fringe. We admired Frantz Fanon and C. R. L. James—activists who each possessed a keen critical sense, tapping into the pulse of the moment in order to offer ways *in* and *out* of the present. It was a sense of possibility that attracted us to their canon. It is easy to criticize but much more difficult to offer a future sense, and we wanted this possibility to infuse our collaboration. We were both drawn to comparative method and empirically saw commonalities between the treatment of Muslims and Arabs in the United Kingdom and the United States, but more cryptically, the recent War on Terror, its effect on Arab migrants in Europe, and the "browning of America" drew our attention to how each could offer insight into the other. We agreed that it was important to situate this treatment historically from a class perspective but not the sterile positivist "class" of social science. It was essential that we reintroduce the subjective in class analysis as drawn out by scholars such as Georg Lukács, Franz Jakubowski, and E. P. Thompson and that we imagine the racist and antiracist state theoretically within the subjective relations of class. As should become clear, we move outside the traditional canon of classical Marxism while remaining committed to democratic transformation inspired by traditions of heterodox political economy.

*Race Defaced* is a critical comparative analysis of different modalities of racism and antiracism in Britain and the United States from the nineteenth century to the current period, situating their development and unfolding within the emancipatory political movements of the modern capitalist world order. As well as providing a critical appraisal of the main theoretical debates in the field, we aim to initiate new lines of analysis and incorporate the interrogation of racism and antiracism in the contemporary context of socioeconomic and cultural change. Our historical focus includes both theoretical and political substantive streams. A key feature of our approach is to unpack the respective influence of *anti-emancipatory* thought on contemporary political and theoretical approaches to "race relations" on both sides of the Atlantic.

*Race Defaced* posits that there is a consensus of thought across the so-called political spectrum (from radical to conservative) underpinned by the contemporary acceptance of the impossibility of human emancipation—*paradigms of pessimism*. This "End of History" development affects negatively the academic and political treatment of racism, which places "problem" and "solution" beyond human hands. A problematic emerges that traps the critical subject of emancipation, rendering us helpless. From the theory that modernity equals racism to studies that set out to criticize an apparently unified mission of hegemonic white unity, we are left without foundation for a radical project. While debate on class, capital, and labor continues to have meaning today in an era of growing capitalist inequality and insecurity, we subvert orthodox debate in order to intervene in what we see as a political climate distinguishable from the context that gave rise to the original critiques. The result is no simple repetition of well-trodden arguments. *Race Defaced* is a heretical intervention aimed at both conservative *and* radical orthodoxies.

The book not only goes beyond the black/white paradigm of racism, but it casts doubt on the prevailing ethnicities approach that generally seeks in response to make visible the oppression of hitherto silenced groups. Our intention is to examine how the presence and absence of emancipatory vision shapes macro- and micro-level approaches to racialized populations and how it determines their position in the British and US "racial hierarchy," as well as shapes forms of antiracist policy. While we treat with analytical specificity the patterns of conflict, subversion, and racialized discourses among increasingly large American and British ethnic minority populations, we do so not to recover silenced histories but to place ethnic fractionization at the center of how capitalist social relations are orientated at present. Our aim is to present a cogent and critical interpretation of how the political economy of class can create new spaces of hope and democratic alternatives. The focus of the book is on the United States and Britain, but we offer analytical links with other parts of Western Europe to highlight our study of the British and US comparisons.

In Chapter 1 we clear a critical theoretical space through which the subject of emancipation can speak in the chapters that follow. We first demonstrate that World War II and the Holocaust set the parameters for how we have come to understand "race" and liberation, circumscribed by paradigms of pessimism. As examples, we draw out the limitations of Hannah Arendt's antitotalitarian thesis and situate Theodor Adorno's immanent critique within a perspective of Left defeat extended through the theory of the influential Authoritarian Personality thesis. Though we are critical of Zygmunt Bauman's holocaust thesis, we draw on tenets of his earlier work in order to engage with Cornel West's Tragic subject—the "prisoner of hope"—and David Theo Goldberg's Foucauldian-inspired scientific subjectification so as to demonstrate their respective limitations as tools for understanding patterns of racism and inequality in the modern capitalist system. Our "Hopeful Subject" counters their respective positions from a Marxism inspired by Ernst Bloch and Georg Lukács and an anarchism inspired by Cornelius Castoriadis. In addition to our conceptualization of the Hopeful Subject, we reverse the well-known idea of inequality rationalized, instead conceptualizing racial doctrine as the *irrationalization of equality* in the system of natural liberty that accompanies the emergence of the capitalist world order. In doing so we offer a dynamic definition of racial doctrine that departs significantly from standard conceptualizations of racism.

Chapter 2 maps the historical emergence of racial doctrine as a social force. We begin by situating racial doctrine embryonically within the counterrevolutionary discourses of the French revolutionary period, illustrating how the idea of "whiteness" was born on already shaky ground, taking shape through the conservative anti-emancipatory movements in Britain and the United States. The so-called "white race" was from the start dogged by a disunity that could not be remedied by processes of racial incorporation. Through historico-comparative UK–US analysis, we map how racial doctrine targeted a "coalition of the condemned" that linked minorities, the urban poor, and radical insurgency. We present case studies of radical agitation and opposition movements, such as the Irish in Britain and the United States (especially the San Patricios), in order to demonstrate how racialization dovetailed with the treatment of the Mexican in the United States and the "residium" in Britain. The irrationalization of equality took its full fruition in the designation of the formerly unequal as nonhumans, thought of as facta, objects, and dead-matter—what Marx conceptualized as the result of capitalist exploitation: the "capital monster." The etiology of social relations was irrationalized, placed within the mystical realm of racialized emotion. This limit point of capitalist equality was expressed most forcefully in the imperialist expansion and rivalries (between putatively white nations) of the nineteenth and early twentieth centuries and domestically within the science of eugenics that incorporated the psychologization of race and its fruition in Manifest Destiny and the White Man's Burden. We draw out how configurations of racialization, such as that of "the Mexican Mind," were developed in the elite's theory of racial revenge, specifically the idea of "oppression psychosis"—a nonstructural explanation that implicated the Jews, the Irish, blacks, and the urban poor as biopsychocultural problems of racial order, degenerates to be policed in the maintenance of white unity.

In Chapter 3 we draw out how the idea of biopsychocultural degeneracy came to influence Anglo-American responses to "race relations," particularly in the acceptance of specific tenets of the "Oppression Psychosis" and "Authoritarian Personality" theses, which set the parameters for how race was to be understood post–World War II. The elites' preoccupation with racial order, especially under the new rubric of the Cold War (the crumbling of the British Empire and the ascendance of the American superpower), came to fashion "race relations" policy. In Britain the focus was on the policing of migration from the New Commonwealth, and in the United States, it was on the civil rights movement, but in both domestic spheres, "whites" were also problematized as potential protagonists of racial disorder. Race relations policies became tools for the integration of biopsychocultural harmony between "whites" and "nonwhites," in which the protagonists were to be subject to an array of policing mechanisms. This chapter demonstrates how the policing of the working class entailed the establishment of the "white victim" that depoliticized while recognizing—a ploy developed by Richard Nixon (paralleling the institutionalization of affirmative action)—but crystallizing in the respective New Right projects of Ronald Reagan and Margaret Thatcher. We revisit the Tottenham and Brixton Riots of 1985 and the role of the local authorities in the establishment of multicultural policies since the mid-1980s in order to situate the racialized place of Muslims and new migrations in the new millennium. Contrary to most schools of thought, we argue that the destruction of the working class as a political force paralleled a redefinition of equality that displaced economics in favor of an "equality of mind." It was under Reagan and Thatcher that multicultural policy was established as part of the mental economy that sought to massage the public sensibility, bringing it into line with the New Right dictum that "There Is No Alternative" to the market. In this respect, multicultural capitalism represented victory of the Right in the political battle and of the Left in the culture war.

In Chapter 4 we explore how the end of the Cold War and the political defeat of the Left had a disarming effect on the Right. Third Way antiracism emerged with the Clinton and Blair administrations as a means of filling the meaning gap at History's End in order to give political purpose and to remedy what was perceived to be the crumbling of racial order. In particular, we focus on the respective works of Amitai Etzioni and Anthony Giddens, demonstrating how a conservative logic rebrands hopelessness as an essential form of human existence. The need to "manage" ethnic anxiety comes through in the evolution of immigration and citizenship legislation. The response to the Los Angeles riots following the assault on Rodney King (Clinton's One America Race Initiative) and the Macpherson report into the police handling of London teenager Stephen Lawrence are analyzed in order to demonstrate how "equality" was therapized, bringing the mental economy under the cosmopolitan agenda of the Third Way. The core point of this approach was to break rigid allegiance to "the conservatism of Left or Right" and to any fundamentalist form of belief system that may hide within a multiculturalist framework. Key is the emergence and management of "hate crime" as a community policing strategy, which defines racism as determined by dangerous emotion. This took on renewed significance with 9/11 and the pairing of terror threat with immigration threat under George W. Bush and Tony Blair, and we illustrate how this dynamic unfolds in relation to the killing of Brazilian migrant Jean Charles de Menezes by police on the London Underground in 2005, Arizona governor Jan Brewer's Safe Neighborhood Act in 2010, and the response of the Obama administration. We discuss how the mental economy continues to utilize key elements of the "Oppression Psychosis" and "Authoritarian Personality" theses, only now devoid of any possibility of solution or economic justice. Rather, current race relations policy seeks to avoid postracial disorder by managing the impact of "dangerous ethnic emotions." In a world absent of alternatives, both "problem" and "solution" are defined according to the anti-emancipation logic of the End of History.

In Chapter 5 we return to theory in order to draw out why radical critique is currently unable to provide an emancipatory answer. On what basis can you, the reader, claim to be antiracist? Put another way, on what basis can it be argued that being antiracist is a good or right "thing" to be? In this chapter, we illustrate through an examination of Left critique and political strategy—how current academic treatments of racism and antiracism neglect these questions. Yet, we contend that this absence undermines projects that seek emancipation as their objective. More specifically, significant theoretical positions of the cultural turn, and more recently of "New Times," that profess antiracism implicitly undermine and deny the possibility of human emancipation. A radicalese pervades the "antiracist" academy of the culturalites that obscures the pessimism of immanent critique celebrated as liberatory by Foucauldian descendants of Althusser. By comparing theorists of the cultural turn such as Stuart Hall, Paul Gilroy, and David Theo Goldberg with Marxist sociologist of racism Robert Miles, this chapter uncovers how anti-enlightenment critiques underscore the collapse of a "Big P" Politics based on the perfectibility of the human subject. The silencing of a historical premise reflects the demise of emancipatory vision in current race theory—the absent prerequisite of social emancipation. Topics covered include Hegelianism and the demise, in theory and practice, of the working-class subject of emancipation; the influence of French thought in the articulation of new social movements analysis, particularly Foucault's 1970s appropriation of the Black Panthers' emancipatory prison struggle divested of its emancipatory force for the French context; and the unwitting theoretical rearticulation of this silencing 20 years later in the United States by theorists such as David Goldberg. We reappraise the so-called race versus class debate in the late 1970s and 1980s through a discussion of Stuart Hall's work and the Paul Gilroy/Bob Miles critical interventions in this contentious period of the cultural turn.

In Chapter 6 we summon our empirical and interpretative research to advance an alternative critical understanding of contemporary racisms and racialized inequalities in Britain and the United States. We provide a counterpoint, from a Left perspective to the argument that we live under neoliberal capitalism. Instead, we argue that the contemporary social and political context is antiliberal and that this cannot be understood within a "neoliberal globalization" framework. Indeed, doing so reproduces the antihuman expression of capitalism turned in on itself. An understanding of the macro-political economy of cosmopolitan capitalism is central to this project, but unless it is linked to the ethical and moral dimensions of people's everyday material and cultural experiences, it will offer little analytical value in our pursuit of a better future. We attempt to go beyond both anti-utopian and parochial debates on multiculturalism and inclusion with a proposal (which is our book) to redirect our political and intellectual analysis within a new language—a Politics of Possibility—that recognizes the exceptional nature of the Hopeful Subject.

# ACKNOWLEDGMENTS

*Race Defaced* was written between late 2009 and 2010 in Los Angeles, Glasgow, London, and Limassol. Having signed with Stanford University Press in September 2008, we spent the best part of one year discussing the book before pen touched paper. This was an intense and rewarding experience. From the start we decided that we did not want to parcel out the writing of this book, so the "US author" wrote the US part and the "British author" wrote the UK part. It was very much a collaborative project in that we were each committed to immersing ourselves in the comparative "domain" of the other. One need not be British/American to observe, think, and write about the United Kingdom–United States. There was significant learning on both our parts, and not only about the "other's domain" but about our own so-called "territory." Swapping terrain kept us fresh. Hopefully this is reflected in the writing of the book.

Visiting trips for each author were made possible by the financial and collegial support of the University of California, Irvine, and Cyprus University of Technology. We wish to thank both institutions for making our cross-Atlantic collaboration possible. Many thanks to our editor Kate Wahl at Stanford University Press for her patience and especially her understanding and continued support even when our project departed from the original proposal. Our thanks to the whole team at SUP. We would also like to thank Leo Chavez for recommending our project to Kate Wahl and the four anonymous reviewers for their helpful comments and recommendations. Special thanks to Mike Davis, Spurgeon Thompson, Evangelos Kyriakides, and Stuart Waiton for reading and commenting on early draft chapters.

Christopher Kyriakides
Rodolfo D. Torres

I wish to express my gratitude to faculty and students at the University of Glasgow who attended my public lectures sponsored by the Adam Smith Foundation. I would also like to thank Satnam Virdee, Department of Sociology, at the University of Glasgow for his support during my several extended visits to Glasgow. I wish to thank several of the participants of the Glasgow Marxism and Racism Workshop, including Mike Cole, Bob Carter, and Steve Fenton, for their engaging conversation. I met Christopher Kyriakides for the very first time at the workshop. His wit, charm, and intellect and our mutual research interests produced this collaborative book project. My thanks to Chris—a premier young scholar. I must thank my two mentors, Mario Barrera and Bob Miles, for their continued encouragement and validation. It was their writings on racism and inequality that inspired me to pursue transatlantic research. Mil gracias to my UC Irvine colleagues in Planning, Policy, and Design, and Chicano-Latino Studies for their continued encouragement. A number of librarians were very helpful, especially, Christina Woo at the University of California, Irvine. Finally, my love to Patricia and my son Jacob D. Torres for a great and full life.

Rodolfo D. Torres

The spark of many of the ideas developed in this book originates from my early political activist years in Glasgow. This influence was retained during my doctoral studies and Fellowship in the Department of Sociology at the University of Glasgow and the Department of Sociology at the University of Bristol. Additionally, a number of scholars contributed to and influenced the trajectory (if not the content) of my academic work. I would particularly like to thank Bridget Fowler, David Frisby, Satnam Virdee, Paul Graham, Tariq Modood, Ruth Levitas, Gregor McLennan, and Hillel Ticktin. I would also like to record my indebtedness to former University of Glasgow PhD buddies, Patricia McCafferty (now at the University of Strathclyde), Stuart Waiton (University of Abertay), Donncha Marron (Robert Gordon University), Jo Buckle (Glasgow Caledonian University), Andy Zieleniec (Keele University), Susan Batchelor (University of Glasgow), Marcia Gibson (University of Glasgow), and Jeanette Hagerstrom (Scottish Executive).

The postcolonial experience, since 2007, of extending and testing my knowledge beyond the British metropolis has been humanized in the "divided" Republic of Cyprus by many good friends and fellow scholars. Special thanks are due to Marios Vryonides and Christos Kassimeris at the European University Cyprus; Dimitra Milioni, Dionysis Panos, Vagia Doudaki, Korinna Patelis, Elena Kyza, Lambros Lambrinos, George Zotos, Nikos Tsapatsoulis, Viky Triga, Stelios Stylianou, and Angeliki Gazi from Cyprus University of Technology; and Nikos Demertzis at the University of Athens. It has been a privilege to work with my three doctoral students in the Postcolonial Communication and Ethnicity and Communication streams at the Department of Communications and Internet Studies—Nikolas Defteras, Maria Avraamidou, and Evros Antoniadis—from whom I have learned the value in acknowledging my limitations as a doctoral supervisor. I would also like to thank the staff and students at the University of California, Irvine, for their warm welcome and support, especially David Feldman and Scott Bollens. John Solomos and Frank Webster at City University London and Robert Miles at the University of North Carolina have always been particularly supportive, and each has my eternal respect. The best thing about this book is that I met Rudy Torres, a unique human being and scholar who is a shining example of all that remains progressive in Western academia—a true friend. To Lubna, Clarabella, and Oscar, the brightest lights in my life, I apologize for the passing of time that should have been yours and thank you for understanding that I endeavored (albeit with limited success) to ensure it was never wasted and always well spent.

Christopher Kyriakides

# RACE DEFACED

CHAPTER ONE

# HOPEFUL SUBJECTS AND THE "SYSTEM OF NATURAL LIBERTY"

I'm a pessimist because of intelligence, but an optimist because of will.

*Antonio Gramsci*[1]

Have pity on the pessimist. He spoils his own existence. In fact, life is endurable only on condition that one's an optimist. The pessimist complicates things to no purpose. . . . What would have happened to us, by Heaven, if we'd been a group of pessimists! . . . How could I have been successful without that dose of optimism which has never left me, and without that faith that moves mountains? . . . One must have faith in life.

*Adolf Hitler*[2]

## PARADIGMS OF PESSIMISM

The belief that another, better world is possible and that Man, not God or Nature, has the power to make this happen, is a distinguishing hallmark of modern political thought. It is also that which is typically dismissed by *End of History* thinkers as redundant, even dangerous. The dismissal also has a long history captured within the constellation of meanings that are usually labeled "utopian," but the negative impulse takes a profound form today. The work of English philosopher John Gray is symptomatic. Taking his cue from ardent anti-utopian postwar liberal Isaiah Berlin, Gray goes further, negatively casting all modern political projects as utopian. In *Black Mass: Apocalyptic Religion and the Death of Utopia*, Gray argues that the Enlightenment humanist belief in progress was a secularized form of religious apocalyptic thought. The secularization of an essential human need for faith is responsible for the deadly belief that human beings can make a more perfect world. We are unable to free ourselves from a conflict-ridden human nature, because "nothing is more human than the readiness to kill and die in order to secure a meaning in life."[3] To the familiar "utopian" sources of meaning against which Gray sets out his stall—communism, National Socialism, and neoliberalism—neoconservatism and al-Qaeda's Islamic fundamentalism are added. Gray's highly conservative appraisal of the need for meaning speaks to a contemporary state of emergency. The current darling of zero-hour intellectuals, he is hailed by writer Will Self as "the most important living philosopher." It is striking that such importance should be placed on a theory that considers human aspiration to be fundamentally flawed, even dangerous. But that Gray begins from one of the architects of postwar liberalism and ends on such a negative view of the Enlightenment tradition, projecting apocalypse onto the present as a warning against the dire consequences of humanism, is particularly revealing, for as the historian of ideas, Russell Jacoby notes, "The defeat of radicalism bleeds liberalism of its vitality."[4]

Gray's philosophical orientation is not particularly helpful; in fact, his antipolitical stance kicks at an open door to a post–Cold War age in which the absence of utopia is generally heralded as a victory to be maintained against the Left-Right ideologies of the past. True, those who still consider themselves on the Left or the Right continue to look for and "identify" their political adversary; however, an alternative reading of the present centralizes not the continuance but the *collapse* of the Left-Right ideological framework, and in this reading neither Left nor Right remains intact. Nor does an unrepentant neoliberalism hold sway. In *A World Without Meaning*, the present, according to Zaki Laïdi, is a period in which "liberal theories [are] made suddenly obsolete." While the end of the Cold War should logically have put liberals "on a pedestal" (and it is on this logic that theories of neoliberalization stand), their relative obsolescence is probably because they and their anti-liberal homologues—though with some nuances—drew their resources from a common well, and ordered their weaponry from the same arsenals, under the illuminated sign of linear progress commanded by the nation-states. The Enlightenment also left its mark here.[5]

Laïdi argues persuasively that the end of communism led to political, ideological, and theoretical fragmentation, an inability globally to find meaning:

. . . if by meaning we imply the triple notion of foundation, unity and final goal: "foundation" meaning the basic principle on which a collective project depends; "unity" meaning that "world images" are collected into a coherent plan of the whole; and "end" or "final goal," meaning projection towards an elsewhere that is deemed to be better.[6]

If "Man," or the belief that Man could radically transform the world, was the critical foundation on which the modern political sensibility was founded (and we will elaborate on this point later), then the absence of foundation alerts us to the presence of a fundamentally new and unprecedented historical context in which the unity (the human race) and final goal (a better world) have not only altered but have dissipated. It is within this context that we seek to situate the idiom of postraciality, now practically synonymous with the election of Barack Obama.

The entry of a "mixed-race" US president into the White House provoked both celebration and skepticism. This was only to be expected, but the casual observer would have been surprised that negative appraisal stemmed not only from the Right but also from the Left. For those who have spent a lifetime canvassing, advocating, and agitating for the rights of minorities, radical "certainty" dictates that one not be too dazzled by star-spangled utopias, carried away in what Tariq Ali has described and dismissed as the "ideological euphoria" that followed the Obama promise to "heal America's wounds at home."[7] Writing amid Obama's first election campaign, Angela Davis had already cautioned against "a model of diversity as the difference that makes no difference, the change that brings about no change" lest the proverbial color-blind flag of racial unity continue to drape the national disunity that has plagued liberal race relations fears since Gunnar Myrdal's dilemma. Davis argues:

[Obama] is being consumed as the embodiment of colour blindness. It's the notion that we have moved beyond racism by not taking race into account. That's what makes him conceivable as a presidential candidate. He's become the model of diversity.[8]

But to a certain extent, both Ali and Davis miss what is different, and crucially so, about the present. Gray's negativity is more clearly representative.

Today, what the Marxist Ernst Bloch once called "the spirit of utopia"—the idea that human beings have an unqualified capacity to dream of and create a better world—is sorely called into question. Ali's cynical yet unreflective jibe at "ideological euphoria" reflects the all-pervasiveness of this negative impulse. Ali cannot situate his own anti-utopianism within the wider political current that he criticizes. One must surely be cautious when interpreting the present as a one-dimensional progressive move forward from, in the words of former British prime minister Tony Blair, "the conservativism of either Left or Right." As we later discuss, however, although the Right may have won the cold (tug of) war over Man, it collapsed and took the belief in human agency—the foundation of hope—with it. In this sense Francis Fukuyama's "last man" was but a shadow of the human subject of history that prefigured modern political thought, at least for the past two hundred years. Today's hopeless subject is not the agent released by "liberal victory." In the absence of meaning, the search for hope, most recently advocated by President Obama and the African American scholar Cornel West, seems to lose itself to an unfulfilled wish.

The absence of hope is the elephant in the room of contemporary human culture. This was not always the case, and it is necessary, as Jacoby recently argued, in an age characterized by the *End of Utopias* to salvage through clarification the relationship between utopian thought and the privileging of human value such that the pursuit of a better world can once again become a legitimate goal but without the trappings of past mistakes. Understandably there is an urgent sense in which the politics of race and the demand for equality suffer from the absence of emancipatory vision. Consequently, in this chapter we lay out the rudiments of a *paradigm of possibility* through which an alternative history of racial politics—from racial ordering to the postracial disorder—is charted in subsequent chapters. We begin by unraveling the strands of contemporary *paradigms of pessimism* via a critical review of some of the key postwar theorists of the Holocaust. We do this not from some putative need to be critical, but rather, we believe the future of the human condition is dependent on our ability to steal hope back from *the* paradigms of pessimism that gave the Hitler movement its barbaric optimistic stance.

## FOOL'S OPTIMISM

The perverse logic that led the human race to the gas chamber 70 years ago continues to dumbfound us, for we were all condemned by it. In what sense barbarism was permitted to unfold while we watched in most part from the sidelines is a question that continues to haunt us, for we are yet to find a satisfactory answer. A sufficient reply to Hitler remains elusive. How could the annihilation of millions of human beings have been a positive goal, the seeming fruition of which validated and generated optimism? In many respects the origin of post–World War II antiracist politics and antiracist theory represents an implicit attempt to grapple with this question. Yet, a crucial distinction between the optimism/pessimism of National Socialism and that of socialism is seldom brought to bear on the search for answers. Where Italian Marxist Antonio Gramsci wanted to move humans optimistically toward a better future, Hitler's denial of a universal humanity underpinned the optimism of racial victory. Where pessimism was for Gramsci the basis of a critical stance directed against the obstacles placed between humanity and freedom, for Hitler this critical stance—the very idea of a universal civilization—was an obstacle to Aryan racial supremacy. The distinction serves to remind us that optimism and pessimism are not simply conditions of individual temperament but of wider philosophical, intellectual, and political significance. It is our contention that the history of racial doctrine cannot be understood without first grasping the *conflict* between these two positions—the radically subjective and the conservative subjective as represented by Gramsci and Hitler, respectively. Contemporary theory ignores their crucial schism.

Following World War II, early pioneers of "official" antiracist thought at UNESCO recognized that "the great and terrible war that has now ended was a war made possible by the denial of the democratic principles of the dignity, equality and mutual respect of men, and by the propagation, in their place, through ignorance and prejudice, of the doctrine of the *inequality* of men and races."[9] Subscribers to the statement held that racism was rooted in the "minds of men,"[10] an irrational force that in the absence of truth gripped individual psychology. The rightfulness of racial inequality was a mistruth; race lies spoke to emotion, offering spurious validity to unrestrained irrational expression and disrupting the rational social order. UNESCO's formulation was underlined by the implicit acceptance that "knowledge of the truth does not always help change emotional attitudes that draw their real strength from the subconscious or from factors beside the real issue."[11] Racial doctrine smoothed the way from gut feeling to reaction, from wrong premise to wrong conclusion. Taking its cue from the spirit of Enlightenment humanism, reeducation could "prevent rationalizations of reprehensive acts or behavior prompted by feelings that men will not easily avow openly."[12] UNESCO's answer was to proffer moral condemnation of those who may be tempted by the lie of race, with the dual antidote of antiracist education. For the team at UNESCO, the Holocaust was an aberration, a deviation from modernity's Enlightened dictum that all individuals are equal—the cornerstone of civilized humane praxis. To modernity, the irrational acts of racial cleansing were antithetical.

Others saw it differently. Hannah Arendt's appraisal of Nazi official Adolf Eichmann delivered a chilling caution to those who interpreted Nazi atrocities as the work of madness. Nor would moral condemnation suffice as a response. On trial in Israel (1961–1962) for his complicity in the Final Solution to the Jewish Question, Eichmann, the *SS-Obersturmbannführer*, showed signs neither of guilt nor responsibility for his actions; he was "merely following orders." What struck Arendt was the absence of anti-Semitism or psychological abnormality in Eichmann's self-defense; in short, his "terrifyingly normal" personality—a point on which psychologists commissioned by the Israeli state concurred—had to be accounted for. According to Arendt, Eichmann's demeanor patently undermined the idea that Nazis were psychopathic or different from people in general. He embodied the banality of evil. Arendt was not simply arguing that anyone could commit such atrocities given circumstances conducive to their enactment but that Eichmann was a fool who had relinquished his will to make moral choices. He had voluntarily abandoned his autonomy to the Fuhrer, renouncing the ethical path open to self-critical free-willing individuals. If the human conscience has a mediating function that tempers the relationship between an individual's universally given empathic drives and his or her willful actions toward other human beings, reasoned Arendt, then "the problem" for Nazis "was how to overcome not so much their conscience as the animal pity by which all normal men are affected in the presence of physical suffering."[13] Eichmann's voluntarism stemmed from the normality of the act and the legitimization of the latter as *duty* by a plethora of German laws. Legalized atrocity erased its immorality, relinquishing the doer of personal responsibility, overriding any deep-rooted revulsion toward human suffering. For Arendt, Nazism was synonymous with conscience surrendered to a higher authority; the subservience of crucial emotional drives to rule-following, although not inevitable, negated individual moral sense.

Arendt's analysis widened the parameters of postwar theoretical deliberations on race, and like UNESCO, her critique reflected Cold War concerns. The establishment of UNESCO should not be conflated with the analyses developed by its contributors, which were by no means consensual, but the institutions' foundation reflected an emerging Cold War framework within which Western liberalism sought a counterpoint to communism. UNESCO's early pronouncements on race were orientated under a Cold War umbrella, where power and meaning were fused in a teleological end-game underpinned by Enlightenment universalism. Each side in the ideological battle offered a vision of social progress predicated on competing visions of the good life. Thus, Laïdi argues, "because Sovietism offered a global meaning, a synthesized representation of the world and its objectives, liberalism was for a long time required to produce a symmetrical counter-discourse, to try to export Locke to check Marx."[14]

It is useful to think about this formulation as a tug-of-war scenario. The communist team collectively believes in socialist Man, and the capitalist team collectively believes in individualist Man. The adversaries are separated by a ditch of fire representing the anti-Man critique catalyzed by Holocaust and Hiroshima. The rope, representing entwined strands of ideology, has a stick of wood (Man) tied to its midpoint that hangs in the balance over the burning ditch and into which each team must pull the other, thereby bringing Man to ideological victory. Weakened by the flames of anti-Man critique, the singed unraveling ideological fibers threaten Man's loss, but on the order to "take up the strain," rope is stretched ideologically taut, the stick (Man) lifted up and out of the ditch to hang suspended in the heat out of fire's reach. Whistle blows; contest begins. Each antagonist vies to wrench power from the other, pulling at the strands of ideology in a bid to bring Man to their side. If both teams pull equally, Man remains suspended, weak but alive. If one team should yield, the stick (Man) falls to the winning side as the victors collapse. The Cold War is represented in the analogy up until the "victorious" end, and we will return to the fall of Man later. But in a real sense, this is what happened. Anti-Enlightenment pessimism resulting from the Holocaust and Hiroshima did have an impact post–World War II, but it was held in check by the Enlightenment liberal-socialist contest to represent the future of Man. It was in this context that antiracist theory and the politics of race developed. Only after the contest ended did paradigms of pessimism come to hold sway both intellectually and politically.

The West's optimism of the individual will did not exist as an internal presupposition of liberalism; rather, it reflected the political imperative of countering the alternative Enlightenment model of human beings—the collective subject—of Soviet communism. This is not simply a question of abstract philosophy; it is predicated on the rise or fall of Western capitalism. Ideological contest drew the international state system in line behind each of two camps, enabling but containing the power of states in the respective but interlocking meaning of East–West divide, under the hegemony of US capitalism against Soviet communism. The nuclear arms race and the uptake of the Soviet model by Third World nationalism were just part of the process by which meaning invoked a future-orientated investment articulated in defiance of mass annihilation and in the name of its counter: hope for a better world. An underpinning universalist principle ensured that state alignment gave a justificatory subjective content to respective national populations between East and West—a ready framework through which the world could be explained and answers could be found. In short, the content of social life was shaped by competing future visions based on the foundation of Man. UNESCO's partial preservation of the Enlightenment project—the retention of a belief in Man with its optimism of the will—was a product of the contest between East and West. This macro context provided the foundation for the battle between Left and Right within the West. Optimism of the will could not be retained without the foundation of Man kept alive by the global ideological contest. What of the intellect? It is here that Arendt's critique of totalitarianism, especially her anti-Marxism, falls into place.

Arendt had no difficulty in accepting that National Socialism was antihuman, a reversal of Enlightenment. The deeper problem was Marxism as embodied in the Stalinist Soviet empire and the workers' movements that emerged reinvigorated under social democracy after the war. Marxism, argued Arendt, although stemming as it did from Enlightenment humanism, embodied an antihuman premise that led to the totalitarian Soviet Union. Margaret Canovan[15] contends that Arendt did not conflate Marxism with Stalinism, but rather, Stalinism was interpreted as the endpoint of a basic flaw in Marx's conception of human beings as laboring individuals. The problem was that Marx universalized humans' relationship with nature through labor. That humans require nature for survival, a relationship devoid of choice, could not be denied, but in extrapolating a theory of Man from this relation to social relations, Arendt believed, Marx ignored and eradicated the power of individual choice and unwittingly provided a blueprint for domination. To Arendt, individuals were more than a universal relationship with nature and had moved on from the "Eat or Die" conditions that had driven the Third Estate to the French Revolution. Differences between individuals could not be universalized. By developing a theory of history in which the labor process—a relationship with nature devoid of choice—was expected to lead humans inexorably and inevitably toward the ultimate end of communism, Marx provided a map to the totalitarian eradication of individual differences: the Soviet Union. But inasmuch as liberalism shared the premise of economic progress through the productive development of natural resources, it, too, was suspect. It was Man's hubris—the belief that "everything is possible"—that connected the principle of human exceptionalism and the attainment of a universal Man to the totalitarian eradication of pluralism, of difference. The saving point of liberal individualism was that it did not obliterate difference. Arendt's position, like that of the UNESCO team, entailed a partial optimism of the will, but its anti-Marxism erased the crucial distinction raised by the critical intellectual pessimism to which Gramsci appealed.

Gramsci's pessimism/optimism formulation saw no communist inevitability, nor was the necessity of conscious choice in its making diminished to a natural unchangeable and determinate relationship. Conscious choice, not natural determinacy, entailed the adoption of a critical stance to the present in making a new future; if revolution was already predetermined by a law of nature, there would be no need for critique. Of this Marx was sure when he and Engels published *The Communist Manifesto* in 1848. Gramsci's position was not a revision of Marx but a critique of the second international's adoption of "natural laws of motion" in a workerist model of human development that celebrated the so-called naturally inevitable, not willfully determined, forward movement of revolutionary change. If progressive revolution was inevitable, what need was there for critique? The "philosophy" of natural determinacy not only paralyzed the German workers movement against the onslaught of Hitler's racial optimism, but it underpinned the absence-of-will formulation employed most forcefully by Stalin—a point to which we return in Chapter 3. We disagree with Canovan's interpretation of Arendt's totalitarian thesis. The existence of the Soviet Union and the workerist celebration of communism's inevitability, which negatively contextualized Arendt's work, meant that she could not grant admittance within her theory to a critical pessimism of the intellect: radical subjectivity.[16] She could not therefore take up Stalinism or social democratic capitalism from a critical Left perspective, nor could Arendt demystify the elision between the Cold War social democratic conception of Man and the Enlightenment's furnishing of the possibility of a critical new human who would later emerge as the mainstay of anticolonial critique vis-à-vis individuals such as Frantz Fanon and C. L. R. James. The possibility of an alternative society to the one that existed when she wrote her book, a world living in fear of Cold War catastrophe, could not be brought out in theory. Such was the impact of World War II on the restriction of human possibility. In effect, Arendt's optimism of the human will *curtailed* critical pessimism of the intellect. Her invocation of individual difference could provide an answer to communism while cautioning against liberal economic hubris.

If anything, World War II demonstrated that the "radically subjective" positing of an alternative society had failed not only to overthrow capitalism in the West but to take a stance against National Socialism in Germany. Nowhere were these twin failures more clearly conceptualized than in Theodor Adorno and colleagues' Authoritarian Personality (AP) thesis.[17] A burning question for the Frankfurt School arose around the complicity of the German working class with National Socialism rather than with the progressive revolutionary politics prophesized by Marxism. Following in the footsteps of earlier studies such as H. D. Lasswell's *The Psychology of Hitlerism* (1933), Wilhelm Reich's *The Mass Psychology of Fascism* (1933), Erich Fromm's *Fear of Freedom* (1941), and P. E. Nathan's *The Psychology of Fascism* (1943), the Frankfurt-Berkeley team's collective analysis of human subjectivity leveled the blame for Nazism at mass society, whereby the working classes, alienated and rule-bound by bureaucratic forces and instrumental reason, followed herd-like behind the dictates of a charismatic leader. Anti-Semitism as "a 'symptom' which fulfills an 'economic' function within the subject's psychology"[18] was particularly crucial to postwar deliberations on race. The idea of the *fascist personality syndrome* as a correlate of authoritarianism underpinned Stanley Milgram's infamous psychology experiments on obedience that were stimulated by the trial of Eichmann and first published in 1963.[19] "Could it be that Eichmann and his million accomplices in the Holocaust were just following orders? Could we call them all accomplices?"[20] Milgram's rhetorical hypothesis drew on the AP thesis and contrasted with Arendt in that it was in effect a challenge to the belief that sovereign free-willing individuals could as a matter of conscience command their own moral choices. For Arendt, Eichmann had *chosen* to follow the rules of atrocity, but for Milgram the determining power of *free* conscious choice was more questionable.

In crucial respects, both originated from the tenets of antitotalitarian critique. Outwardly Arendt's thesis seemed more open than AP theory to the possibility of an alternative outcome to the Holocaust. Despite its limitations,[21] Arendt's theory encapsulated her belief that all individuals had the capacity to self-reflect and, thus, to change. Nor did the Holocaust represent for her the *relinquishing* of a believed-in historical proletarian subject of social change; as a student under Heidegger, a proletarian path had been ruled out. By contrast, at least for the Frankfurt school side of the AP team, the proletariat had failed, and both capitalism and modernity were heavily implicated. The point on which they agreed was that the movements represented by Stalin and Hitler not only cast a shadow over any liberationist philosophy that stood on the premise of freeing Man, but as projects of modernity, they were culpable in their conflation of technological progress with human progress:

> Universal history must be construed and denied. After the catastrophes that have happened, and in view of the catastrophes to come, it would be cynical to say that

a plan for a better world is manifested in history and unites it. Not to be denied for that reason, however, is the unity that cements the discontinuous, chaotically splintered moments and phases of history—the unity of the control of nature, progressing to rule over men, and finally to that over men's inner nature. No universal history leads from savagery to humanitarianism, but there is one leading from the slingshot to the megaton bomb.[22]

The difference between this formulation and Arendt's was that where Adorno interpreted the Human-Nature relationship of "dominance" as primordial and thus a profoundly negative barrier to any theory of human liberation, Arendt did not see the Human-Nature relationship in such an all-determining way; rather, it was only one part of the human condition underlying pluralism. But Arendt and Adorno both understood humans' relationship to nature as *domination* validated by modernity's glorification of economic progress by extraction of natural resources. For Adorno, the human-nature relationship of domination ultimately led to human-on-human domination and to self-directed domination: the historical theory of Man's liberation from natural limitation catapults Man to self-destruction. There could be no optimism of the will without eventual annihilation. Nevertheless, Adorno did attempt to maintain a critical stance. His notion of immanent critique laid all the minutiae of everyday life—from astrology to opera—open to critical analysis, while demanding that we do not adopt any liberationist universal project that seeks to transcend the present as its final goal.[23] This *optimism* of the intellect (the opposite of liberationist critique) understood the idea of human' liberation as dangerous. Thus, Adorno partially embraced Georg Lukács' Marxist theory of reification as a means of understanding consciousness in a capitalist society. On Adorno's reading capitalism's incessant drive to commodify all in its path includes the commodification of human consciousness; humans take up social positions as objects, their expression of will reduced to the expression of the competitive drive. For Adorno this made perfect sense in explaining the impact of mass consumer culture on proletarian failure and National Socialist "success," and so he rejected the crucial addition to Lukács' theory that proletarian subjectivity, the radically subjective, could break the process of reification. For Adorno this was a workerist fetish. Critical pessimism of the intellect was diminished not only in Adorno's philosophical take but within the theory of AP. Any posited radical project of change was not only suspect but reeked of impossibility.

Reflecting on her student experience and politicization in the 1960s, Angela Davis recalled:

> In Frankfurt, when I was studying with Adorno, he discouraged me from seeking to discover ways of linking my seemingly discrepant interests in philosophy and social activism. After the founding of the Black Panther Party in 1966, I felt very much drawn back to [the United States]. During one of my last meetings with him (students were extremely fortunate if we managed to get one meeting over the course of our studies with a professor like Adorno), he suggested that my desire to work directly in the radical movements of that period was akin to a media studies scholar deciding to become a radio technician.[24]

In contrast, Davis' decision to study under Herbert Marcuse had a radicalizing effect. Marcuse held open the possibility of social transformation; utopian dissent infused his approach. In *One Dimensional Man*, he outlined the forces of conformity unleashed in advanced capitalist society, forces that diffused the revolutionary ferment of the working class, but he maintained a critical focus on the capitalist contradiction represented by unprecedented wealth, poverty, racism, and imperialism. As Douglas Kellner notes, Marcuse may have begun from a position of despondency, but this was transformed by the new social movements' Great Refusal.[25] The utopian impulse was kept alive in the New Left's pursuit of an alternative society free from the forces of domination. In maintaining the possibility of liberation through dialectical critique, Marcuse's pluralistic distance from the Old Left could not only accommodate but could also inspire radical movement. Davis took this fusion of radical philosophy and political movement with her into the Panthers. The emanicipatory vision of the Panthers drew its force, for example, by inverting the Enlightenment promise of equality contained in the US Declaration of Independence in order to expose the exclusionary domination of antiblack oppression hidden within that declaration. The "self-evidence of Man's equality" symbolized American hypocrisy that eclipsed the fascist totalitarian tendencies of the US state.

As Davis points out, "The thinkers associated with the Frankfurt School were motivated in many of their intellectual endeavors by the desire to develop oppositional—which at that time meant antifascist—theoretical work."[26] The difference between the Old Left and theorists such as Marcuse and Adorno lay in their distancing from the privileged site occupied by industrial workers as the Stalinist subject of historical change, and Marcuse's invocation of pluralist *transformative possibility* added extra distance between his liberationist project and that of Adorno's immanent critique. But what is not drawn out by Davis is the extent to which *oppositional* antifascism dovetailed with the dominant liberal and socialist tendencies of the moment. In laying bare the continuity between fascism and liberalism as a critique of US capitalism, neither Marcuse nor the Panthers fully appreciated the antitransformative power of antifascism as a mainstream critique. Commenting on British antiracism, Paul Gilroy would later argue:

> This simplistic anti fascist emphasis attempts to mobilise the memory of earlier encounters with the fascism of Hitler and Mussolini. The racists are a problem because they are descended from brown- or black-shirted enemies of earlier days. To oppose them is a patriotic act; their own use of the national flags and symbols is nothing more than a sham masking their terroristic inclinations.[27]

Of course, we would not argue (and neither would Gilroy) that the Panthers worked with a simplistic understanding of racism, but as we will go on to demonstrate in Chapter 3, the state's own brand of liberal capitalist antitotalitarianism, more in keeping with the antitransformative tenets of AP theory, isolated and cut off the opposition. This formulation would have a crucial impact on the political reduction of human liberation predicated on the idea that "universal equality is possible" to a notion of equality delimited by "economy of mind" in the latter half of the twentieth century and beyond.

## MAN AFTER THE COLD (TUG OF) WAR: PERFECTION VERSUS PERFECTIBILITY

So far, we have laid out some basic rudiments of Cold War approaches to racism. Competing interpretations of human subjectivity were underscored by moral and political questions that the Holocaust made it impossible to ignore. But the search for an alternative to the barbaric outcome of racial doctrine was restricted to the orbit of East–West standoff; theoretical development was, in some respects a Cold War casualty. Hiroshima's afterglow lowered the horizon of critique, while the conflation of Stalin, Hitler, and modernity narrowed the analytical focus, eclipsing the qualitative distinction between the two quotations with which we opened this chapter. The pursuit of an alternative, better society was not such an immediate concern when four decades later the Cold War ended and Zygmunt Bauman synthesized such currents into a more comprehensive sociological analysis.

In *Modernity and the Holocaust*,[28] Bauman argues that Nazi atrocity was no anomaly but rather symptomatic of modernity's dual face: the rational and the irrational. The most rational of acts in a world where social organization was premised on rational calculation, where all individuals were judged equal on the basis of their common rationality but where that very rationality suppressed the irrational, the latter must break through—must manifest. Where moral worth was exacted instrumentally and bestowed only on the rational individual, a "theory" of ascription, anti-Semitism, resurrected the emotional connections buried by instrumental rationalist individualism—a regrouping of modernity's fragmented individuals. And it is from this putative human need to belong that moral proximity between group members developed as the mirror of those who did not belong. Drawing on Arendt's notion of animal pity as the source of spontaneous moral sense, the distancing effect and anonymity of modern bureaucratic forces, argues Bauman, cut off and divided human beings by breaking the potential for moral proximity. With science and technology placed at the helm, humans, like nature, were classified and observed as objects of discovery. The rational pursuit of civilization resulted in the objectification and dehumanization of those who could not be incorporated; ascription of group boundaries worked in congruence with technology and rational calculation to reconstruct social value as individual worth. The need for efficiency and cost-effectiveness enforced by military hardware bred *moral indifference* directed by an anonymous bureaucracy over which no one could exert authority. Extermination of the Jews was therefore implicated in the smooth, normal running of the modern world order.

Bauman's thesis presents some dilemmas. For one, moral proximity is not necessarily a condition of group belonging. Evidently, moral distancing can occur within so-called emotionally bound groups. It would be hard to account for instances of domestic violence or child abuse, including murder, that take place between emotionally connected family members. One could, taking a cue from Wilhelm Reich, presumably argue that the victims, predominantly women and children, consigned to modernity's patriarchical private sphere, are denied the validity of rationality as a condition of their modern worth and that this denial supports the perpetrators' violence. But a move from this level of analysis to a generally useful interpretation of National Socialism's barbarity is difficult to sustain. For one, moral proximity can exist between peoples of different nations even while anonymous, and again, there are evident tensions between class and national group formations, cracks that cannot easily be smoothed over. Even if they proved redundant in the case at hand, which is doubtful, some explanation not offered by what can be interpreted as a primordial need for group boundaries with its attendant moral proximity would seem necessary. But perhaps more problematic is an identification of modernity with the Holocaust that makes it hard to see how one could resist modernity's totalizing power. History, as Bauman is well aware, is replete with examples of human beings taking a stand against repression, and his early works, such as *Socialism: The Active Utopia*, capture the basis of this agency very well. Despite being intrigued by those instances of resistance to the Nazis in Nazi Germany, acts of defiance cannot easily be understood in a "Modernity equals Holocaust" framework, even if, as Bauman notes, racism is not inevitable.

Unfortunately, totalizing conceptions of modernity's relationship to racism have become somewhat orthodox at "History's End." One of the clearest adherents of this view, David Theo Goldberg, utilizes Michel Foucault's deconstruction of the medico-scientific gaze to demonstrate the emergent force of scientific epistemology and its interpellative power in the construction of racial subjects.[29] The principal medium for this development, argues Goldberg, is Enlightenment thought as personified in the various works of Hume, Locke, Rousseau, and Kant (among many others), which crystallized in the twin principles of empiricism and reason. Accordingly, the pursuit of objective facts—of absolute truth—was the source of scientific complicity in racial subjectification. For Goldberg the very idea of objective truth is an ethnocentric production of the "Enlightened" West. Under a regime where sensory perception provided *the* gaze for investigation of human beings, bodies were forcefully ascribed through measurement of height, weight, skull size, and so forth—a means of getting closer to the truth. Behavior revealed an individual's degree of rationality; outer appearance and behaviors signified his or her inner world—that is, the ability to reason; inner and outer worlds were homologized and homogenized. Capacity for civilization was measured by whether or not a given society had developed systems of legal-rational governance. Interpreted within a linear developmental trajectory of social evolution, the inhabitants of various parts of the world where no such state existed came to be known as irrational. Because of the privileging of sensation as an empirical tool, skin color, and so pigmentation as a visible marker, signified a measure of rational capacity. White skin meant rational and black skin meant irrational. Racial hierarchy developed into a technology for exercising the scientific gaze—a technology of rationalized racial power.

Goldberg's "Modernity equals Racism" thesis differs in important respects from Bauman's analysis, most specifically in that it is *completely* totalizing. For Goldberg, irrationality is a discursive construct of modernity; rationality is the "other" of irrationality—two sides of racial discourse within which constructed human subjects are raced and positioned. For Bauman, irrationality *actually exists* as part of the Modern condition: Humans live in an oppressive state of being where their irrationality is suppressed and must therefore forcibly manifest. If the human subject was singularly an invention of modern scientific subjectification, Bauman might concur with Goldberg's thesis. However, as we will go on to demonstrate, for Bauman, science, its instrumental rational kernel and human subjectivity cannot be so conflated. Although historically related, they are not mutually reducible. We are simply not dealing with a one-dimensional "abstracted, universal subject commanded only by Reason" as Goldberg would have us think of modern subjects.[30] If this *were* the case, it would be difficult to account for how human beings have stood against oppression carried out in the name of reason historically without replicating the cause of their own domination. This is exactly Goldberg's conclusion. As we will later demonstrate, human beings in Goldberg's analysis are not ontologically sentient beings living in a condition of oppression against which we can measure the denial and realization of liberation in the name of an alternative human condition based on freedom. Despite this important difference, in a parallel sense Bauman's "Modernity equals Holocaust" thesis presents us with a similar problem: If the irrational is part of the modern human condition, how can we account for those modern humans who stood against the

Nazis' "rationalism," both outside and inside the Third Reich? If rationality and irrationality are implicated in racism, then surely something else beyond their totalizing power, something other than animal pity, accounts not only for defiance but for the existence of an alternative stance to that of the dominant. Perhaps it is only when that transcendent basis of defiance—the possibility of an alternative stance and thus social action—is considered that we can build a fuller understanding of racism. This is at least what we want to argue. Luckily, Bauman's earlier work is helpful in directing us to an answer, but it is an answer he does not provide vis-à-vis race.

Bauman's *Socialism: The Active Utopia*,[31] published in a very different historical period but just 15 years prior to *Modernity and the Holocaust*, situates hope and freedom as utopian manifestations inherent to the modern condition:

> Utopias entered the historical stage as important members of the cast only after the stage had been set by a series of social and intellectual developments usually identified with the advent of modernity.[32]

Utopia is not used here as a negative pejorative trope by which to undermine a set of ideas or actions as unrealistic; rather, utopia is used to explicate the modern transformation of social existence from the static feudal order. The emergence of the modern world was characterized by intensified pace of social change within an individual's life span, linked to but not determined by the development of modern technology, and this speeding up of change provoked a "drastic adjustment of cognitive and moral standards."[33] The concomitant application of skills through craftsmanship entailed by developments in agricultural and later industrial production centered human action, at least in the developing "European" economies, as a conscious transformational force in overcoming the limits of natural time that until then had been experienced as the external power of divinely ordained seasons. Change was no longer experienced by human beings as lying beyond their control, and changes were now more *immediately* evident such that the *expectation* of human-determined transformation deepened, and that expectation was driven by the proviso that the end result was never completely knowable even when imaginable.

The *absence* of a knowable fixed end result is crucial here. Francis Bacon's distinction between perfection (as a knowable end) and perfectibility (as an open-ended process) relied on the positing of human beings as creators surmounting the limits of natural time (the seasons). Perfection was essential to the feudal Great Chain of Being. A theory that rested on the belief that "humans" inhabited a world of plenitude in which nothing new could be added to the fixed natural hierarchy of continuity, from rocks to plants, apes, serfs, nobles, kings, angels, and at its pinnacle God, the perfect form was timeless and untouchable. Degrees of perfection were preordained, as were brutes, savages, and people of high intellect. None could change their allotted place, nor could they attain future perfection; human time stood still. Argues Bauman, where the notion of *perfection* had reflected the prior dominant idea of development representing an immutable preordained unchangeable social condition that justified the condemnation of any attempt to transgress its boundaries, *perfectibility* stressed movement, unlimited development, and no fixed endpoint. Perfection placed a limitation: Social relations were determined by fixed hierarchical position beyond which it was impossible to tread. The idea of perfectibility, by contrast, animated utopia, both as the human creator's elevation over natural limitation *and* in the social sphere, such that:

> This new and emancipating belief flourished in all its numerous aspects throughout the seventeenth and the eighteenth centuries until it took solid root in the European mind to the point of becoming a part of common knowledge, the constant backcloth against which to paint innumerable utopias, ideologies, political programmes.[34]

Perfectibility, not perfection, stressed the open-ended development of human society. The claim against the permanence of a static social order animated early bourgeois ideology against the fixed preordained divine right to rule of feudal monarchs. Without an open-ended orientation, there could be no legitimate basis for overthrowing feudalism's fixed social hierarchy.

Perfection and perfectibility are generally conflated when race and modernity are at issue. The outstanding legacy of historian George Mosse, particularly that of *Towards a Final Solution*, illustrates the deep penetration of Greek ideals of beauty as an aesthetic of European modernity. The "perfect form" against which all must compare revealed itself most catastrophically in the negative comparison and subsequent extermination of the Jews. But the perfect form is a limitation on universal aspiration that must be accounted for, and it is quite different from the idea of perfectibility that Bauman places deep in the modern European mindset. They are at odds. In this sense a specific antipathy between utopian and conservative thought becomes apparent: The former centralizes human-centered activism in bringing about change, the latter subordinates human activity to the maintenance of eternal laws. Utopian aspiration does not possess the conservative "luxury" of predetermination and requires by default active engagement with the present in order to change it. "Whatever the nature of man as such," states Bauman, "the capacity to think in a utopian way does involve the ability to break habitual associations, to emancipate oneself from the apparently overwhelming mental and physical dominance of the routine, the ordinary, the 'normal.'"[35] In short, breaking from the *determinate* past relativizes history in response to the question "What may I hope?" This quality of hope is modernity's existential cognitive internalization, projected onto the world in the pursuit of *freedom*, which in the words of Ernst Bloch is hope's final destination.[36]

This is somewhat different to that quality entailed by Cornel West for whom hope emanates within "the tragic linked to human agency," an existential form connoting the "wrestle with despair yet never to allow despair to have the last word."[37] For West hope begins at the point of severance of the umbilical cord; the first hunger cries of an infant are hope's fundamental expression of mortality. Yet, the key word is "allow." Where does the power to prohibit despair's victory come from? For Bloch, the human condition is constituted by conscious engagement with nature, so humans live with nature, but they can consciously transcend natural limitations, and it is here that Adorno and Arendt's concern for the relation of human domination over nature strikes the pulse of pessimism. Recall the argument that the ideology of human exceptionality and mastery over nature cannot easily be distinguished from the act of human-on-human domination. But human mastery over nature and the psychological internalization of this "power" externalized as a social relation of domination between humans raises a problem that can be fruitfully answered by Bloch. As sentient beings, *we*, not nature, can consciously direct our actions. Consciousness distinguishes humans from nature. The latter is dead nonhuman matter in that it has no conscious power over humans, so it cannot be "dominated," nor can nature dominate. The source of human-on-human domination is qualitatively different and must therefore lie elsewhere. Our oppressive acts cannot be extrapolated from human use of the natural world that neither "knows" nor "understands" the human conceptualization of domination.

This is not to say that acts of oppression have not been justified historically on the oppressor's presumption that the target knows nothing nor understands the act of oppression as domination. The reduction of some human beings by others to the realm of nature, to material dead matter, as a justification for domination cannot be equated with human use of nature. It is the reduction that is at stake and that must be explained. In this sense, hope begins not with the biological impulse of hunger but with its social *satisfaction*, which may or may not be possible. Hope is not existentially tragic or inevitable but is contingent on the *outcome* of a defiant human stance, first as an attempt to overcome reification—the "power" that natural hierarchy is assumed to have over humans[38]—and then against those who seek, for reason of presumed necessity, to limit that outcome through imposition.[39] Hope, therefore, is neither a neutral cognition nor merely a psychological phenomenon; the qualifying "may" entails that hope is permitted, and, if not, it is demanded. As a principle, it is inherently critical, and it is hope's critical power that is qualitatively extended by utopia's "Yes, I can!"—a demand that underpinned Gramsci's optimism of the will, pessimism of the intellect formulation. The alternative, we might add, is that the absence of utopia lowers hope's horizon.

The shaping of the modern life world included two additional conditions: impersonalism and plebiscitarianism.[40] Impersonalism implies the interaction of standardized, anonymous individuals, their condition of existence universalized as a socially nondistinct public persona. Personal idiosyncratic differences, although suppressed, continue to be expressed, shaped by social impersonalism. Equal for as long as they were indistinguishable, difference was the indispensable private mirror of modern impersonal public cosmopolitans.[41] Hence, difference retained a determinate potential, but it did not constitute an inevitably dominant force in social relations. Plebiscitarianism expresses the transformation from subjects of monarchs into citizens of state, their collective will positing and striving for an idealized autonomy. Both impersonalism and plebiscitarianism influence how Bauman reads the social. We add that the fusion of impersonalism and plebiscitarianism entails that the pursuit of autonomy (freedom), as hope's vision, is not simply a reference to a fixed idealized individual, aka laissez-faire liberalism. As Cornelius Castoriadis once argued, the modern positing *of* autonomy entailed by radical utopia represents Politics with a capital P—the pursuit of real human freedom.[42] Where the "small p" political merely denotes a series of negative and positive injunctions in a social network of prohibitions representing an explicit dimension of power (in the sense that Foucauldians may conceptualize power), the most important signifier that implicitly animates the institution of society is that pertaining to its origin, its foundation appealed to in justification of power (a foundation denied in Foucauldian conceptions). Whether the foundation be God, Nature (racialized and/or gendered), Man, or, as we will later explore, the postmodern foundation of anti-Man, "no material coercion has ever been lastingly—that is to say, socially effective—without this compliment of justification."[43] More than this even, if the appealed to foundation of any given society determines hope's raising or lowering, then "awareness of this fundamental fact: institutions are human works"[44] provides modernity's legitimizing foundation for hope unbridled by external nonhuman constraints. Plebiscitarianism, then, emerging as a direct challenge to the Divine Right of Kings, entails that social action be infused by "Big P" Politics—a permanent rupture to the historical constellation of predestined hierarchy. The *radical utopia*, by challenging the premodern doctrine of nonhuman social foundations, makes Politics.

Autonomy, as conceptualized here, is not patriarchical or masculine;[45] rather, it is in deep opposition to heteronomy (human action founded on appeals to laws of nonhuman determinacy). The latter is the hallmark of a conservativism that establishes and aims to preserve limits. What emerges with modernity's radical utopias is that:

> The institution of society renders possible the creation of individuals who no longer see anything as untouchable but succeed rather in putting the institution into question, be it in words, be it in deeds, be it through both at once.[46]

This entails that we are not bound by modernity's limits. In this respect, our analysis must depart from Bauman's rationality-irrationality couplet. The iron cage of bureaucracy developed by Max Weber and utilized by Bauman in his analysis of the Holocaust presents a limitation on human freedom, a limitation that Weber thought insurmountable. In utilizing such a formulation, Bauman reproduces, in theory, a helplessness that he ascribes to the modern condition. Weber's theoretical limit point produces a conservative result that takes shape in the "Modernity equals Holocaust" thesis. In our contrary perspective, subjectivity "as agent of reflection and deliberation (as thought and will) is a social-historical project,"[47] yet it remains fully unattained in the modern world:

> Politics properly conceived, can be defined as the explicit collective activity which aims at being lucid (reflective and deliberate) and whose object is the institution of society as such. It is, therefore, a coming into light, *though certainly partial*, of the instituting in person; a dramatic, though by no means exclusive, illustration of this is presented by the moments of revolution [italics added].[48]

The political expression of a social system in which human equality is inherently curtailed is in this sense anti-Political; it is pessimistic of the will, and its pessimism gives rise not only to a series of negative injunctions, regulations, and prohibitions that curtail the pursuit of freedom, but also to theories of society that limit aspiration. The bourgeois revolutions broke terminally with the Great Chain of Being. But as we will later elaborate, just as the permanence of the Chain offered a sense of optimism[49] to those who occupied positions of esteemed status in their high degree of proximity to perfection (God had, after all, ordained their fortuitous rank), the later modern purveyors of racial doctrine drew optimism from the fruition of their predestined position within the racial hierarchy. The modern world is at once the product of radical utopia that ignites hope in the social imagination, leading to widescale rupture—the American, French, and Bolshevik Revolutions being such moments—calling institutionalized heteronomy into question. Put differently but no less dramatically, utopias "help to lay bare and make conspicuous the major divisions of interest within a society."[50] But there are no guarantees of success. In the post-1789 polity, the pursuit of autonomous subjectivity (freedom) was cohered through conflict: laissez-faire liberalism's equal and anonymous individual opposed by socialism's now conspicuously unequal collective subject. Informal and unequal power relations hidden by the atomizing formal equality of the market were laid bare by utopia's "activating presence."[51] Partisan aspirations, the expression of social antagonisms, relativized the future; hope collided with conservative despair such that the emerging European nation-states enclosed a tension inherent to their performative modern incantations. Radical utopian universalism stood apposite conservative limitation that placed the present beyond human hands.

To summarize thus far, the Hopeful Subject does not seek perfection but utilizes perfectibility. Perfection is the antithesis of an open-ended requisite for overcoming appeals to external determinants in justification of constraint. Not a goal but a qualitative tool used to counter conservative imposition, perfectibility is implicated in a subjective stance toward the world that challenges constraints justified through appeals to natural limitations. In apprehending that humans make nature meaningful, nature is socialized, natural constraint deprivileged. Where the modern social is replete with landed interest founded on the conservative maintenance of constraint, utopia's radical work makes visible those interests that presage the Hopeful Subject's passage to freedom. In short, utopia gives hope vitality. However, one more fundamental quality of our aspirational subject requires attention: *possibility*.[52]

## TOWARD A PARADIGM OF POSSIBILITY

When we bring utopia into our framework, it becomes apparent that there is a sense in which anti-Enlightenment critiques of racism must remain partial. This becomes clearer when we pair our perfection/perfectibility distinction, where the latter undermines the former's determinate evolutionary teleology, with an understanding of the difference between "possibility" and scientific "probability." Back to Bauman. Although probability signals the likelihood of an event's occurrence based on past experience, it can say nothing of the future event:

> Probability belongs to the realm of facta, to the realm of events which have already taken place, which can be relished or regretted, but cannot be changed; events in relation to which men have neither will nor liberty of action, neither power nor influence. Precisely because of this quality of facta, which puts men in a position of passive contemplation, they are "knowable" in the scientific way.[53]

Goldberg's thesis is supported inasmuch as he would argue that modernity's scientific gaze activates power through racial subjectification—the creation of racial subjects. In this regard, Foucault's invocation of the state's knowledge of its subjects as statistics is central to his argument on modernity and racial neoliberalism.[54] However, scientific investigation (and we include here statistical analysis as the lingua franca of positivistic social science), predicated as it is on uncovering probability, can only rely on *the past* as a source of knowledge about the present. In this sense, science, when applied positivistically to the *future sense* of the human subject—the social animal—ascribes passivity; humans are thought of, treated as, and reduced to objects whose actions are predictable. As Adorno illustrates, "To call for a 'solution of the Jewish problem' results in their being reduced to 'material' for manipulation."[55] What Adorno does not consider fully is that such ascription cannot automatically create passivity of *actual* human beings even where inequality is naturalized. The pacification of human beings requires that they first accept their own brutalization as unchangeable; they must internalize the imposed external social constraint as personal limitation. For Foucault, modern subjectification is not underpinned by any distinction between sentient human subjects and objectified passive humans—a condition to which we are reduced; consequently, Goldberg's Foucauldian premise cannot provide a basis for overcoming our reduction to the state of helplessness (we will return to this question in Chapter 5).

In stark contrast, utopia "defies this reduction by legitimizing the status of 'the possible' in valid knowledge."[56] We can, and therefore do, argue that as a category, *"the possible" signifies an event that has not yet occurred and whose future occurrence cannot be predicted scientifically on the basis of past events. Science can neither account for nor extinguish the power of possibility. The very positing of the possible as an ideal and the actions garnered in the ideal's enactment distinguish human subjectivity from the realm of facta—the gaze of science—because the posited ideal is integral to whether or not the future event will be realized (even if it never materializes).*

This is crucial! As Erich Fromm once argued, authoritarianism engages in activity in the name of a higher or external power but never in the name of the future. The latter is to be extinguished as an object of terror, since authoritarianism fears freedom.[57] Utopia dereifies and thus frees subjectivity from objectification. Possibility distinguishes "being" (what we are) as given to us from "becoming" (what we could be) as the unique lived modality in which humans exist in and transform the world; an open-ended inconclusive orientation underpins what we refer to as the Hopeful Subject such that "to measure the life 'as it is' by a life 'as it might or should be' is a defining, constitutive feature of humanity."[58] Possibility defies the scientific gaze, the reduction of humans to predictable facta.

The problem in conceptualizing the universal human subject as a construction of the scientific gaze, as Goldberg does, is that the analysis does not allow for aspiration or desired change premised on the possibility of human becoming. Thus, Cornel West is surely correct in his conclusion:

> Optimism adopts the role of the spectator who surveys the evidence in order to infer that things are going to get better. . . . Hope enacts the stance of the participant who actively struggles against the evidence in order to change the deadly tides of wealth inequality, group xenophobia, and personal despair.[59]

But he is right for the wrong reason, for Hitler was no spectator. Evidence—that is, conclusive facts drawn from past events—though integral to science, is certainly not of utopia's kernel and reflects the narrowing of possibility—the reduction of humans to facta. The distinguishing feature of radical utopia lies in human engagement with and transcendence of the naturalized, the dead aconscious matter of nature to which the Jews were reduced. Thus, "possibility" places hope in human hands and paves the way toward "Big P" Politics. In West's (irrationalist) Nietzschean/Chekhovian inflected argument that "a sense of the tragic is an attempt to keep alive some sense of possibility. Some sense of hope. Some sense of agency,"[60] overcoming the reduction of humanity to material dead matter (facta) and thus circumventing dehumanization is not, despite West's good intentions, theoretically possible. Indeed, dead passive matter is inherently and essentially part of what he sees as the subjectively tragic: In West's formulation, at an existential level the tragic cannot and should not be negated, since fear of mortality—that is, our cognizance of inevitable death—provides the basis of hope. Tragedy must remain a constant feature of our existence; without tragedy there is no hope. Tragedy (representing the threat posed by the lifeless material world) cannot therefore dynamically engage the lifeless material world of which it is a part and on which it is sustained. Consequently, pursuit of human betterment suffers because material limitation (and thus inequality) assumes an essential part of what it means to be human; it provokes (for West, at least) a wishful, not (for us) a hopeful, stance. Hence, West celebrates the *tragic subject's* "prisoner of hope" status, while our *hopeful subject* wants no master—theological or scientific—and is therefore, but for quite different reasons, also the antithesis of that determinate gaze entailed by Goldberg's modern scientific subjectification. Without possibility as the antithesis of probability derived from facta, it is difficult to valorize actions and beliefs that counter racism because there can be no universal ethical foundation beyond the constructed Enlightenment subject's rational kernel. Thus, Goldberg argues characteristically:

> . . . The modern obsession with race . . . was deeply predicated on an appeal to reason, to a deeply racial sense of rationality, that representational expressions of resistance felt bound to emulate. Reaction suffers having to employ the very same terms and conditions of denigration and subjugation as a condition of their being understood as proof of their rationality initially denied.[61]

Goldberg's delineation of an all-encompassing rationality, like West's tragic premise, closes from view and thus incarcerates that described by Castoriadis, Bauman, and Bloch as integral to the modern human condition—radical utopia—embodied in what we have called the Hopeful Subject. Hope is neither one-dimensionally rational nor tragic, and it can only become so reduced when utopia as an open-ended challenge to social limitation is diminished, placed beyond human hands. As will be demonstrated in Chapter 2, nineteenth-century racial doctrine represented reaction *against* perfectibility and the possibility of an equal world, and it was partially "successful" in reducing universal equality to the "economy of mind." Perfection entailed the transformation of the pursuit of human freedom into a system for the maintenance of natural inequality, and it was the pursuit of such a *perfect* world, the limitation placed on human universality, that provided Hitler with a sense of optimism.

## THE IRRATIONALIZATION OF EQUALITY

One of the central problems with "Modernity equals Racism" is that too much is laid at the sacrificial altar. That which is to be analyzed is narrowly framed. There are a number of senses in which the modern world can be understood beyond the rationality-irrationality couplet. Conversely, as a concept modernity's baggage can overwhelm those who seek to unpack it. On this point, Kenan Malik is helpful:

> On the one hand there is modernity in the sense of an intellectual or philosophical outlook which holds that it is possible to apprehend the world through reason and

science—an outlook that came to be associated with the Enlightenment. On the other hand modernity has also come to mean the particular society in which these ideas found expression—in other words, capitalism.[62]

If racism is to be framed as a modern phenomenon, then it is incumbent upon us to unravel those constituent elements of the modern world that gave rise to racial doctrine; with this proposition few would disagree. Here, capitalism is often left undertheorized in terms of its explanatory significance. Usually interpreted as purely an economic system, although some qualify this by accepting a link to social relations, economy can no longer be analyzed as a foundational determinant. Marx's identification of modern society as capitalist society was in this sense crucial in that it attempted to situate the human population in relation to how it adapted to, used, and transformed the natural world so as to procure a means of subsistence without which very little else, *including individuality*, is possible. For Marx, capitalism entailed an exploitative and oppressive system that was irrational when viewed through the Enlightenment lens of universal equality. This irrationality expressed itself in the crisis-ridden drive to accumulate for profit, rather than to produce for human need; capitalism and its inherent crisis entailed a limitation on the Enlightenment promise. In other words, capitalism imposed a condition of impossibility on the modern condition of possibility. Not only does this contradiction set limits on social relations, it narrows human consciousness in the sense outlined by Lukács' theory of reification.

In his now almost universally ignored work from 1954 on the philosophical roots of the Holocaust, *The Destruction of Reason*, Lukács identified the narrowing of consciousness with the intellectual expression of capitalist limitation as irrationalism. One of the deciding hallmarks of irrationalism is its stress on *impossibility*. Not only is a solution to a problem deemed unachievable, acknowledgment of this "certainty" is acclaimed as a superior form of knowledge:

Irrationalism is merely a form of reaction (reaction in the double sense of the secondary and the retrograde) to the dialectical development of human thought. Its history therefore hinges on that development of science and philosophy, and it reacts to the new questions they pose by designating the mere problem as an answer and declaring the allegedly fundamental insolubility of the problem to be a higher form of comprehension. This styling of the declared insolubility as an answer, along with the claim that this evasion and side-stepping of the answer, this flight from it, contains a positive solution and "true" achievement of reality is irrationalism's decisive hallmark.[63]

Modern irrationalism developed as a reaction against the Promethean spirit of the Enlightenment. Its first incarnation was aristocratic reaction in opposition to the equalizing march of bourgeois progress; later, it would cohere the bourgeoisie's ideological legitimation of capitalism's unequal social order. This is the central qualification that Marx placed on progress under capitalism. Though capitalism furnished humanity with indispensable tools for economic development and equality, its downward trajectory, precipitated by profit, competition, and crisis, entailed the continued immiseration of the majority of the human population; individuals who were "free" to sell their labor for a wage were simultaneously cut off from their creative power and from one another, thus assuming the persona of objects in narrow exchange relations: what science conceptualizes as facta. If, as Marx wrote, "Communism . . . equals humanism,"[64] then under capitalist social relations the real "living labor" of human beings was transformed into "dead labor," the capital "monster which is fruitful and multiplies."[65] Human beings were assigned the status of facta. The overcoming of natural limitation entailed by liberalism's utopian impulse suffered accordingly. The task of human liberation therefore fell to socialism; a collective overthrow of the fetters to individual freedom lay in the abolition of competitive market individualism. In this sense, socialism was the active utopia, the carrier of social progress that could elevate human beings to a position no longer subordinate to the naturalized world of limitation.

It is here that the contest between Left and Right becomes clear. Where the "Big P" Politics of liberals and socialists held different conceptions of the human subject—one as individual, the other as collective subjects—both were incarnations of the *possibility* and demand for human freedom. While the contest between these radical *parties of movement* was underpinned by the first principle of human freedom—hope—the anti-Political conservatism of capitalist society acted as a limiting paradigm on hope's realization. The conservative *parties of order* operationalized the limit point.[66] The dynamic finds an early expression in the United States in the tenets of Jacksonian democracy.

The liberal extension of suffrage predicated on a universalist understanding of equality was paralleled by the ideology of Manifest Destiny, a conservative appeal to nonhuman forces such that early capitalist territorial expansion was justified on the basis of white supremacy. Both possibility and limitation were expressed in the ideological pursuit and hindrance of freedom. The conservative interpretation of social inequality—that it was natural—imposed a potentially profound influence on the modern expression of hope. From this dialectical interpretation we understand that nineteenth-century racial doctrine was *not the rationalization of inequality, but an attempt to systematize the irrationalization of equality; that is, the unequal social relations of capitalist society were interpreted as insoluble race relations, and this insolubility, the futility of solution, included an appeal to external (nonhuman) determinacy, the reduction of human beings to color-coded facta; absence of solution made visible and knowable; knowledge presented as virtue.*

We do not, therefore, understand racism as essential to capitalism; irrationalism is, and racial doctrine is but one historical incarnation. The social inadequacy of the capitalist system as a means of providing for human need gave rise to the irrationalization of equality that placed limits on the perfectibility of the human species; human exceptionality could not be maintained. Gradually the emerging open-ended orientation of the modern ethos was subsumed within definite developmental endpoints. The human as a desired but ultimately unknowable entity was expelled in favor of knowable distinct and predestined races. When the eighteenth-century French conservative counterrevolutionary Joseph de Maistre mocked, "There is no such thing as *man* in the world," only "Frenchmen, Italians, Russians, and so on,"[67] his particularist essentialist claim was in its day a moribund critique of universalism that would reappear in many guises over the coming two centuries, especially when quests for social equality threatened the established order of *things*. When the German philosopher Johann Gottfried von Herder coined the highly influential idea of the national *Volk*, he opposed racial differentiation while conceptualizing national cultures in as dire a way as racial determinacy eventually would. National *Volksgeist*, from intuition to sentiment, to language, to thought, was organically unique to a people, making cultures incommensurable. People were determined intergenerationally by an inner voice, not by outward physique. The nation was the teleological endpoint of an organically founded and continuous spirit. Herder's *Volksgeist* could very easily translate into a theory of the incommensurability of races, and it did so in the era of *Herenvolk democracy*. In this respect, the French Revolution and the rise of comparative anatomy under its orbit were instructive of things to come, a point to which we will return in Chapter 2.

The Enlightenment promise of equality personified in hopeful subjectivity contradicted by the inability of the capitalist system to deliver on that promise provoked ruling elite reaction. The agitating masses of Europe in 1848 and India in 1857 are but two examples of the radical subjective that led to a symptomatic post hoc reappraisal and reconceptualization of bourgeois rule. The doctrine of racial (i.e., nonhuman) determinacy and its nationalist homologue came to permeate a now secularized and collapsing public-private order. Those feudal particularisms, antiquated prejudices privately acquiescent, were publicly recast under the guise of a scientifically validated social hierarchy. In turn, the challenge to bourgeois social progress precipitated the reactionary irrationalist elevation of natural limitation. In other words, the validation of limits to social progress endowed nature with powers beyond human control. The earlier nineteenth-century works of antirevolutionary Thomas Malthus, who believed that population growth, specifically of the urban poor and working classes, outstripped natural resources and should be curtailed, gained currency of explanation.[68] Malthus' anti-utopian critique was leveled at the utopian works of William Godwin and the Marquis de Condorcet.[69] Through later notables such as Herbert Spencer and Thomas Huxley in England, Ludwig Gumplowicz in Austria, Nicholas Danilevsky in Russia, and William Graham Sumner in the United States, neo-Malthusian antihumanist arguments laid the Social Darwinist groundwork for future policies of eugenics. Irrationalism provided the ideological basis for setting limits on human development, not as a consciously directed bourgeois conspiracy but because the real limitations of the human condition of existence under capitalism appeared insurmountable. Attempts to surmount suffered accordingly, social order recast as a virtuous moral mission expressed through legalized barbarity. Thus, eugenics could be validated as a necessary instrument for the maintenance of racial health. As we will go on to show, it is the *limit point* of equality that expressed itself through the irrationalist doctrine of race and that allows us to conceptualize what we call "the racial order."

## FROM RACIAL ORDERING TO POSTRACIAL DISORDERING

In this chapter, we cleared a space for and set out the basic rudiments of our analytical framework. We begin as Hopeful Subjects from a position of pessimism of the intellect, optimism of the will, and we "measure" radically according to this standard. We understand racism as a subjective limitation. Consequently, our focus is on the antagonistic interplay between the radical subjective and the conservative subjective as expressed historically in their respective parties of movement and order. Their adversarial development reveals the changing limit point of capitalist inequality; they make it, and they move it, and in doing so they give it meaning.[70] Meaning is imbued with the project of "Big P" Politics—founded on the project of autonomy, contested by that of heteronomy, and institutionalized via the "small p" power politics—the injunctions, sanctions, and prohibitions—of modern statehood. For this reason, the irrationalization of equality is neither static nor unchanging. As we go on to elaborate, historically racial ordering sought to impose regulation on the impact of social inequality when the determinants of that impact were presumed to be racial in origin. Circular "logic" bellies the irrationalist premise of racial doctrine, for the "impact" attested to included no less than the legitimate retaliation both within and outside colonial metropoles against the failures of, and in the name of, universal equality. Radical subjectivity, the subject of hope, was curtailed, suppressed, maimed, and murdered by the limit point enforced by conservative reaction.

In Chapter 2, we attempt to unwrap how racial ordering has played out historically in Britain and the United States. Through a discussion of the reactionary response to uprisings of freedom on both sides of the Atlantic, our story takes us from Gabriel's Rebellion in Virginia and the Chartist movement in London, through the treatment of the urban poor and Irish Migrants in Britain and the *San Patricio* mobilization in the Mexican-American War. We also examine the emergence of the eugenics movement on both sides of the Atlantic and how its favored diagnosis of "feeblemindedness" not only set a precedent for how the deviant human subject was to be conceptualized but how the humanness of the hopeful subject was reduced to facta and, especially in the United States, sterilized. The fusion of sexuality, gender, and "dangerous migrants" comes to full fruition in the collapsing public-private order through which Chinese and Mexican migrants to the United States and Jewish migrants to Britain are received in the late nineteenth and early twentieth centuries. The subsequent rise of Bolshevism and anticolonial agitation were met by the quest for racial order embodied by the authority of the modern imperialist state and its ideology—scientific racism—crystallizing through National Socialism in Germany.

Since then, the West's attempt to come to terms with itself has been configured within the collapsing philosophical, intellectual, economic, and political currents that underpinned the maintenance of racial order. Enter multicultural capitalism, the subject of Chapter 3. The emergence of multicultural capitalism out of the postwar social democratic compact that crystallized in the Thatcher-Reagan era embodied the political defeat of the Left and the cultural defeat of the Right. This is a period in which the vitality of the human subject expressed most vociferously in the Kennedy era gradually gave way to a growing sense of futility. The crescendo or seeming high point of individual Man represented in the 1980s battle with socialism's collective Man at home and abroad made a place for the "ethnic block" in corporate and council structures. Ethnicity was more than ably squared with the idea of victims' rights, which emerged with Nixon's call to the "white" silent majority, in turn, championed by Reagan. Ultimately, equality is transformed from the arena of economy to that of recognition: the mental economy, a reduction in aspiration, an economy of mind.

What we enter after Thatcher-Reagan is not a neoliberal hegemony, as most "Left" analysts argue today, but a quest for meaning ushered in by the Clinton-Blair administrations' need for a world-view that lies beyond Left and Right. The need to make the present without alternatives bearable results in therapeutics. For Third Way political elites, multiculturalism embodied potentially disastrous rigid systems of belief that were to be broken by the tolerance of cosmopolitan nationalism. Under the rubric of what we call Third Way antiracism, rigidity of strong belief systems came to represent all that was dangerous about the world—the embodiment of hate. In this sense antifundamentalism was really the hallmark of the Third Way. We do not here use postraciality to demarcate the end of race or of racial inequality; rather, it is to signal a crisis of racial ordering that has been such a hallmark of Western capitalist modernity. The postracial disorder is therefore not the other but the unraveling of the racial order, the outcome of the disintegration of the contradiction between human exceptionalism and its limitation that together figured as constitutive conceptual elements of racial doctrine, but it is more than this. Postraciality is forced to search for a basis of its own legitimacy, and it is the very absence of this basis that presents us with a sense of uncertainty. At the level of political debate and public policy, current "postracial" elites seek to hold center ground against what they perceive as threats to postraciality, and in Chapter 4 we subject these posited threats—immigration and terror—to scrutiny, focusing on the killing of Jean Charles de Menezes by British police on the London Underground in 2005 and the emergence of the "other than Mexican" migrant category in the United States under George W. Bush. The specificities of the mental economy of fear are further drawn out in a discussion of the Obama administration's response to the policing of the Arizona-Mexico border and "hate crimes." But in a historical period in which capitalism is now hailed as the only viable social system, the crumbling legitimizing basis of bourgeois society—a belief in human exceptionality unbridled by external constraints—galvanizes a sense of uncontrollability, of helplessness, over our world. It is from this understanding made possible by pessimism of the intellect, optimism of the will, that we, throughout the chapters that follow and especially in Chapter 5, take up theoreticians of past and present.

It should by now be apparent that we do not here mean to imply that racism is determined by or is a consequence of economics or market forces. Rather, we are conscious of an epistemological break in social thought, developing in the late nineteenth century, that severed the links between economic and social theory such that any attempt to situate an understanding of society within the parameters of the capitalist system of development is easily branded and therefore discarded as economic determinism. It should also be clear that our analysis does not fall within a structuralist framework. In rejecting both economic determinism and structuralism, we privilege history as an open-ended *process*, made by thinking, acting human subjects in their individual and social incarnations. Along with E. P. Thompson, we reject all theories that maintain:

> 1. . . . However many variables are introduced, and however complex their permutations, these variables maintain their original fixity as categories: with Smelser, the "value-system," the factors of production, "political arrangements," and (the motor) "structural differentiation"; with Althusser, "the economy," "politics,"

"ideology," and (the motor) "class struggle." Thus the categories are *categories* of *stasis*, even if they are then set in motion as moving parts.

2. Movement can only take place *within the closed field* of the system or structure; that is, however complex and mutually-reciprocating the motions of the parts, this movement is enclosed within the overall limits and determinations of the pre-given structure.[71]

While the "postmodern gaze" may indeed provide a robust analytic method in a world deeply imbued by fragmentation,[72] this does not mean that Marx's method cannot usefully explain the very fragmentation under study.[73] It is certainly true that economic determinism eradicates the human subject as a key actor, but it is more than doubtful that the separation of economic and social theory into distinct fields of analysis provides a satisfactory alternative. Perhaps it is telling that Adam Smith, usually identified as the father of modern economics, referred to capitalism as the "system of natural liberty." His chief concern with what we now call capitalism was that it was by far the closest match to that which was then commonly thought of as human nature. There could be no separation between human need, desire, morals, and economy in Smith's formulation. *Our* aim in the following chapter is to identify how that cardinal *quality* of modernity, the *sentient* desire for universal human freedom, found its pessimistic limit point of racial doctrine in the emergent social "system of natural liberty": *capitalism*.

CHAPTER TWO

# THE WEAKNESS OF WHITENESS

## A HOUSE DIVIDED

Racial doctrine is no *Hindenburg*. It was not invented, nor did it explode onto the modern world arena ready-made as an object of technological wonder, advance, catastrophe, and retrogress. Rather, the meaning of race materialized within the wider orbit of social antagonisms, themselves instrumental players in the emerging narrative of modernity's making. Any analysis of this making requires cognizance of a historical process that gives centrality to the conservative inhibition of radical subjectivity, for it is within this antagonism that the limit point of capitalist equality is laid bare as the central protagonist of racial ordering. In this chapter, we use historical comparative method to illustrate how the emergence of racial doctrine as a worldview in Britain and the United States was counter to the pursuit of equality, placing it beyond human hands and into the economy of mind. The conservative correlate of radical subjectivity read the impossibility of the egalitarian development model unleashed in the Age of Revolutions through its own developmental despair. Ultimately, the "invisible force" of racial order signaled both the advance and decline of whiteness as a ruling ideology, a defeat built into the theory of its own inception—a defeat made visible by the empirical absence of "white" unity.

The "assumption of permanent difference," writes sociologist Michael Banton, "is the capital error and the central issue with which the history of racial thought must be concerned."[1] Few would disagree. Nineteenth-century racial doctrine drew on explanations of human variation underpinned by a theory of "types." Classificatory schemas divided the human population into fixed, separate biological groups. In 1812, the eminent Parisian anatomist Georges Cuvier extrapolated a theory of distinctive human types from the fossilized remains of the paleontological record. Although Cuvier considered, among other hypotheses, that individuals were descended from Adam[2] and of the same species, each, he believed, could be classified according to the bone structures of three distinct subspecies or types: Caucasian, Mongolian, and Ethiopian. The human population had emerged in the separate geographical locations of Mount Caucasus, Mount Altai, and Mount Atlas as survivors of the great floods of Noah chronicled in the Old Testament: Natural catastrophe explained their distinctive development and migratory patterns. Types could be ranked in a developmental scale. Beginning with the assumption that physical constitution explained cultural capacity, the larger skulls of Caucasians accounted for their greater civilizational progress. Although Cuvier advocated the abolition of "negro" slavery in America, by merging biological difference with separate lines of descent, the theory of types was pivotal in grounding later claims that distinct biological groups originating from different geographical locations could be ranked in a racial hierarchy and that such a hierarchy was *permanent*—beyond possibility.

Analytically, Cuvier's theory of catastrophe gave primary weight to the power of nature as a defining force—a natural scientific orientation that diminished human agency. The inclusion of divine origin, even as only one of several possible explanatory factors, further mystified the basis of human action, while fixed nonevolutionary hierarchical descent (that each type was unchangeable, its social position predetermined) undermined the possibility of conscious social change. But how should we account for the seemingly arbitrary inclusion of natural hierarchy in the schema of permanent types?

Cuvier's "discovery" cannot be extricated from the historical and political circumstances in which it arose—namely, the Napoleonic and Restoration periods. In effect, prerevolutionary ideas were fused with the rationalist orientation of the new bourgeois order into a conservative interpretation of humanity. As

Stephen Jay Gould notes, it has been argued that Cuvier, part of an elite circle at the Paris Museum of Natural History in postrevolutionary France, personified "the underlying consistency of a true political and biological conservative: after a bloody and traumatic revolution, any hierarchical order, proceeding from any source holding promise of stability, must be preferred over potential anarchy and populism."[3] As we have already pointed out, postrevolutionary struggles around the Declaration of the Rights of Man had thrown up counterrevolutionary arguments of great import. Effectively, the fledgling French nation-state was interpreted by those on the pro-Royalist Right as being comprised of groups whose ordered position in the prerevolutionary social hierarchy had been unleashed by the bourgeois demand for equality. "The negroes in our colonies and the servants in our houses," Rivarol forewarned, "could, with the declaration of rights in their hands, chase us from our inheritance."[4] Counterrevolutionary arguments drew on the feudal conception of the Great Chain of Being, under which social position was ordained by God, ordered accordingly through monarch down to peasant. Under the restoration, the ultra-Royalist Comte de Montlosier defended the *ancien régime*. In his *De la monarchie français*, published in 1814—acclaimed by the Right and detested by liberals—Montlosier contended that French history was essentially a struggle between two irreconcilable races: the superior Nobility (descendants of the Franks) and the Third Estate (descendants of the Gauls). The former he characterized by their love of war, courage, honor, service, and the open rural landscape, and the latter by their tyrannical love of money, industry, science, and beliefs such as that of liberty, culminating in the overthrow of monarchy and the rise of revolution.[5] The publication had immediate appeal and influence from which the patrons of the Paris Museum could not have been immune.[6]

In the second edition of his *Le règne animal*, published in 1817, Cuvier introduced what seems like a somewhat arbitrary Aryan-Semite classificatory distinction within the Caucasian race where the Semites, composed of Aramaeans and Syrians, were deemed culturally inferior to the Aryan descendants of Germans, Indians, and ancient Greeks. It is unlikely that a clear separation can be drawn between Cuvier's Aryan-Semite distinction and the restorationist political context in which the theory was developed. Postrevolutionary France required a stabilizing force, and Cuvier provided a theoretical advance, potentially both socially restorationist and conservative, that fused ecclesiastical claims of divine origin and aristocratic desire for social hierarchy under the leadership of the bourgeois scientific gaze *against* the antagonistic equality-claims of the (also Caucasian) plebeian classes unleashed by the revolution. Cuvier's Caucasian split, intended or otherwise, validated permanent and unchangeable internal and external divisions not only between but within types. It is not that Cuvier believed that sections of the French population were Jewish, with all the connotations that such a distinction would later have under German National Socialism, or that Semites were a separate type, but the characteristics that Montlosier attributed to the Third Estate resonate with the later stereotype disfigurement of Jewish peoples, especially the Hitlerite signification of Jews as money-grabbing *conduits* for communism and disorder. Rather, in effect, Cuvier provided a postrevolutionary scientific justification for the social fixity revered by the *ancien régime*'s feudal hierarchy against which the 1789 bourgeoisie had rallied the masses, and this validated the conservative endorsement of natural hierarchical inequality *within* the nation. The bourgeoisie could adopt and transubstantiate the theory for its own use against the equality claims of the working classes. Only by bringing the nobility's claims into modernity do we enter the bourgeois epoch of racial ordering.

Hannah Augstein, though alert to this distinction within the Caucasian type, argues that while the Caucasian hypothesis was accepted widely in North America, it received a more mixed response in Europe "as it did not allow for sufficient distinctions to be made among the Europeans themselves."[7] For Augstein, the Caucasian hypothesis "was based on physical analysis rather than on the history of linguistics which lay at the basis of the Aryan theory of race."[8] Augstein's claim is problematic. It is clear that Cuvier's Aryan-Semite distinction within the theory of types was also cultural in that the Aryan branch was deemed to have outclassed the Semites in "philosophy, sciences and arts"[9] and that this entailed some form of natural hierarchy. Moreover, the Aryan theory of race cannot be so easily differentiated from the physical spectrum of race when placed within the historical context of revolution/counterrevolution.

Cuvier had extrapolated a theory of the division of human types from the paleontological record—that is, from fossilized dead matter, from facta. His method represented an understanding of human beings at odds with the belief in the universal capacity for change and advancement. Arguably, such a theory was as useful to the Right as it would later be to a bourgeois liberal intent on not relinquishing power either to the Right or to the incumbent masses, but it was, for obvious reasons, more problematic for liberalism. Montlosier's theory could be reversed and adapted *only* as a justification of limitation within the parameters of bourgeois progress, and it was, for the bourgeois epoch would require a validation of its own inequality-wars, both of the exterior and the interior, and it found such a justification, partially, in those characteristics previously articulated as noble. The English anthropologist James Cowles Prichard, a humanist monogenist who contested what he wrongly saw as the polygenism of his contemporary Cuvier, argued that although all people belonged to one species, class hierarchy was essential to a civilized society. As we will argue next, the relationship between physicality and culture that lay at the heart of nineteenth-century racial doctrine posited homologous cultural differences *within* inequality-fractured European nation-states, explanations for which were drawn from theories of racial proximity and distance. Crucially, some "whites" were deemed more racially distant from blacks than others, and it is here that we begin to see the significance of gradations of whiteness within racial hierarchy. At its inception, the intellectual validation of mystified fixed descent in the emerging modern capitalist order included the white race as a house divided, and it is this internal split, the weakness of whiteness, that would ultimately influence the differing trajectories of racial doctrine in Britain and the United States.

It was not until midcentury that racial typology began to emerge as a significant force, and as Banton notes, the theory of types was developed most systematically in the United States where people met within the power dynamic of white-on-black enslavement. What Banton does not dwell on to any great extent is that the doctrine of racial types included a pessimistic interpretation of development and migration. Writing in the United States, Josiah Clark Nott and George Robbins Gliddon broke with the premise of common descent. In their 1854 publication *Types of Mankind*, they argued that different types did not originate from Adam. While all races were mixed due to migration, permanent types remained unchanged, and although populations could, through racial mixing, diverge to a degree from pure type, and had done so, the essential primitive core of each race remained immutable, unchanged over time. Environmental relativism stressed that all types were best suited to specific geographical areas, and although *proximate* races (closer by degree) could interbreed, the hybrid offspring of races deemed farther apart were less fertile and doomed to extinction. Because permanent types had distinctive attributes, any social relationship that did not allow pure typological characteristics to flourish would perish. Inasmuch as racial intermixing could not be stopped, and was a normal characteristic of the period, the success of the "white type" was not assured.

The idea of racial proximity would become crucial in that it provided a basis for interpreting the rise *or* fall of the white race brought by the radical subjection entailed by the Rights of Man. Distinctions retained within whiteness allowed for the probability that some groups of whites, due to their apparent differences, would be seen as the conduits of chaos and degeneration. Banton is therefore correct in pointing out that racial doctrine included a theory of race relations, but what is equally important is that while racial typology was underpinned by a theory of biological permanence, its advocates were as much concerned with interpreting change, and their interpretation reflected the pessimistic condition of a society that they saw as being newly and wrongly constructed on the basis of human equality. Hypothetically, change can be theorized either positively or negatively. Early racial doctrine extracted and built upon the observations of social relationships in a crumbling hierarchy. More particularly, in the United States, knowledge was drawn from a historical context in which white-on-black enslavement was increasingly open to challenge.

For advocates of racial doctrine, the negative social condition supported the conclusion that contact induced by migration (forced or otherwise) of biologically distant "types" beyond their natural climatic zones was wholly damaging and would lead to racial chaos. This is key for our discussion. Racial doctrine was inherently underpinned by social pessimism, and this pessimistic kernel of knowledge infused early theories of race relations as a *struggle* among races. Consequently, *preservation* of the racial order subsumed the *permanence* of types, for to preserve entailed action with the aim of arresting the inevitable repercussions of negative change, and it was the latter that shattered any illusion of a static social order. "How can we preserve?" was a perplexing question, the answer to which would be conservative at best and wholly reactionary when taken to its most brutal conclusion. Invasion and mass extermination were, after all, the strategies through which Hitler's Third Reich aimed to preserve the "pure Aryan type"; a Final Solution to the problem of racial order underpinned the optimism of National Socialism.

Of the roots of pessimism we have said a little. The French Revolution of 1789 and the forward march of liberty, equality, and fraternity provided a new footing through which development, migration, and intimate contact between different groups could be interpreted—based on the assumption that all men are the same and that social position is not determined by divine ordinance. It was this prior claim to universal rights with which supporters of the old order had to contend and that underpinned their conservative reaction. The newness of racial doctrine must be grasped within the contradiction between the radical demand for equality and the continuance of inequality. The continued absence of equality permitted a space through which a racist worldview developed by the conservative ideologues of displaced nobility could emerge. That the permanent pure type was destined to continue unaltered by racial interbreeding was by no means a forgone conclusion. This was the central concern of French aristocrat Joseph Arthur Comte de Gobineau, a key protagonist of racial doctrine:

> It has already been established that every social order is founded upon three original classes, each of which represents a racial variety: the nobility, a more or less accurate reflection of the conquering race; the bourgeoisie, composed of mixed stock coming close to the chief race; and the common people, who live in servitude or at least in a very depressed position. These last belong to a lower race which came about in the south through miscegenation with negroes, and in the north with Finns.[10]

According to Gobineau, only the nobility had maintained its racial purity. The superior social structures of European feudalism and the nobility exemplified the distinction between Aryan and all others, including those inferior branches of the Caucasian. As a Christian and a scientist, Gobineau lamented the loss of the prerevolutionary feudal order and the privileged status of the nobility now vanquished by the emergent bourgeoisie. Though he believed, in congruence with the Old Testament, that all men shared a common origin and could, regardless of race, attain the cultural virtues offered by Christianity, he was antidemocratic and opposed to equality, which he saw as unnatural. As Alexis de Tocqueville pointed out at the time, Gobineau could not reconcile his race theory with Christianity, but while later adherents to racial doctrine would castigate as naive his refusal to relinquish Genesis, in allowing for the belief that "lower races" were uncivilizable and suited only to be slaves, Gobineau stood within the racial science camp. He applauded slave owners of the American South, and Josiah Nott, while revising and updating Gobineau's work, agreed with its central propositions. In establishing a method through which human history could be interpreted as the history of race struggle, both Gobineau and Nott naturalized the imminent demise of the ruling race. Though Gobineau's prediction was framed by the loss of a static order of being that placed the nobility above that of the bourgeoisie, it was the latter that would carry racial doctrine forward as a scientific theory of its own preservation.

## OFF-WHITES

The emerging formulations of racial doctrine as a worldview can be clarified, in part, by their utility as explanations of disorder. In the early nineteenth century, the continuance of inequality was as self-evident, if not more so, than that of equality. The contradiction was only *made* self-evident by those who were on the receiving end. The bourgeois promise of equality was increasingly used by the oppressed as a clarion call to arms against their oppressor. Those exploited, whose history of exploitation swept back to mercantile colonialism, found justification in fighting the purveyors of inequality. The black Jacobins of French San Domingo were but the most indefatigable pioneers of revolutionary self-determination, succeeding first in forcing their colonial masters to abolish slavery, then in defeating Napoleon's 25,000-strong expedition to reestablish slavery, and finally in proclaiming the Independent Republic of Haiti (meaning "higher place").

In taking on the Spanish, British, and French empires, the black Jacobins elevated the rights of man to a conclusion beyond that of the American and French Revolutions; now they were the true representatives of universal man.[11] The Haitian Revolution (1791–1804) established the first black-led postcolonial nation and delivered a bitter shock not only to the French colonial regime (of which the aforementioned anatomist Cuvier was an esteemed scholar) but also across the United States, where fears of black slave revolt loomed large in the white imagination. North American elites were alarmed by the success of the

San Domingo slave revolt, especially as fleeing French planters sought refuge on the southern shores of the United States, bringing with them, where they could, their own black bondsmen. The presence of blacks who had tasted the spirit of revolution in Haiti, it was feared, would embolden an already overly empowered slave consciousness in the southern states, where white planter authority had been significantly weakened by the revolutionary theory of the American patriots. As Douglas Egerton points out, the "institution, slavery was in a dangerous state of chaos by the end of the eighteenth century,"[12] and it is precisely this chaos that fanned the flames of white fear. On this, Thomas Jefferson intuited correctly:

> Perhaps the first chapter of this history, which has begun in St. Domingo, & the next succeeding ones, which will re-count how all the whites were driven from all the other islands, may prepare our minds for a peaceable accommodation between justice, policy & necessity; & furnish an answer to the difficult question, whither shall the colored emigrants go ? and the sooner we put some plan underway, the greater hope there is that it may be permitted to proceed peaceably to its ultimate effect. But if something is not done, & soon done, we shall be the murderers of our own children. The "murmura ventures nautis prodentia ventos" has already reached us; the revolutionary storm, now sweeping the globe, will be upon us, and happy if we make timely provision to give it an easy passage over our land. From the present state of things in Europe & America, the day which begins our combustion must be near at hand; and only a single spark is wanting to make that day tomorrow. If we had begun sooner, we might probably have been allowed a lengthier operation to clear ourselves, but every day's delay lessens the time we may take for emancipation. Some people derive hope from the aid of the confederated States. But this is a delusion. There is but one state in the Union which will aid us sincerely, if an insurrection begins, and that one may, perhaps, have its own fire to quench at the same time.[13]

The future presented a stark choice for one of the principle architects of American independence. A solution to the problem of the "colored emigrants" required the enactment of a strategy that did not unleash their radicalized revenge upon the future generations of whiteness. The "greater hope" was the containment of imminent decline. Taken at face value, it is, of course, ironic that one of the key protagonists in the historic overthrow of a colonial power should in little more than a decade so fear the downfall of his own revolutionary credo—and at the hands of unfree men. Liberal capitalism required individual free-wage laborers. But neither the American Revolution nor the French Revolution was opposed to property rights—the cornerstone of the capitalist enterprise. The propertied had rights that no others could claim, and slaves were property, pure and simple. The contradiction presented the emerging bourgeois worldview, especially in the United States, where the Declaration of Independence proclaimed a political distance from old England's feudal order of privilege, with a sense of urgency that was part of a wider impulse reverberating across the world. For early advocates of racial doctrine, fear of racial revenge manifested in a reactionary theory of natural disorder, the system of natural liberty now disturbed. The racial chaos they saw before them was a product of folly—the imposition of universal equality on a naturally unequal racial order. Thus, the kernel of racial doctrine can only be understood as emerging within a historical context where the value of human equality was proclaimed as self-evident universal truth and where its absence was open to challenge. This for us is the central dynamic with which the history of racial thought must be concerned.

The dynamic is well captured by the impact of one North American slave revolt that coincided with the Haiti Revolution: the foiled uprising of 1801 in Richmond, Virginia, led by black slave Gabriel "Prosser."[14] Literate, articulate, and highly politicized, Gabriel had come of age in the age of revolutions. Well acquainted with ex-bondsmen, radical white artisans and inspired by the revolutionary zeal of sworn enemy of America Haitian leader Toussaint L'Ouverture, Gabriel, aided by two French co-conspirators and a select group of black collaborators, planned to unite an almost 1,000-strong slave army in the violent overthrow of white Virginia. That the planned insurrection was never executed—having been usurped by informants and torrential rains that broke the rebels' tread—is overshadowed by the reaction that followed. Egerton illustrates vividly the panic set in motion. Disbelief that "docile Negroes" could hatch, let alone pull off, such a fantastic scheme gave way to terror as officials learned more, especially when it was revealed that patrolling town militias would have presented no match for the rebels. The possible involvement of Frenchmen aroused deep-seated alarm. Gabriel had given instructions that no women, Quaker or French, were to be harmed in the uprising. Quakers were vociferous opponents of slavery, but for white elites the French "republican" population had long constituted a source of anxiety, since they were considered to cavort more freely with blacks. Fears were bolstered by the revelation that Gabriel had expected the involvement of white artisans who stood against the aristocratic privilege of Virginia planters. Gabriel's key objective was to clear the feudal remnants of parasitic planter privilege so as free men, both blacks and whites could enjoy the natural liberty of their universal manhood in the emerging capitalist market. The reaction of white privilege to this possibility was no less than a frantic, desperate attempt to restore order.

In total, 35 men, including Gabriel, were publicly hanged. Legalized murder was brought to a halt only by the intervention of Jefferson, who, along with Virginia elites, seriously contemplated the alternative of a forced emigration scheme for freed blacks (otherwise known at the time as colonization) to be implemented as part of a policy of gradual emancipation. A few of Gabriel's co-conspirators, found guilty, avoided the birch only by being sold into forced emigration: a strategy to isolate and expel guilty blacks. Authorities were hostile to the possibility of further insurrection posed by the presence of a large free black population in their state, but Jefferson did not give the go-ahead to a "liberalized" policy of gradual emancipation. Now determined to harness what they perceived as the racial chaos in their midst, white elites implemented more "suitable" methods of preserving racial order. The result was the introduction of a series of laws intended to drastically reduce any possibility blacks might have to experience that which white elites believed could ferment and ignite racial chaos: a sense of entitlement to equal treatment.[15] It was clear, they presumed, that blacks had enjoyed too much leniency since independence and must be put in their place. Greater freedoms of movement, communication, commerce, assembly, leisure, education, and worship were overturned, the reversal reinforced by state-backed violence.

The importance of this reaction was that it occurred long before the doctrine of racial typology had taken hold. Yet, each legal injunction could have been later justified by the kernel of knowledge contributed by racial typologists. The reader will recall that the doctrine of racial types acknowledged racial mixing and interbreeding as normal if kept within and between biologically proximate groups. Black-white intimacy did not fall within this category. For Nott, writing midcentury, such mixing would bring about the "probable extermination of the two races." In the state of Virginia, black-white intermarriage was illegal; nevertheless, intimate and long-term relationships between black males and white females (as long as they were of a low class) had been increasingly tolerated since the war. After Gabriel, this could no longer be, and the proposed penalty was 39 lashes of the whip, heavily laid on each of the offenders. No trivial aside, Nott had later argued that dark-skinned whites such as those he observed in Mobile and New Orleans seemed to enter into productive sexual relationships with blacks. The blood of these whites—French, Italians, Spanish, Portuguese—he proffered, was closer to that of blacks and explained their greater social affinity.[16]

A widely held view in early-nineteenth-century Virginia was that Europeans who freely mixed with blacks were party to moral decline. This was especially the case with the French because of their presumed role in stimulating republican black insurrection, having legally abolished slavery in 1794. Both Gobineau and Nott agreed with the view that biology determined culture, of which interbreeding between the inferior Negro and proximate dark-skinned Southern European was proof. It is no coincidence that Nott offered a dismissive racial type justification for why their relationships were successful: Their high tempers proved their racial proximity. Inferior as this proximation may have been in the white planter imagination, it posed a threat to racial order, to the maintenance of white-on-black oppression. If the white type was to truly flourish, then the black type should not be led to question his station. This questioning implicated impure whites. Black aspiration for freedom only led to chaos, and if race-mixing was inevitable, pure whites were sure to fall. Gabriel's Rebellion brought this home to the white elites of Virginia, and though they would do all within their power to stem the tide of racial chaos, they correctly intuited, along irrationalist lines, with the later racial typologists that no amount of racial ordering could preserve the cultural purity of white power indefinitely. Uprisings in Louisiana in 1811, Denmark Vesey's conspiracy in 1822, Nat Turner's Rebellion of 1831, and the Black Seminole Rebellion of 1835–1838 would only confirm the fears of the racial typologists and their constituents. The political reaction against black dissent, against radical subjectivity, and the intellectual interpretation of that dissent as being fostered by impure whites (as if blacks could not do it all by themselves) fused in the formation of a worldview that underpinned the weakness of whiteness after "emancipation."

While the remnants of feudal absolutism's static social order could not withstand the radical venture unleashed by the bourgeois revolutions, threats to aristocratic privilege triggered conservative counterreaction. These political and ideological changes were underpinned by the real conditions of existence vis-à-vis relations between humans and how those relations were orientated with the nonhuman world of nature, relations in which all must participate if they were to survive. The capitalist drive to accumulate through extraction of natural resource and class exploitation, once unleashed, could not be stopped. The procurement of free-wage labor drove the juggernaut of industrialization; this machine in the garden was such that the institution of slavery could not withstand the dynamic formation of modern nation-states based as they were, in theory at least, on the plebiscitarian contract of free-willing subjects. Theories that stressed the divinely ordained unnaturalness of universalism, the necessity of inequality, could not hold firm against the forward march of progressive movements. But while all fixed, fast, frozen relations of the feudal order would melt into air, the new order would have to come to terms with the persistence of inequality. The deterritorialization of the feudal order replaced by capitalist reterritorialization reconfigured unequal social relations. The possible-impossible attainment of equality unfolded within the emerging international system of nation-states. Though still generalized as a law of natural determinacy, the irrationalist limit point drew in new tenets of ideological validation. Key to our discussion is how the radical stance against inequality was interpreted and included in racial doctrine as a cause of disorder. It is this chink in the bourgeois armor that exposes the link between early and later racial doctrine, providing us with a conceptual framework for the making of equality's limit point in the latter half of the nineteenth century.

The abolition of slavery did not produce a concomitant eradication of the presumed need to preserve racial order, as epitomized in the United States by its continuance in Black Codes and Jim Crow following the Civil War, and specifically the emergence of "separate but equal." Rather, apologia found a justification of inequality within the psychology of types. Irrationalism set a new limit point that focused on the expression and curtailment of will, determined by invisible forces lying deep within the racial biopsychoculture of individuals.

Theories of invisible drives signaled *impossibility* in two senses. First, invisibility rendered futile the possibility of changing or halting inequality; the force of inequality was unreachable and beyond control. Second, it explained the *probability* of white victory when faced by challenge. Theories of inner force developed in parallel with imperial expansion, the success of which gave validity to the superiority of "pure white" mission, but it also expressed elite disquiet about the dangerous unequal—blacks and impure whites—in the emerging nation-states. Here, color-coding as an external ascription of race was complemented by fear of the masses, whose putative whiteness could be no cover for inner degenerative force. The later eugenicist action of enforced sterilization was symptomatic of this development, especially in the United States, but the logic of degeneration, that of an invisible force that determined a person's social status, found its early expression in the ideology of Manifest Destiny. As we will discuss later, the invisible force theory of race, which drove the ideology of Manifest Destiny, was later developed most fully by ideologues of German National Socialism such as Houston Stewart Chamberlain, but the transition can be more readily illustrated in a discussion of the formation of the British nation-state, and so it is to Britain that we now turn our attention.

## FROM RACIAL DEGENERATION TO COLLABORATIVE FIT

Although the transatlantic slave trade provided the mercantilist motor and, by the nineteenth century, the wealth accumulation for industrial capitalism on both sides of the Atlantic, the transportation of black slaves overwhelmingly to the Americas tends to overshadow that there has been a historical black presence in Britain that can be traced back to their participation as soldiers of the Roman Empire, although in what nonpresentist sense that historical formation can be called "Britain" and its population referred to as "blacks among whites" in the way commonly understood today is dubious. Despite Britain's role predominantly as a carrier of slaves between Africa and the Americas, the trade settled blacks in England, and by the late eighteenth century, there was a visible African population in the port cities of London, Bristol, and Liverpool, numbering around 10,000 within a greater English and Welsh population of 9 million.[17] In comparison to forced labor in the American colonies, black slaves did not in terms of sheer numbers constitute a similar presence *within* Britain, and it was not until after World War II that black subjects of the empire were contracted on a large scale for work as free-wage laborers in British metropoles.

Lack of black should not be taken as an indication that the enslaved were treated more favorably than in the colonies, although as Peter Fryer notes, there were differences of nuance:

> Black people were tolerated, after a fashion, if they had money, knew their place and kept it. For black to marry white was, in the eyes of many, not just stepping out of place; it was contrary to nature.[18]

According to Alastair Bonnett, British colonial elites from the late eighteenth century onward were responsible for importing black-white representations into Britain, especially from America, that were subsequently used to signify sections of the British working classes not initially thought of as white. In the early-nineteenth-century reactionary romantic imagination, Irish migrants and the industrial poor were contrasted with "the valued purity of the rural past,"[19] thereby signaling a hierarchical trajectory in British society that shared key elements of a naturalizing discourse of race. It was only through the emergence of welfare capitalism, argues Bonnett, that significant sections of the working class were gradually included and began to think of themselves as white, a mirror to inferior colonial black "others." We are sympathetic with Bonnett's position. The arbitrariness of race is well illustrated by the argument that imperialism and welfare were key components in the formation of cross-class whiteness throughout the twentieth century, but discussion of how this process worked itself out in the nineteenth century does not attend adequately to the emerging antipathies, the gradations of whiteness, of the Victorian era.

David Cannadine's contention that Victorian elites often considered themselves part of the same class or aristocratic pedigree as nonwhite ruling elites[20] cannot easily be accommodated in Bonnett's argument. According to Cannadine, metropole-colonial relationships were not straightforwardly cast within white/black, superior/inferior binaries but were additionally ordered according to status hierarchies. Nor were Cannadine's subjects merely expressing a self-loathing cultural relativism derived from Gobineau's doctrine of racial defeat, described by Robert Young as "Romantic dislike of the egalitarian industrialized West."[21] They did not, as is often thought, simply interpret the world through a black (other) and white (self) lens. There were distinctions made within the British interior that impacted the meaning of race. For one, as E. P. Thompson noted, "The sensibility of the Victorian middle class was nurtured in the 1790s by frightened gentry who had seen miners, potters and cutlers reading *Rights of Man*. . . . It was in these counter-revolutionary decades that the humanitarian tradition became warped beyond recognition."[22] Elite fears of threat to the social hierarchy that emerged in the aftermath of the French Revolution clearly impacted the ideological development of the notion of humanitarianism, and these fears could not be divorced from the conscience of social welfare, later to be subsumed under the orbit of racial hygiene. There is a tension, then, between the view that posits a cross-class British whiteness forged in the late nineteenth century through welfarism and the view that British elites did not in the same period hierarchically homogenize all colonial peoples by skin color. It was not that class broke color in the national social hierarchy, or vice versa, but rather that racial doctrine encapsulated a spectrum of naturalized differentials that came to the fore amid the dynamic antagonisms precipitated by capitalist development both within and outside the emergent European nation-states.

It has been argued that national sentiment was more than a unifying impulse prior to the nineteenth century. As Linda Colley observes:

> What most enabled Great Britain to emerge as an artificial nation, and to be superimposed onto older alignments and loyalties, was a series of massive wars between 1689 and 1815 that allowed its diverse inhabitants to focus on what they had in common, rather than on what divided them, and that forged an overseas empire from which all parts of Britain could secure real as well as psychic profits.[23]

Ingredients of national belonging were certainly forged through global commerce and trade expansion, not to mention a domestic military-fiscal apparatus.[24] Historic victories and defeats entailed that despite local differences, a significant unity of ideals and philosophical premises, albeit embryonic, undermined regional parochialisms that prefigured the fractionalized class society from which Bonnett begins.[25] But if we accept along with Hobsbawm that the earliest most systematic use of the term "nation" stems from its origin in the Age of Revolution where the most frequent meaning invoked a political identity of citizenry, sovereignty, and state,[26] then it is this definition that most befits comparison with the British state's mid- to late-Victorian nationalist adjunct. We should not infer popular enthusiasm for nationalism among the working classes in Britain during the late eighteenth and early nineteenth centuries. British nationalism, initially a weapon against parochialism and later an assertion of imperial will, had to contend with popular enthusiasm for the French Revolution and the concomitant absence of support for the war with Napoleon. The trial of Thomas Hardy and other leading members of the Corresponding Society on the charge of high treason was symptomatic, as were demonstrations 150,000 strong against starvation and antimonarchist mobilizations against King George III.[27] The forging of the British nation entailed the repression of domestic agitation and movements.

That elite fears emerged significantly with the appearance of an industrial working-class threat is exemplified by the most significant early challenge to British social hierarchy: the Chartist movement. Constituted by shifting working-class and lower-middle-class alliances, and driven by English, Irish, *and* black agitators,[28] they demanded their six points through mass peaceful protest and bloody violent confrontation with the state. Their escalating collision with ruling elites, underpinned by the demand for equality denied, drew Chartists into wider connections with revolutionary nationalists across Europe and America, activated government reform, and provoked state repression.[29] Crisis and reaction intensified with the European revolutionary uprisings of 1848, and conservative interpretations of "the masses" via the naturalized categories of social stasis were symptomatic. Aristocratic elites feared that the unruly could be incited by radicalism, as had been the case across the European continent. The subsequent defeat of radical insurrection in Britain, including the suppressed Young Ireland Rebellion of 1848, compared with its continental neighbors in that it was largely facilitated by the empire. The radicalized vanguard of insurrection was pacified. Increasing calls "for state-assisted emigration as the means of averting Chartism and socialism at home"[30] fused with Malthusian concerns. Transportation of the "dangerous criminal class," the urban poor, and political prisoners, including Irish nationalists, paralleled schemes to remedy the perceived perils of overpopulation. The targets were the "unrespectable," "degenerate" sections of the working class, and the ethos to get rid was so successful that "by 1852 over half of those emigrating from Britain and Ireland were going to British dependencies."[31] In addition, the shifting of high taxation from metropolis to periphery appeased both middle- and upper-working-class discontent, tying their economic position to colonial interests. As Miles Taylor notes, the British Empire was an important internal "safety valve" through which "the rhetoric of British radicalism" was undercut. As will be demonstrated next, however, that rhetoric was interpreted through the racialized lens of "degeneracy" legitimized by science.

Scientific discourses of race intensified in response to the Indian Mutiny (1857), the American Civil War (1861–1865), and the Jamaican uprising (1865). Key targets of such discourses were specific sections of the urban working class residing within the metropolis. Henry Mayhew's infamous mid-Victorian four-volume social investigation of the "non-respectable" working classes, an urban "race apart," is but one example.[32] As Malik notes, liberal elites could simultaneously interpret slavery in the Americas as immoral, while castigating the "residuum" of the English factory system as an undeserving, violent, unruly, and inferior race distinct from the "respectable working class."[33] It may be, as Catherine Hall argues, that early-nineteenth-century Baptist missionaries and liberal abolitionists drew on the Jamaican experience to pair "a belief in brotherhood and spiritual equality . . . with an assumption of white superiority,"[34] but whiteness could not have encapsulated the British interior in toto. Only a paradigmatic assumption that interprets racism within strict black-white polarities and class as an economic category could miss the explanatory significance that racial doctrine provided for the elite classes vis-à-vis the weakness of their ruling position in Britain.[35]

"Proximity" and "distance" fueled the emerging polygenist argument. Those deemed closer in "racial stock" were presumed to produce more fertile offspring than those signified as racially further apart.[36] Evidently "distant races" did interbreed and produce fertile "hybrids," but they were, according to the Scottish anatomist Robert Knox, generationally time-limited: destined to naturally degenerate over time. Their progeny would either die out or revert back to the originally dominant species, thus securing the latter's preeminence. In one sense this was wishful thinking, but in another sense we can argue that natural time was reawakened as a determinate social force in theory, thus placing change, in the form of (de)generation, beyond human hands. Aided by the "scientific observation" that England was an amalgam, a "mongrel" assemblage of "proximate races," Knox, in a move that would have salience throughout the latter part of the century, merged familial heredity, cultural (de)generation, and national belonging such that *proximate* races and their descendants were valorized as regenerative national (but not human) assets—the "racially proximate" generated the future of the nation—a "scientifically probable" outcome. What Knox represented in theory was the bourgeoisie's alignment against challenges to the inequality of capitalist development: The domestic national limit-point to equality was established in concert with British imperial expansion, and the impoverished and anticolonial Irish were key to that limit.

Ridding England of unfit elements gained credibility in the mid-Victorian metropolis, preparing the ideological terrain from which late-century colonial scrambles drew their force. Interpretations of national democratic participation that fused plebiscitarian contract with biological determinacy were increasingly adopted: Rights of citizenship would be granted to those "racially fit" for governance.[37] The 1866 Reform Bill introduced by Gladstone's Whig government explicitly excluded "the residium" from the proposed enfranchisement. And although the bill was defeated, the subsequent 1867 Reform Act that extended the vote by defining a larger proportion of the population as "respectable" (specifically artisans and shopkeepers) did not extinguish the residium's "race apart" status. Not only did the 1867 Act defuse protest and demonstration, the major shift from the now marginalized Chartist demand for full suffrage reflected the nationalist sentiment of the League's leadership.[38]

Despite its avowed demand for suffrage, the League *in fear* of transportation and *in favor* of racialized nationalism rejected civil war, specifically amid opportunity to combine with the Irish Nationalist cause. One League contemporary was more perspicacious. "You will have seen what a scandal 'our people' have caused in the Reform League," wrote Marx. "I sought by every means at my disposal to incite the English workers to demonstrate in favor of Fenianism."[39] This was not to be, and as Maurice Cowling notes, the Act was in effect an aristocratic reward for good behavior, subservience, and conformism.[40] In refusing the Irish cause for which there was considerable support in the movement, the League missed what Marx saw as a historic opportunity to undermine capitalist limitation by building solidarity between English workers of the colonial heartland and those fighting for the independence of Britain's first colony. Since the defeat of the United Irishmen in 1798 (the Irish bourgeois revolution) and the subsequent 1801 Act of Union, Irish migration to industrializing Britain entered an increasingly competitive position vis-à-vis British workers. The social and economic threat posed by Irish Catholics, and the anticolonial radicalism they were associated with, permeated an elite discourse that distanced them as a breed apart from the civilized white race. They were a threat to racial order. As Robert Knox summated:

The Celtic race does not, and never could be made to comprehend the meaning of the word liberty. . . . I appeal to the Saxon men of all countries whether I am right or not in my estimate of the Celtic character. Furious fanaticism; a love of war and disorder; a hatred for order and patient industry; no accumulative habits; restless, treacherous, uncertain: look at Ireland.[41]

The source of all evil lies *in the race*, the Celtic race of Ireland. There is no getting over *historical facts*. . . . The race must be forced from the soil; by fair means, if possible; still they must leave. England's safety requires it. I speak not of the justice of the cause; nations must ever act as Machiavelli advised: look to yourself. The Orange club of Ireland is a Saxon confederation for the clearing the land of all papists and jacobites; this means Celts.[42]

In the midst of defeat, the "respectable" sections of the British working class chose tradition, aligning with anti-Irish British chauvinism, the relinquishing of universalism, and the particularistic legitimization of scientific racism. The "respectable" were "racially proximate" in that their behavioral and cognitive traits proved nondegenerative—that is, conformity signified their culturally British credentials. Where nationalism posited a notion of universal political rights, it was progressive. The right to vote epitomizes an act of perfectibility, a striving for betterment in which each vote cast has an equal hand. But the Reform League's demand for political rights did not undermine the natural determinacy that entailed the dehumanization of both the enfranchised and the unenfranchised through the institutionalization of racial heteronomy: laws of nonhuman determinacy. Where one section of the human population is enfranchised at the expense of another, the justification can only be that the acquisition of rights is not by human design but determined by nonhuman factors—in this case, race. For the elites, enfranchisement became a means of conserving racial perfection against degeneracy. Reformism was the British state's policy tool through which racial proximity and distance were institutionalized. The achievement of the franchise at the expense of specific sections of the working class and the defeat of Irish anticolonialism were as unprecedented as they were a double-bind. The nonrespectable would continuously hold a mirror to the dystopic weakness of whiteness. On this, the last word should go to committed socialists Sidney and Beatrice Webb, who wrote the following during a visit to Dublin in 1892:

We will tell you about Ireland when we come back. The people are charming but we detest them, as we should the Hottentots—for their very virtues. Home Rule is an absolute necessity *in order to depopulate the country of this detestable race.*[43]

We have little to add to the historiography uncovered by Curtis. However, three key points emerge from our discussion of nineteenth-century British national formation. The first is that the theory of proximity signaled the expected probability that groups of people deemed racially close, even if regionally different, as in the case of the Scots and the English, would assume a set of expected behaviors and actions that maintained rather than threatened the racial order. Second, rules, regulations, injunctions, and laws, developed in response to social antagonisms, imposed hierarchy and collectively enforced an explicit dimension of power, the limits of which individuals should not and could not transgress if they were to be thought of as naturally white. Any alternative course of action or set of behaviors were therefore considered unnatural and the culprit treated accordingly; based on the idea of degeneration, the transgressor was deemed to be a contaminant who could be legitimately got rid of. The idea of race incorporated the bourgeois response to challenges mustered against social hierarchy within the capitalist metropolis. Racial science developed in congruence with that response.

The third point is that evidently peoples who would today be considered white were guilty of such transgressions. This is undoubtedly the reaction exacted upon Irish Catholic migrants, placed within the ranks of the lowest urban poor in mainland Britain, especially when that set of practices with which they were identified included the added and ultimate transgression of anticolonial radicalism. The Great Famine of 1845 produced by the British colonial exploitation of Ireland precipitated forced migration of two types that cannot easily be separated: those who were ruined in the famine but who could still flee the prospect of starvation and those whose fight against British colonialism resulted in transportation, such as the Young Ireland agitators. In a real sense, the experience of both migrant groupings was that of defeat. One of the possible consequences of defeat is that it gives power to limitation, and while defeat signaled victory for British capitalism over the Irish pursuit of independence from British rule, it reinforced the race-apart status of Irish Catholics and the British working classes, the limit point of a system of natural equality as that limit was enforced in the British context. The result was that the basis of the bourgeois order—freedom of human will from external compulsion—was diminished in favor of oppression. Racism was the form taken by national oppression within the oppressor nation, and in the imperialist epoch, the fate of the British working classes was tied to the "success" of overseas expansion. However, periodic crises in the interior could never eradicate wholesale the immiseration of sections of the otherwise white working class. It was this very immiseration that provided their status within the social hierarchy of facta. Therein lay the weakness of British whiteness.

## PUMPKIN VERSUS POTATO

The weakness was articulated most clearly within the tenets of the eugenics movement. The argument that nineteenth-century British eugenics targeted class and not race has been taken up by Dan Stone, who argues that "race thinking, so often overlooked by historians, was integral to the worldview of the British eugenicists."[44] Stone makes his case for the influence of race-thinking by illustrating eugenicist claims made against the assumed degenerative threat posed by blacks and foreign migration such as Jews. Such claims are set against the "class-view" that support for eugenics was a middle-class movement against the expense of taxes paid for the amelioration of working-class poverty and other ills. Stone's exploration of race-thinking retains a class-race distinction, where class-based eugenics are economically grounded against social groups within the nation-state and race-based claims are targeted at extranational groups. The class-race distinction is not helpful here. It retains the notion that racial doctrine was not the underlying framework through which Britain's urban poor, Irish nationalists, and other radical insurgents were targeted. It is clear from our discussion of the residuum, Chartists and Irish radicalism, that their assumed common biocultural characteristics entailed racial distance and proximity.

Writing in 1873, Francis Galton, the father of eugenics, observed racial degeneration as follows:

> Visitors to Ireland after the potato famine generally remarked that the Irish type of face seemed to have become more prognathous—that is more like the Negro in the protrusion of the lower jaw. The interpretation of which was that the men who

survived the Starvation and other deadly accidents of that horrible time were generally of low and coarse organisation.[45]

For Galton, it was not that poverty had transformed the Irish into Negroes and that this could be reversed through social intervention. More acutely, only those who were naturally suited to such brutal conditions could survive them—the connection between blacks and the impoverished Irish lay in their ability to survive the natural conditions to which they were best suited. Those who survived had reverted to natural type. Galton's claims cannot be viewed in isolation from those of Knox, whose interpretation of the Irish presence in mainland Britain was not framed on clearly drawn lines of class (as economy) *or* race (as foreign or skin color). Stone rather misses an opportunity to go beyond the race-class analytical distinction offered by his excellent observation of Edwardian aristocratic and Tory revivalism against organized labor:

> It is no coincidence that the 19th Baron Willoughby de Broke, the leader of the "Diehard" peers against the Parliament Act in 1911, and against Irish Home Rule in 1913–14, was also a theorist of aristocratic society. His vision of an organic society, based on the concept of *noblesse oblige*, had room for the "working man," just as long as he knew his place.[46]

But what of the working man who did not know his place? How would this Tory supporter of aristocracy, an antidemocrat opposed to Irish self-determination, interpret working-class defiance and nonconformity? Would his interpretation be class or race based? There is little sense in designating eugenicist arguments as class and/or race-based, since it is practically impossible to ascertain where each begins and ends within the spectrum of racial typology. By the time ardent British eugenicist Karl Pearson was claiming that there existed "a hereditary nobility, an aristocracy of worth . . . a caste scattered throughout all classes,"[47] the "observation" of racial de/regeneration was an implicit irrationalization of equality premised on European nation-state rivalry in the international capitalist competition and carve-up of imperial territories. What is at play here is the irrationalization of equality as an interior/exterior divide within the spectrum offered by the doctrine of racial struggle, and this imposing of limits on the universal human condition cannot be laid bare by *sociological* categories of class *or* race.

Degeneration doctrine implied the probability of regeneration if nature was not unduly interfered with by the artifice of equality. Galton's mission was to artificially *restore* natural balance in Britain, where it was assumed that social intervention, premised on human equality, had gone too far. For Galton, writing in 1869, four years after the American Civil War, the physically and mentally weak, such as hereditary paupers, imbeciles, and criminals, were reproducing at an alarming rate, whereas the superior minded and bodied were prone to marry later and produce fewer offspring. This imbalance, thought Galton, had to be reversed if national degeneration was to be avoided. Galton and eugenics took a powerfully conservative stance in the nature-nurture debate that was erupting in Britain over the question of social reform—and that debate drew on the tenets of racial doctrine.

Eugenicist claims cannot be separated from the racialization of the British interior. The well-known debate between utilitarian John Stuart Mill and essayist Thomas Carlyle over Ireland was symptomatic. Writing during the Irish famine, Mill argued against innate determinacy as the cause of Irish pauperization, which he believed could be ameliorated through social intervention. Carlyle saw it differently, tying the status of the Irish "potato people" to that of the Jamaican "pumpkin people," both of whom he considered naturally lazy and in need of compulsion to work. Carlyle's romantic quest for a return to the natural order of feudalism was set against the utilitarian freedom of industrial capitalism: The lack of compulsion to work entailed by free-wage labor let loose "savage impulses," squalor, and an undisciplined urban poor. Mill and Carlyle would again come to blows over the 1865 Jamaican uprising, where Mill stood on the side of blacks and Carlyle supported the brutal retaliations, including the execution of blacks instigated by British governor Edward John Eyre, who was subsequently acquitted of any wrongdoing.

What is crucial is that the eugenicist claims of Galton and his peers provided scientific validation for the conservative naturist argument within the context of industrial capitalism. Exploitation of the interior and oppressive imperial expansion determined the limit to equality, now refashioned such that the targets of eugenics were those whites whose behaviors differentiated them from respectable Anglo-Saxons in that they presented a threat to the naturally endowed health of the nation. The instability of whiteness underpinned the eugenicist claim that the cause of racial degenerative external manifestations—behaviors, mannerisms, habits—was a racially unique invisible force internal to the individual. As noted above, the fear of invisible force has a history. The respective works of Cesare Lombroso in Italy, Benedict Augustin Morel in France, and Henry Maudsley in England reveal that skin color was not integral to the presumed hereditary biological traits used to identify "degenerate groups" across and within European nations. The alleged cause of civilizational decline was located *within* "the degenerate" delineated as a nationally *internal* population.[48] This dual force of internal decline was an invisible disease, a social pathology that threatened the bourgeois social order, revolutionary upsurge being its most extreme incarnation. Hence, under the discursive terms set, any emergent doctrine of white racial superiority, of race as determinant of national health signified by skin color, would have had to account for *internal* national "degenerates."

Although not a eugenicist, French pioneer of social psychology Gustave Le Bon differentiated the human population into physiological and psychological races—primitive, inferior, average, and superior—arguing that each had its own immutable race soul.[49] This antiobjectivist irrationalist claim took its most distressing form in the work of Houston Stewart Chamberlain, the philosophical architect of German National Socialism.[50] Though he was not a Social Darwinist, Chamberlain followed their rejection of Darwin's theory of evolution in favor of teleology where origin and endpoint were racially fixed, unchangeable. Mankind did not exist, only permanent races, and though race could not be objectively defined, it was intuitive. The external world was but necessary myth, and the scientific gaze of empiricism was vital in validating such myth. But the essential myth of race was underpinned by racial beings who could *feel* their own existence as a vital force emanating from within, carrying them toward their racial destiny. Those who could not intuit racially were degenerates whose existence was determined by miscegenation predicated on the false humanist doctrine of Judaism and Rome. The Old Testament was part of a wider Jewish conspiracy, unwittingly smuggled into Gobineau's racial historiography. Christ was no Jew but the Aryan descendant of a long line originating in the racially pure aristocratic culture of ancient India and culminating in the Germanic race. Aryans alone were "truly human," and it was up to the Teutonic branch of the Aryan race to save the human, as Chamberlain defined it, from the chaotic tribal miscegenation forces unleashed by raceless Communistic Judaism established via Roman territorial dominance. The abolition of the Jew was simultaneously the abolition of the idea of universal reason, the enlightenment's common predicate of Man. In this formulation, Chamberlain replaced Gobineau's feudal aristocratic pessimism with the industrial optimism of Aryan superiority—the ideology of German imperial expansion in the era of limitation imposed by monopoly capitalism. But what is clear is that the internal invisible force of race placed the limits of capitalist equality beyond rational intervention.

The mystification of human action predates Chamberlain in its eugenicist incarnation. While Galton's contribution to psychology was hard materialist, nonidealist, the extinguished Cartesian subject that took center stage in eugenicist theory—the subject driven by hard biological brain matter—underpins the erosion of human consciousness as a determining power. Human agency was rendered mystical within the materialist doctrine of racial degeneracy. Taken together, in Britain the fear of imminent national demise, real or imagined, caused by sections of the population in the nation-state, such as Irish Catholics, radicals, and the urban poor; the defense of bourgeois inequality through the incorporation of the respectable as opposed to the dangerous at home and abroad due to imperial expansion; and the fusion of biological and psychological theories of causation in racial doctrine mutually reinforced the historical resonance of a Caucasian split previously laid out by the likes of Cuvier as cultured-Aryan/uncultured-Semite. "Aryan" was interchangeable depending on the imperialist national formation—in Britain Anglo-Saxon, and in the United States Anglo-American. Although phenotypically proximate, the behavioral manifestations of *biopsychocultural* drives exposed these "other whites" as unfit contaminants: the conduits of white degeneration.

It was this internal invisible cause of biocultural degeneration and regeneration that facilitated the visible demarcation of phenotypically "white" groups such as Irish Catholics, the urban poor, and late-century Eastern European Jewish migrants as threats to racial order. A closer look at significations of threat conjured in late-nineteenth-century British medical discourses mobilized around the figure of the Jewish migrant reveals that anti-Semitism drew discourses of white degeneracy into a coherent form of racial deviance. As Bernard Harris notes, concerns were less about the physical health of European

Jews—which was considered as good as, if not better than, the native British—and more about the Jewish psychological condition. The high number of Jews in Prussian lunatic asylums and the high proportion of Jewish insane compared with Germans in the German empire alarmed the establishment, as did the purported role played by unrestricted Jewish migration in the national degeneration of Poland. Dr. John Gray, secretary of the British Medical Association's Anthropometric Committee, concluded that the biopsychological differences between Jew and Gentile indicated "that the insanity is connected with degeneration."[51]

What is mostly left undeveloped by interpretations of late-nineteenth-century Jewish migration to Britain is the significance of the idea that Polish national degeneration was *caused* by Jews. It was, of course, widely known that Jewish migrants were fleeing persecution during and after the Russian Pogroms (1881–1884) and also amid the anti-Jewish Warsaw riots and continuing repression in Poland. In effect, Jews in Russia and Poland were blamed for the brutalized reaction instigated against them. Their problematic presence was signified through Jewish association with radical politics and agitation. The Jewish enlightenment Haskalah contributed to a growing number of radical movements for Jewish emancipation and against repression. The emergence of Zionism and the participation of Jews in the socialist movement in Poland also contributed to the elite view that Jews who did not know their place constituted a threat. Observations that Jewish migrants to Britain were primarily impoverished migrants fleeing the political turbulence they were deemed, at least in part, to have caused, and the idea that Jews were better suited to living impoverished urban lives on low wages, which undercut British workers, brought the three strands of biopsychocultural degeneracy together in the signification of the Jewish migrant as a threat to national health. The legislative result was the Aliens Immigration Act of 1905, introduced as a means of insulating British welfare from Jews.

"National health" was not merely sought in terms of physical regeneration; it included social and political concerns that came together in the color-coded spectrum of racial doctrine. The Jews were white, but they were degenerates. Whether caged in the insane asylum or barred through immigration controls, the diagnosis of Caucasian deviants reflected the mystified invisible force of destiny, at once nonrational but emotional, through which white racial superiority was both threatened and galvanized. The absence of a human solution to inequality was theorized as a triumph, and the move ensured that there was no objective basis, nor was one needed, for the validity extolled on the drive toward white perfection. The biopsychological *force élan*—the mental and physical condition of racial type—imposed its own hierarchical teleology that could neither be proved nor disproved; rather, its self-evidence was manifest in the brutalized empirical world of natural inequality: a devastating proposition that summoned helplessness.

Midcentury polygenism encapsulated the emerging attack against universalism. It is true that the preceding monogenist worldview, underpinned by the belief in the universality of human beings, also fused with a scientific classificatory system. But what is important for our story is that monogenism—the belief that all human beings were of the same species—did not undermine the "Big P" political call for human perfectibility. All humans *could be* equal regardless of difference; the possibility was left open, and the probability held in check by a humanist anchor. Science could not extinguish the purchase of humanism. Hopeful subjects could not be reduced to mere facta. Polygenism, by contrast, stressed the particularity and thus the incommensurability of different races. A conservative developmental trajectory was implicit such that specific races were valorized as possessing a destined perfection—a fixed beginning and endpoint—bioculturally built in and generated from their distinct origins. The possibility of human improvement was gradually subsumed within the pessimistic paradigm of "racial destiny," laying the basis for the institutionalization of the belief in nonhuman determinacy. In short, polygenism represented the transformation of the possibility of human perfectibility into the probability of "racial perfection," but this transformation was the result of social and political conflict and the implications of such for the preservation of the new irrationalist imperial order.

It should be of little surprise, then, that while plebiscitism—the move from subjects of monarchs to citizens of state as an ideal—was integral to the bourgeois worldview, the racialization of rights tied to welfare and biological fit was by the late nineteenth century an antiautonomous requisite for the rehabilitation of the British monarchy against insurrection, resistance, and Anglo-Saxon defeat. British crown subjects would gain their status under the tutelage of Queen Victoria, conferred Empress of India through the Royal Titles Act of

1876 introduced by Conservative prime minister Benjamin Disraeli. Working from Disraeli's dictum that "all is race," celebration of monarchy through the mythic artifacts of pomp and pageantry paralleled and gave heteronomous validation to political, economic, and social reforms,[52] including the Artisan's and Laborers' Dwellings Improvement Act of 1875, the Public Health Act of 1875, the Education Act of 1876, and the 1878 Factory Act. Peaceful picketing was made lawful under the Conspiracy and Protection of Property Act of 1875, and the Employers and Workmen Act of 1875 gave workers legal redress in the event of an employer's breach of contract.[53]

Such reforms were clearly victories for the working classes; they cushioned the irrationality of capitalist inequality (at least in the domestic British context). But for Disraeli, an arch-Conservative inspired by Burke and therefore more patricianist than populist,[54] reform was part of a wider crusade to enervate and restore English traditions against what he considered divisive continental radical cosmopolitanism. Identification with a mythical common past was the chosen antidote to socialism's active utopia. The 1867 Reform Act had converged with wider concerns over Russian and French imperial expansionism and with an aristocratic crisis of leadership in the face of perceived internal threats. Imperial war was the chosen antidote based on the aristocratic belief in the cross-class mobilizing power of honor, prestige, and victory, and it is for this reason of internal rallying that Britain confronted Abyssinia in 1867.[55] Maximizing working-class identification with the Conservatives as "traditional English leaders" through reform was compatible with Disraeli's pro-imperialist views, especially in relation to India—jewel in the crown of the British Empire.

Disraeli blamed the British government for the 1857 Indian Mutiny and was critical of anti-Sepoy media hysteria that followed. Increasing centralization and bureaucratization associated with utilitarianism were to his mind decidedly un-English developments that went against England's "noble system of self-government."[56] The extension of such un-English tendencies to colonial rule undermined England's apparently benign assertion of global power. As Parry notes:

> [One limitation of] unaccountable bureaucracy was when it became infected with moralistic whig Westernization. Disraeli believed that this was in the ascendant after 1848, under Dalhousie and contrary to the traditional policy of governing a multi-

racial empire, which was to respect the traditions, property, and above all religions of all its elements. Disraeli blamed the Indian Mutiny of 1857 on this new-fangled English intolerance of Hindu and Moslem religious customs, ignorance of traditional laws, and contempt for property rights, which had rallied the different races and religions against imperial rule.[57]

Disraeli's "multiculturalism" pinpointed unaccountable bureaucratic tendencies 150 years prior to Zygmunt Bauman's rationality thesis, albeit as an explanation for rebellion *against* the ruling section of the white race. The conservative restoration of English tradition against radicalism at home—that is, against the degeneration of England—demanded respect for presumed cultural difference in the colonies. The traditions of the "racially proximate" were tied more closely and paternalistically to the color-bound binaries of imperialist national oppression. Racial ordering developed characteristically. Colonial and metropolitan disarray were to be held in check through the fostering of emotional identification with Queen Victoria's symbolic embodiment of England's sovereign guarantee to "protect" distinct traditions and races both at home and abroad. While imperialist expansion suffered humiliating defeats at the hands of those refusing British colonial rule—Zulu victory at Isandlwana in 1879, Afghan at Maiwand in 1880—which reinforced metropolitan fin-de-siècle fears of decline, by the beginning of the twentieth century, Britain's empire had "successfully" oppressed the aspirations of a quarter of the world's population and subsumed the will of the British working classes to the realization and maintenance of white rule. With universal impulse now denigrated, the capitalist drive to accumulate through territorial expansion subjected the ideal of equality to irrationalist limitation. The "racially fit" were to be harnessed for a race war in which the outcome—victory—only proved the probability of white perfection. The future was placed beyond conscious human hands, given over to mythical destiny.

To summate our discussion of British national formation and its interplay with racial doctrine, we make the following points: Skin color signified race prior to the mid-Victorian period, but the meaning of race as biopsychocultural permanence, probability, perfection, and destiny could only take hold when a significant polygenist challenge was mounted against the humanist canon within postrevolutionary metropoles. For it was precisely this humanism that exposed the unequal position of persons who were phenotypically white. In getting rid, or through treatment, the eugenics movement sought to restore the balance of natural hereditary so as to regenerate a decaying racial order. Theories of degeneracy were underpinned and facilitated by a diminished universalism. Bourgeois social organization allowed for the emergence of particularist ideological currents of nationhood that could not have prefigured the universalist impulse now under attack. Elite pessimism and conservatism infused the meaning of inevitable advance and decline, a meaning that had antecedents but could not have circulated prior to the particular conditions described. A constellation of historically specific events, ideas, and antagonisms within the social organization of British capitalist development elevated the Anglo-Saxon, not the Human, to center stage, and in the remainder of this chapter we examine how this constellation worked itself out in the United States.

## WARFARE OF THE CRADLE

If white-black representations had by the beginning of the nineteenth century been imported into Britain, then anti-Irish significations of racial separateness that developed within the British colonial relation were imported into and established in the United States, where freedom was already a white-delimited category: The condition of whiteness signified the limit point of equality vis-à-vis enslaved blacks. The respective works of Theodore Allen, David Roediger, and Noel Ignatiev have subsequently, and in different ways, drawn much needed attention to the relationship between the emergence of whiteness and the incorporation of the working classes, including Irish migrants into that construct as a mirror of the social position of blacks, and their contribution need not be exhaustively reviewed here. However, just as Bonnett's problematization of whiteness in the British context vis-à-vis imperialism and welfare required qualification that drew out the limitations of whiteness as an all-embracing category related to phenotype, it is necessary to highlight some limitations of the whiteness thesis in the United States, and for this we must begin by returning to eugenics.

While eugenics in Britain has been predominantly thought of as class-based, the obverse is the case in the United States, where it is usually conceptualized as race- and gender-based.[58] This is an understandable interpretation, specifically when we consider that the Immigration Act of 1924 strongly supported by Deep South legislators in both the House and Senate was driven by Oregon and California lawmakers primarily opposed to Chinese and Mexican immigration. The Act, justified by eugenicist claims, restricted the immigration of persons from southern and eastern Europe: countries presumed to send high numbers of mentally defective migrants. However, this leaves significantly undertheorized cases where those targeted by eugenicists in a bid to maintain the purity of the Anglo-Saxon race were phenotypically white—otherwise known as "poor white trash." In the state of Virginia, for example, from the time of the passage of its Sterilization Act in 1924 to the end of forced sterilization in 1979 approximately 8,300 Virginians were sterilized, 4,000 of whom were phenotypically white. The infamous case of *Buck v. Bell* in 1927 is instructive.[59] Speaking as a witness against 18-year-old Carrie Buck, who had been forcibly institutionalized after giving birth due to being raped by a family member, arch-eugenicist Harry Laughlin explained to the court that "these people belong to the shiftless, ignorant, worthless class of antisocial whites of the South."[60] As is well known, Carrie Buck was ordered by the US Supreme Court to undergo forced sterilization on the basis of her alleged "feeblemindedness," for which there was no objective basis. Matt Wray argues that the stigmatization of poor whites such as Carrie Buck has a history that goes back to treatment by British American colonists suspicious of poor whites' potential to act as allies with black slaves. In drawing out the various historical forms taken by stigmatization, Wray reveals how social boundary definition was operationalized vis-à-vis "poor white trash" as targets of the eugenicist movement. However, the initial significance of the relationship between whites and blacks and how this might illuminate the development of the color-coded spectrum of racial limitation is lost when it comes to the discussion of eugenics. We are unsympathetic with Wray's claim that in "the latter half of the nineteenth century, the analytical object of scientized prejudice and the focus of popular discourses about inferiority and natural hierarchies shifted from people of color—primarily blacks and Indians—to poor white Americans, 'foreigners,' and immigrants."[61] There is little evidence for any "shift from people of color."

Self-ascribed "pure white" elites interpreted the vulnerability of their racial order through biocultural degeneracy, the conduits for which were presumed to be those infected by racially mixed blood. Thus, so-called interracial marriage or procreation, outlawed as part of a wider policy of white-black racial segregation, fused the presumed biological and cultural determinants of white collapse, the conduits for which were "white trash." In reality those targeted were the impoverished, who, due to the limit point of equality fixed by the irrationality of capitalist development, stood on the fringes of white rule, along with blacks, Indians, and other apparently nonwhite migrants. This coalition of the condemned was ascribed its status from the conservatism underpinning notions of racial proximity and distance.

While it is true that many eugenicists considered their movement as a progressive bid to improve human well-being, it is essential that we do not lose sight of how they defined the human being whose welfare was presumed to be at stake. The highly ambiguous catch-all category of "feeblemindedness" under which the presumed conduits of "white racial death" were forcibly sterilized drew on theories of the innateness of psychological defect, not as an attribute of human consciousness which would have entailed free will. The bio and the psycho fused in the reduction of human beings to biopsychocultural degenerates/regenerates. The feared invisible force of degeneracy undermined libertarian conceptions of free will—hence the state's authoritarian policy measures such as forced/involuntary sterilization. The irrationalization of equality necessitated by the inability of capitalism to deliver the Enlightenment promise of equality gave rise to the weakness of whiteness in two respects: first as embodied by those whose very existence held a mirror to the limit point on which they stood by force of circumstance and that some crossed in defiance, and second, as a reaction by white elites against that embodiment presumed to divide and diminish the power of white rule. The solution to "white weakness" was genetic extermination.

It is this biopsychocultural degeneration that leads us to question the "Irish became white" thesis. We do not here intend to suggest that people of Irish descent did not attain cultural and political inclusion in the top echelons of the white racial order, as Roediger makes clear, for example, in the case of the Democratic Party's designation of a White-Celtic Irish American. Rather, our argument is that just as whiteness cannot be conceptualized as a homogeneous force of racial stability in the nineteenth and twentieth centuries, neither can there be conceptualized a homogeneous Irish population that was incorporated. In addition, the heterogeneous categorization of the Irish by religion, class, or gender does not fully deproblematize the idea of a homogeneous Irish population vis-à-vis the development of racial doctrine. As Peter Quinn notes:

> By the 1920s, some eugenicists seemed ready to admit the Irish, or "Celts," to a racial status close to Anglo-Saxons. But not all. In *The Passing of the Great Race* (1920), a widely read and highly influential attack on "racial mongrelization," the eugenicist Madison Grant waffled about where the Irish stood.
>
> Grant observed that a physical change had occurred among the Irish in America. The "Neanderthal physical characteristics of the native Irish—the great upper lip, bridgeless nose, beetling brow with low growing hair, and wild and savage aspect"—had largely disappeared. The Irish apeman of Nast's cartoons had evolved a more human form. Yet, with the Irish, in Grant's view, looks could be deceiving. When it came to intellectual and moral traits, "the mental and cultural traits of the aborigines have proved to be exceedingly persistent and appear in the unstable temperament and the lack of coordinating and reasoning power, so often found among the Irish."[62]

Feeblemindedness as a cornerstone of eugenic thought, Quinn points out, connects the idea of unstable Irish temperament to the historical response of Irish migrants who refused to accept their "allotted place." "Their chronic resistance and restiveness," argues Quinn, "led some English observers to detect a racial bent toward querulous insubordination."[63] The historical record allows us to draw out a significant continuity between Irish retaliation and the idea of biopsychocultural mongrelization institutionalized via state authoritarian racial ordering, and this continuity has implications for how we understand the racialization of the human population, both migrant and "native."

As Michael Carroll notes, Irish Americans of the prefamine era, both Ulster Scots and Irish Catholics, supported and participated in the American Revolution with great fervor. Two main reasons for this are extended. The generally held view among historians is that experience with English rule and the colonial yoke prepared the Irish Americans for revolution against the British. The second more nuanced view is that while recent Irish migrants surely supported revolutionary agitation due to English colonial experience, established Irish settlers from earlier migrations were influenced more by the promise of autonomy and democracy that could facilitate their procurement of rights that until then had been reserved for Anglo-Americans.[64] Both explanations build from the experience of oppression, but the distinction between pre- and post-revolution periods, where the former situates Irish migrants in relation to the war of independence as a dual liberation from Anglo-American domination, is as important to the signification of the Irish in America as the defeat of the United Irishmen was to the reception of the Irish in Britain. Viewed through this historical lens, one could delineate three Irish migrations: migrants with a longer history of American settlement prior to the war of independence, those who arrived after the defeated United Irish uprising, and those driven by the colonial-induced famine. Three historical groups of Irish separated by different experiences of the fight for universal freedom and its suppression—one successful, the other defeated, and the last defeated and hungry—are apparently incorporated and merge into American whiteness by the end of the twentieth century. But such a wholesale incorporation into whiteness makes it difficult to understand instances where, for example, people of Irish descent in America sought common cause, not with the British or later with the Confederates, but with the oppressed, and to such an extent that they took up arms against US imperialism. In short, theorists of whiteness need to account for the San Patricios.

The San Patricios, otherwise known as the Saint Patrick's Battalion of the Mexican army, consisted of deserters and defectors from US forces during the Mexican-American War (1846–1848). Estimates of their numbers vary, with the highest being 700; however, their impact far exceeded their numbers, for they were no ordinary absconders. Under the lead of Irishman Captain John Riley, the San Patricios were the first deserters in US history to organize an enemy battalion.[65] Renowned for the ferocity of their fight against the armies of Generals Taylor and Scott in all major battles of the war, especially those at Buena Vista and Churubusco, it is that very reputation that underpinned the intense reaction that followed their defeat and capture. Of the 85 San Patricios taken prisoner, 72 were tried for desertion and 48 were hanged.[66] As Hogan notes, the punishments were not in accord with military codes, and they far exceeded in level of brutality those imposed on other deserters. Of the 5,000 who deserted during the war, only the San Patricios were hanged.[67] Most historians and commentators view the battalion through an Irish Catholic lens, and this is certainly in part how the US military saw them, since at least 50 percent were Irish and they marched into battle under a green flag emblazoned with Mexican and Irish republican imagery, including the image of Saint Patrick.[68] But we cannot ignore the many other European immigrants who fought under the flag: Germans, French, Spaniards, Italians, Poles, Swiss, English, Scots, and Canadians. And, most significantly, they were joined by Mexicans and blacks.[69]

Given the sensitivity of Anglo-American elites to black insurrection in the United States, especially where it was suspected that antiwhite rebellion found solidarity with "dark-skinned" Europeans, as in the case of Gabriel's Rebellion, the brutal force used to extinguish such threats was wholly in keeping with white weakness. The interpretation of the San Patricios, European migrants taking sides with "inferior races" against Anglo-Saxons, spelled disaster for the prospects of continued white rule: The "traitors" reflected the existence of an enemy within who was willing to break with Anglo-Saxon hegemony. While a number of theories have been offered to account for their desertion, ranging from Catholic solidarity, to reaction against nativist mistreatment, to financial gain, the events that led to the Mexican immortalization of the San Patricios as heroes of the Mexican-American War testify to the existence of Irish, although not only Irish, in America who fought for the defense of an enemy state where slavery was outlawed, thereby defending its independent status against US expansion into the slave state of Texas and across the Southwest. Their participation was part of a broader fight-back in solidarity with Mexicans, who were already signified as a "nonwhite" racial group in the United States. They represented resistance against, but ultimate defeat by, those who believed they had the force of Manifest Destiny on their side. Though Mexico was defeated, the Caucasian split could never be completely bridged, since inequality, inherent to the emerging capitalist system both within and outside the European nation-states, would always lead to differentiation within the "white race."

Manifest Destiny is usually thought of as a confident expression of the belief in Anglo-American progress. Coined in 1845 by the journalist John L. O'Sullivan, the ideology followed two periods of economic crisis—1818 and 1839—in the United States. While territorial expansion was a key response to economic limitation, the ideology of expansion—that it was the predestined outcome of a privileged Anglo-American creed ordained by providence—is not a universalist or rationalist justification; rather, it is an irrationalist argument that transforms the limitation of an irrational crisis-ridden, albeit emergent, social system into a particularistic legitimation of white privilege. Progress was not therefore the universal condition of all human beings but the invisible condition of Anglo-Americans made visible, no longer an objective scientific fact but a mystical force determining the volition of the white race. War with Mexico provided an opportunity to test and prove the truth of this reactionary credo. Nonetheless, victory would have to come to terms with two important responses: Mexicans fought back with ferocity (after all, this was a war) and Europeans expressed solidarity with the Mexican cause. Where both responses merged, the unity voiced a refusal of the imposed limit point of capitalist expansion.

Our argument is not that the whiteness thesis is disproved by the existence of "race traitors" but that the thesis wrongly assumes an internally cohesive whiteness that expands exponentially, without splitting, in order to accommodate new "recruits." The historical record suggests otherwise. Whiteness is intrinsically weak—fractured in its origin—and it is only after we are able to grasp the internal weakness of whiteness that we begin to understand the relative strength of racial doctrine. The power of limitation it placed on possibility was related not to the strength of whiteness but to the prior defeat of the radically subjective.

If the revolutionary struggles of 1848 were significant for Europe, the Mexican-American War provided a catalyst for the emerging form of racial doctrine in the United States. It is well known that the war ultimately crystallized into the antagonistic forces of the American Civil War. Continued racial segregation and black immiseration, as evidenced by the stripping away of the gains made by the Civil War, reflected the concern that the cause of racial degeneration, of racial mixing, must be held at bay. The irrationalization of equality took its cue from that deemed to initiate white superiority, the external manifestation (territorial and material expansion) of internal drive: Manifest Destiny. The elusive quality of internally ordained destiny reflected a shift from revolutionary democratic conceptions of the nation built on the rights and choices of individuals—stepping-stones to a universal society—to particularistic conceptualizations where nations were the natural consequence of historical evolution. In the latter sense, a perfect, fixed, and predetermined national endpoint was envisaged in terms of an exclusive culture withheld from those deemed culturally apart. The modern "Enlightened" idea of autonomous choice, implicit in the belief in human-determined social change, was undermined, for example, in Ernest Renan's culturalist transhistorical conception of nationhood. Renan's formulation shared an antihumanist conservativism inherent to racial determinism's rejection of the universal human capacity for change in favor of a culturally fixed "end state"—the culmination of an evolutionary predestined process.

Manifest destiny as a conservative ideology embodied, albeit in a provisional sense, one component of what Etienne Balibar calls "theoretical racism": "a philosophy of history which makes history the consequence of a hidden secret revealed to men about their own nature and their own birth."[70] It "makes visible the invisible cause of the fate of societies and peoples." An "ideal synthesis of transformation and fixity, of repetition and destiny . . . substitutes the signifier of culture for that of race," attaching the secret "of heritage, ancestry, rootedness."[71] Of course, whites, including the slave masters of old, were exclusively privileged in the process of Reconstruction, and "off-whites" previously excluded from such privilege joined them. However, San Patricio action had indicated that there were sections of the so-called white race that could not be trusted as automatic national regenerates. The fear precipitating conservative reaction to slave uprisings after the revolutionary war was extended throughout Reconstruction. Reaction ensured that emancipation would not affect a loss in white privilege. In effect, separate but equal was a metaphor for nondilution: legitimized retribution against blacks and any white transgressors (through the ascription of guilt by association). Preserving the color line was a strategy of prevention; averting the race suicide of Caucasian split was a presupposition of racial doctrine that included the invisible force theory of race war later instrumentalized by American eugenics and promoted by Theodore Roosevelt's "warfare of the cradle."[72] Roosevelt condemned Chamberlain's theory of Aryan/Teutonic supremacy as inconsistent, historically flawed, feebleminded, insane, and irrational not because he disagreed on the question of white superiority but because acceptance of such a theory would have undermined the contribution made to civilization by the non-Germanic Anglo-American creed, which, of course, served as a justification for American imperialism.[73] As we will later discuss, interwhite antagonism was propelled by interimperial rivalry, but for now it is important to underline that eugenics secularized the invisible force of Manifest Destiny, substituting the mysticism of the divine for that of the hard material of mental causation located in the heads of both the racially clear-minded and the degenerate feebleminded—a catch-all diagnosis for biopsychocultural degeneracy. "Unwhite" temperament was signified in the pathologization of *refusal* to accept one's place in the color-coded spectrum of racial hierarchy, the limit point of equality. It was a refusal shared by many, and it terrified the white ruling class.

## RACIAL REVENGE

It is in such a context that we need to situate "the problem of the Mexican." As Gilbert Gonzales and Raul Fernandez explain, the colonial exploitation of Mexico by the United States in the late nineteenth century undercut Mexico's independent socioeconomic development, precipitating Mexican migration into the United States. Moreover, colonialism justified itself through an assemblage of dismissive racial stereotypes: "A critical mass of pathological cultural norms affecting Mexican society known generally by the term 'the Mexican Problem'" had, by the 1920s, taken root in the United States and framed the reception of Mexican migrants.[74] Significations of the Mexican as degenerate built on the assumption that the population of Mexico was in large part a mongrelized biopsychocultural hybrid of Indian and European types. The Mestizo "mixed-breed" exemplified the worst of each type, differentiated from the minority of white Mexicans at the top of the racial hierarchy and "full-blooded" Indians at the bottom. The attribution of the Mexican "mind as essentially Oriental"[75] drew on and reinforced so-called similarities with Asiatic, Mongolian, and/or African peoples, and was only superseded by the designation of Mexican migrants as peons, low-class Mestizo workers. The peon was additionally signified in the common parlance of racial doctrine, likened to plantation blacks of the US South. The "lazy Southern darkey" was included within a more extensive array of inferior traits "prone to excessive drinking and promiscuity, lethargic, unambitious, docile, unintelligent, fatalistic, superstitious, cowardly, cruel, uneducated but trainable under the right influence."[76] Such significations underpinned the distance between Mexicans and Americans such that their segregated presence in the United States as unequal was legitimized, the Mexican placed beyond the limit of equality.

It was precisely the key ideological link between Manifest Destiny and fears of "the Mexican problem," the invisibility of drives as an explanation of social advance and decline, that underpinned reaction. This was exemplified in Wallace Thompson's widely read book *The Mexican Mind: A Study of National Psychology*. In it we find the Mexican mind as a hybridized result of two races—the "white and the red," meaning the European and the Indian—and it is within this hybrid that we are alerted to the negative impact of interracial miscegenation, of "races which in mind and in living were as far apart as the globe which separated them."[77] Following in the footsteps of Gobineau's history of race struggle and the environmental relativism of Nott and Gliddon, Thompson redrew a history of transatlantic colonialism through the prism of heroic white racial conquest over the red by the Anglo-Saxon in the North and the Spanish in the South. But the Mexican, aka Mestizo, provided a cautionary lesson of what happens when the white and red races amalgamate despite the biocultural influence of superior European values: revolution. In his book, Thompson states the following:

> Millions of the Mexicans, mixed blood and Indian, remained red, and red they are to this day, and red they have shown themselves to all the world for these past ten bloody years. They do not dress in war paint and their tomahawks are great long corn knives which readily disembowel their adversaries but do not lend themselves to the more gentle art of scalp-taking. But Indian they are and today, behind the flimsy curtain of their Spanish language and religion, behind the tattered, flapping blinds of what was once a copy of the American Federal Constitution, behind the blatant Marseillaise of modern socialism, they leap in savage war dances and look forward to the day when Indian communism (not Marxian socialism) shall rule, when the white man with his mines and oil wells shall be forgotten and Indian demagogues and Indian priests shall rule their ways and their thoughts.[78]

This reversion to "strange Indian psychologies" spelled the demise of white rule.[79] But although Thompson thought the "Indian in physical type and in spiritual and mental temperament" was inferior to the "mind of the black man, . . . the brown man of the Mediterranean, . . . even the yellow Oriental," such negative racial significations drew the oppressed together in a biopsychocultural matrix of national advance and decline.[80]

The relationship between Asian migration and criminality had already been established by the 1875 Page Act, when Congress excluded from entry "persons convicted of 'crimes involving moral turpitude' and prostitutes."[81]

The implication of racial degeneracy carried by immigrant, specifically Chinese, prostitution due to presumed immoral influence on white male patrons was made explicit in the 1882 Chinese Exclusion Act. But an 1877 congressional report on the proposed Act explicitly tied controls to the filtering of mental capability: "There is not sufficient brain capacity in the Chinese race to furnish motive power for self-government. Upon the point of morals, there is no Aryan or European race which is not far superior. . . ."[82] The charges of decline came together most explicitly in the quota and literacy restrictions of the 1924 Immigration Act, and although the families of Russian Jews fleeing religious persecution were exempt from the literacy test, no such exemption was entertained for those escaping political persecution. Anti-American political acts had already been paired with immigration threat in the 1903 Anarchist Act and the 1917 and 1918 Immigration Acts. The 1917 Act "exclude[d] from the United States not only individual advocates of violent revolution but also those who advocated sabotage or belonged to revolutionary organizations" and allowed for the deportation "of any alien who at any time after entry was found preaching such doctrines."[83] The biopsychocultural cause of white decline had a history that brought political resistance against oppression into the orbit of race war, but it would only explicitly come of age when white panic surfaced in debates over the presumed psychology and theory of *black* racial revenge following World War I and the Bolshevik Revolution.

One of the main weaknesses with the ideology of white supremacy was that it had to increasingly come to terms not only with nationally internal divisions represented by blacks, browns, reds, and yellows, but also with those divisions experienced as racially internal to whiteness. White division expressed itself most forcefully in the interimperial rivalries of European nation-states competing for new territories and resources in the emerging reach of global capitalism. Competitive international state rivalries unleashed a drive for capitalist expansion that did not serve the cause of white racial unity. The idea of a unified and superior white race was difficult to defend when white nations went to war with and destroyed one another. And this is precisely one of the key factors that elevated the liberation confidence of oppressed peoples in the period running up to and including World War I. Related to the confidence of oppressed groups, and potentially more cataclysmic for white elites, was the defeat of a white nation by a "racially inferior" nation, as in the case of Ethiopian victory over Italy in 1896 and Japanese victory over Russia in 1905. As Paul Lauren argues, such defeats had a devastating effect on European and American white racial arrogance, for they inspired the confidence of blacks and elevated the prospect of their racial revenge. As one French reporter commented, Japanese victory signaled "revenge which effaced the centuries of humiliations . . . ; it was the awakening hope of Oriental peoples, it was the first blow given to the other race, to that accursed race of the west."[84] The spark of black confidence expressed itself in William Du Bois' cogent critique of the color line and the formation of movements that took their force from the principle of equality, such as the Niagara Movement, the NAACP, the Pan African Congress, the Pan-Asian Society in China, the National Congress of British West Africa, the Union Intercoloniale and Ligue Universelle pour la Défense de la Race Noire by intellectuals from the French colonies and the West Africa Students' Union in London. A key development was the empowered black soldier, enlisted in the *war to end all wars*, a witness not only to whites killing whites but to his own moral authority in killing white enemy soldiers in the name of universal freedom. Riots and public lynching were symptomatic of the white response awaiting uniformed black soldiers in southern US cities. In this respect, the anticolonial clarion call instigated by the Bolshevik's support for the right to self-determination, which put Western imperialists on the defensive, was significant.[85] The perception that the "color-blind" Soviet Union occupied the moral high ground on race and that its authority would appeal to and catalyze the growing confidence of the oppressed against the racial order had a major impact on how European and American elites interpreted their domestic and colonial populations. Taken together with the growing experience in the colonies of blacks fighting back, the early twentieth century ushered in a new era of fear of imminent white decline on the part of the transatlantic Anglo-American elite, and the fear of racial revenge emerged in the interpretation of radical blacks as the carriers of white racial ruin.

Diplomatic concern following World War I was that black reaction to white supremacy would dissolve white rule. This was confirmed in the Red Summer riots of 1919 across the United States[86] as white supremacy was confronted by black confidence, embodied in the returning rights-conscious black soldier, and the demand for equality denied by Woodrow Wilson's veto at the Paris Conference. Riots erupted simultaneously across Britain, directed at resident blacks and Lascar seamen in the port cities of Cardiff, Liverpool, and Glasgow.[87] The false portrayal of black activism as communist activism—for instance, such as that leveled at Marcus Garvey's Universal Negro Improvement Association and African Communities (Imperial) League—grew in currency and paralleled the later stigmatization of the Jews in Nazi Germany. As Frank Furedi makes clear, elite fear manifested in the response to what was interpreted as the dangerous race consciousness of the oppressed, especially that of Pan-Africanism. The interpretation of race consciousness depoliticized the demand for equality. Furedi cites Herbert A. Miller's widely read and influential 1924 study *Races, Nations and Classes: The Psychology of Domination and Freedom* which argued that the oppressed were mentally disturbed. The diagnosis of Irish, Jews, and blacks as suffering from "oppression psychosis," an inferiority complex, assumed that they constituted a socially dangerous destabilizing force instigated by their hypersensitive exaggerated response:

> [By] focusing on the subjective disposition of the individual, the wider structural influences became marginal to the analysis. The main point of discussion was the mental state of the oppressed rather than the experience of oppression. Oppression psychosis, which masqueraded as a scientific description of mental symptoms, became a condemnation of those who questioned the legitimacy of racial domination.[88]

The diagnosis was characteristic of white defensiveness: locating the problem not within the structural maintenance of white supremacy but within the abnormal psychologies of the inferior races. Emboldened black retaliation took its place within the interpretative "color problem" framework of racial proximity and distance, the pseudoscience of classification developed as a self-interpretation of white weakness—eugenics—and the crushing blow instigated against white rule. The irrationality of capitalism's inequality-ridden world system of exploitation and the reaction against it gave rise to an interpretation of the demand for equality that presumed the irrationality of those who fought back.

The psychologization of race would set the parameters through which transatlantic elites framed race relations, especially after World War II, but medical diagnosis could not stem the tide of demand for universal equality. In the twentieth century, social democracy institutionalized an ambivalent subculture of revenge that gained leverage from the reach of the Bolshevik Revolution. While the Holocaust and Hiroshima represented the full crystallization of the dystopic destruction of hopeful subjects, the rise of "Third World" movements for self-determination and of cold war civil rights epitomized hope's vitality in *transcending* the conditions of inequality; possibility infused the passing of the British Empire co-opted by American hegemony. The demand for equality held a mirror to reaction embodied in the class compromise of twentieth-century welfare capitalism, contesting the "permanent, predictable, inevitability" of white rule, insetting the demise of imperial national cultures built on the reduction of the human race to facta. It is within this demise that we, in Chapter 3, situate the postwar politics of "race relations."

CHAPTER THREE

# FROM SOCIAL DEMOCRATIC RACE RELATIONS TO MULTICULTURAL CAPITALISM

## THE ANTIRADICAL ROOTS OF POSTWAR RACE RELATIONS POLICY

In this chapter we set out to demonstrate how the contest between radical subjectivity and conservatism played out in relation to racial doctrine in the twentieth century. We focus specifically on the post–World War II era stretching from the Macmillan/Kennedy to the Thatcher/Reagan administrations in Britain and the United States. Our aim is to demonstrate how the concept of equality was gradually redefined such that economic considerations diminished in importance, being substituted by the politics of recognition. The latter was to become the hallmark of an economy of mind delimited by ethnic considerations. Not only was the emergence of multicultural capitalism in keeping with market discipline in that capitalist crisis entailed the greater immiseration of working people, but the irrationalization of equality—that is, the equal economy of mind—made a new virtue out of the absence of economic well-being for the majority of the human population. As we will demonstrate, just as social democratic race relations drew on the historical legacy of racial doctrine while transforming its basic tenets for a post–Holocaust era, multicultural capitalism would subvert those very terms of reference within the renewed contest between radical and conservative subjectivity entailed by the intensified and collapsing capital-labor postwar settlement.

Two key developments discussed in the preceding chapters must merge in any exploration of the social democratic welfare capitalist response to race: the interpretation of reaction against racism as oppression psychosis and of racist perpetration as authoritarianism; both developments informed the policy target of postwar approaches to "race relations." We do not wish to imply that these analytical constructs easily translated unchanged into a state response to race; they did not. Nor do we intend to argue that there existed a single unchanging state response. But they did provide a framework that was readily drawn on by policy makers, specifically because they both in different ways provided explanations for what the political classes understood as the dynamic of race relations.

Writing in 1921, one exponent of the oppression psychosis theory, sociologist Herbert A. Miller, laid out terms that would encapsulate the future race relations policy concerns of the transatlantic elite:

> In America we have inherited all the oppression problems of Europe and out of them we are trying to build up a cooperating democracy in which men may rise to their full human dignity. One-tenth of our population is Negro with its actual or potential psychoses, and approximately one-third of the remainder is either foreign born or of foreign-born stock. Counting the Irish, it is no exaggeration to say that there are in the United States more than twenty million people who are more or less psychopathic on account of one or all forms of oppression previously or at present experienced in Europe.[1]

Victims of oppression were psychopathic or potentially so. Moreover, such victims were not necessarily black; rather they shared a common link with Europeans, who had also been oppressed. These were no isolated musings, and Miller was no segregationist or eugenicist. Indeed, he lost his university position in 1931 for purportedly holding liberal views on race. The ever-growing popularity of Alfred Adler's theory of inferiority complex stressed the social determinants of inferiorization against which the individual may aggressively overcompensate by asserting a sense of superiority over others. Influenced by Nietzsche's "will to power," Adler's sense of optimism brought irrationalism into interpretations of race, and its influence on the later theory of the authoritarian personality provides a bridge to social democratic approaches to "race relations."

Whether we like it or loathe it, Miller's "diagnosis" included a remedy. He believed there was a "cure" for oppression psychosis, a prescribed treatment for the individual that doubled as a social intervention. For Miller, writing before World War II and Auschwitz, individual feelings of inferiority/superiority and social discrimination were mutually reinforcing. If human dignity was to be salvaged, then society would have to change. Miller's interventions were part of a broader emergence of American Left liberalism increasingly disaffected with capitalist individualism and enamored by the Soviet Union, especially its stand against Western foreign policy and the reflection of such on domestic injustice. Miller advised:

> Some day minorities will assert themselves in Africa. A solution of the whole problem can come only as the result of the application of the principles being used in the Soviet Union. . . . Consciousness that the present menace of minorities is based on irrationality and injustice is the beginning of wisdom.[2]

The pairing of injustice with irrationality brings politics into the remit of psychology. A series of injunctions are justified via the purported effect of mental abnormality, and a solution is presented that alters the terms of emancipation. Socialism as practiced in the Soviet Union was the antidote to the psychopathology caused by unfettered capitalist individualism. However, as Fred Siegel[3] notes, left-leaning liberalism really took off during the Great Depression of the 1930s. It emerged from and included within it the dual streams of cultural libertarianism and economic statism, both of which had roots in the antipathies that emerged out of World War I against Wilsonianism. Modern liberalism, argues Siegel, was epitomized by the founder and editor of *The New Republic*, Herbert Croly, and the writer and public intellectual Randolph Bourne. In his book *The Promise of American Life*, Croly envisioned a political nationalism that would replace what he saw as the narrow individualism of Jeffersonian democracy. In an industrial society, argued Croly, the federal government should provide for the amelioration of poverty. The bargaining power of labor unions must be strengthened, large corporations should be nationalized, and the power of the middle class, including the small business sector, should be held in check. Likewise, Bourne railed against the political corruption of puritanical middle-class capitalism, advocating state administration by a new aristocracy, a priestly class of intellectuals, poets, and social scientists. The tension and convergence between cultural libertarianism and economic statism contained an antimodernist sentiment that drew on Nietzsche. Bourne, writing during World War I and against war with Germany, held a disdain for American popular culture as the secularized degradation of the urban masses, the epitome of laissez-faire capitalism, from which the individual should be liberated. He took an antiassimilationist stance, arguing that immigrants to the United States would always retain a spiritual link to their distinct culture. Both his advocacy of a "Trans-National America" and antiwar sentiment drew on admiration for the "folk cultures" of Europe, especially the German, approval for which was buttressed by an idealization of the German welfare state. Bourne's writing and ideas predated the rise of German National Socialism, and he did not live to experience Hitler or subsequent developments in the Soviet Union after the Bolshevik Revolution. However, both National Socialism and Stalinism would have a significant impact on the development of liberalism in the 1930s and beyond.

Roosevelt's New Deal was, of course, as ideologically significant as it was economically essential in providing capitalism with a response to the Great Depression. The Soviet Union increasingly hailed by the liberal Left as *the* model for the future prosperity of mankind—"a future," proclaimed Lincoln Steffens, "that works," provided a modifiable blueprint through which the exigencies of capitalist inequality could be held in check or, as some believed, eradicated. In 1934 during a visit to the Soviet Union, H. G. Wells interviewed Joseph Stalin. Though Wells was enamored with the Soviets, he put it to Stalin that Roosevelt and the New Dealers were in fact building socialism in America without a violent revolution and, in this respect, provided a more satisfactory route to egalitarianism. In effect, the United States had taken on board the communist venture into state planning and nationalization, thus making redundant any need—undesirable to Wells—for a proletarian dictatorship. Of course, Stalin disagreed not with Roosevelt's use of state planning but with the contention that socialism could succeed without a dictatorship, which *had*, after all, put Stalin in his current position. (As is discussed in Chapter 5, Stalin would eventually dispense with the proletariat [but not dictatorship] as the agent of history.) Wells' departing words were as follows:

> At the present time there are in the world only two persons to whose opinion, to whose every word, millions are listening: you and Roosevelt. Others may preach as

much as they like; what they say will never be printed or heeded. I cannot yet appreciate what has been done in your country; I only arrived yesterday. But I have already seen the happy faces of healthy men and women and I know that something very considerable is being done here. The contrast with 1920 is astounding.[4]

Though Wells' commendation of Soviet prosperity was shared by many in the West, and not only by the Left, it is important to grasp the peculiarities of the Stalinist incarnation of communism that so enthused Western pro-statist elites of the interwar period. Although not directly drawn on, most salient was Stalin's *socialism in one country* (SIOC) thesis, developed in 1924 amid the defeat of international proletarian insurrection, specifically those of the German and Hungarian workers' movements. It was such defeats that catalyzed the move from the Bolshevik Revolution based ostensibly on the overthrow of minority by majority working-class rule, to the establishment of a ruling elite oligarchy. Stalin saw his mission as that of turning the pessimism of international defeat into a legitimization of his own power position in the Soviet Union. Consequently, SOIC supplanted Lenin's call for international revolution with a nationalistic momentum through which workers could be disciplined domestically. If communism was by its very nature a call to the international brotherhood of man, a breaking of bourgeois capitalist nation-state boundaries to be implemented by the proletarian majority, then SOIC, intuited Leon Trotsky, was its antithesis: a political defeat of the working class transformed into Stalin's iron fist and presented as the virtuous revolutionary strategy of national defense. While SOIC became the official policy of the Soviet Union under Stalin, the adoption of state planning and nationalization of industry in the capitalist West provided the impetus for an incorporative nationalism that to no lesser extent included the pessimistic stance of defeated international socialism: a need to keep workers in their place. For the New Dealers, social democracy—in effect the potential defeat of *international* socialism—presented an optimistic vision for the *national* rehabilitation of America beyond the perils of laissez-faire individualism.

The logic of social democracy provided a working class buy-in to capitalism that satisfied the liberal elites' fear of revolutionary socialist challenge. Although social democracy was a step forward in terms of the everyday living conditions of the working classes in the West, as an elite strategy for social rehabilitation, it included a deep-rooted suspicion of the urban masses, an antipathy that dovetailed with, but inverted, the anticapitalism of cultural libertarianism. Working-class revolution was rarely entertained with much validity by Left liberals. The theory of a mass urban consumerist mindset, put forward by Bourne as a challenge to capitalist degradation not so much as a defense of the working classes but as an attack against the decadent middle class culture of capitalism, could quite easily be inverted when the working classes apparently complied with their own degradation, especially when the very same working classes that the Marxist Left had idolized as historical agents of human emancipation were seen to support Hitler. By the end of World War II, it was this deep suspicion of the working classes that found an ally in the theory of the Authoritarian Personality (AP).

As we noted in Chapter 1, the AP thesis was in part founded on the need to account for the rise of National Socialism despite the powerful position of the German labor movement prior to World War II. On this account, which was shaped by its wartime context, the failure of the proletariat to revolutionize Germany was located within the personality structure of authoritarians who, due to pathological patriarchical child-rearing patterns, were thought more inclined to follow the dictates of a charismatic leader, hence Hitler's "success." AP's American significance lay in the critique of modern mass society, its rational calculation and puritanical discipline, which AP exponents believed made it probable that "the masses" would comply slavishly with the ethos of the most extreme example of mass-market consumerism—the United States—thus making it likely that fascism would eventually overturn America. It was this indictment of the masses that fused with the theory of oppression psychosis and came to exert a key influence on the development of postwar race relations theory and policy. The key to their fusion was domination. If domination in early childhood was the root cause of authoritarianism, then by virtue of their experience, the oppressed could become authoritarian. The merging of what on face value look like contradictory tenets—suspicion and celebration of the working classes—within the social democratic compact made sense to elites whose aim was to hold capitalism together, and it was a fusion that would manifest in various political guises throughout the welfare era.

## HATE IN BLACK AND WHITE

In her seminal study of the influence of psychology on US social policy, Ellen Herman vividly illustrates how political elites "depended upon explanations for racial crises that were founded, as theories of Third World development and revolution were, on such psychological basics as personality development, the roles of frustration and aggression in motivating behaviour, and the logic of identity formation."[5] As Herman notes, champion of the Swedish welfare state, Gunnar Myrdal paired social policy intervention with psychological explanations of "race relations," including, for example, "Psychic traits . . . The Protest Motive and Negro Personality, [and] The Psychopathology of Lynching."[6] Moreover, the central tenets of Myrdal's *An American Dilemma*, widely hailed as a monument to "good race relations," heavily influenced the Truman administration's *To Secure These Rights*, the pivotal *Brown v. Board of Education* 1954 court ruling, the Moynihan Report's extension of a legal equality framework, and the Kerner Commission's response to urban "race riots" across America in the mid-1960s. Irrational tendencies would be tackled through state intervention; removing discriminatory barriers would in turn facilitate greater autonomy and racial integration. One did not have to buy in wholesale to all the tenets of AP, but its significance was that in its identification of a "new 'anthropological' species . . . the authoritarian type of man,"[7] AP provided the most developed Left critique of illiberal behavior, and to a liberal establishment keen to bolster its moral authority against the Soviets, the accommodation of Left critique as a mainstay of what Mary Dudziak has called "Cold War civil rights" provided a crucial step toward the rehabilitation of the West.[8]

After Auschwitz, the biological basis of "race relations" was discredited to all but a few isolated extremists; however, the legacy of race endured in its psychocultural form. Nowhere is this more clearly articulated than in the 1959 five-part television documentary titled *The Hate That Hate Produced*, which introduced the American public to the Nation of Islam (NOI), featuring interviews with Malcolm X and other black leaders and footage of their political speeches and rallies. Researchers working at the University of Columbia make the point that the documentary was instrumental in pairing the NOI "with hate in the public mind, playing on white fear and contrasting the 'Black racists' of the NOI with more moderate, 'sober-minded Negroes'—a binary that was subsequently reinforced in countless media portrayals."[9] This is most certainly correct, but it is important to add that the program's title, while demonizing NOI and black radicalism, represents the appeal of their hate as being an effect, a reaction against white hate. What strikes us about the documentary, particularly the interview with Malcolm X, is the extent to which black reaction is framed within the theory of oppression psychosis and consequently, due to its inherent irrationalism, as authoritarian—a vicious cycle by which authoritarian treatment breeds an authoritarian reaction through its oppressive dominance. Moreover, Malcolm X works within this rubric. It is worth exploring in detail some of the interview exchanges. For example, when reporter Louis Lomax asks Malcolm X if a white man can join his temple, he replies:

> That's one of the reasons why most people think Mr Muhammad teaches hate. But, if there is a rattle snake in the field who has been biting your brothers and your sisters and you go and tell them that that's the rattle snake, and all of the harm that's ever come *to* them, has come from that particular source, well then that rattler will think that the warner is teaching hate, he'll go back and tell the other snakes that "this man is teaching hate, this man is teaching hate," but it's not hate it's just that when you study people who have been harmed and discover the source of their injury, the source of all of their defects and you begin to point out that source, it's not that you hate the source, but your love for your people is so intense, so great, that you must let them know what is wrong with them, what is the cause of their ills and this is one of the basic factors I believe [is] involved when people think, or when the propaganda is put out that Mr Muhammad teaches hate, he teaches black people to love each other and our love for each other is so strong that we don't have any room left in our heart.[10]

Malcolm X attempts to break from the signification of authoritarianism by arguing that "it is not that you hate the source." Additionally, that black people are being taught "to love each other" signifies compassion and virtue, which breaks from authoritarianism. However, if the experience being described is interpreted within the framework of "oppression psychosis," it automatically becomes dangerous to the liberal order, for oppression must explode in the face of the oppressor. This, of course, feeds into Myrdal's "American dilemma," but it is embellished within the AP framework. In the documentary, host Mike Wallace informs us that:

> This is the psychology of the Muslims; they know that the American negro is angry because he's been cast in an inferior role, and they seek to convert him to the Muslim cause by drenching him in a doctrine of black supremacy. These, then, are the Muslims; these are the things they're saying, preaching, teaching their children, and they are the most powerful of the black supremacist groups.[11]

Let us adapt Wallace's quote to our discussion. Look at what happens when we substitute "Nazi" for "Muslim," "German" for "American Negro," and "Aryan" for "black":

> This is the psychology of the *Nazis*; they know that the *German* is angry because he's been cast in an inferior role [*to the Jews*], and they seek to convert him to the *Nazi* cause by drenching him in a doctrine of *Aryan* supremacy. These, then, are the *Nazis*; these are the things they're saying, preaching, teaching their children, and they are the most powerful of the *Aryan* supremacist groups.

The logic could have been lifted without much alteration from the AP thesis, illustrating just how easily the discourse of antioppression can be turned against the oppressed. That the oppressed or hard-done-by adopt a stance of hatred toward their oppressor and that this hatred is passed on to their children is a recipe for the development of later authoritarians. But equally significant is that the presenter accepts that blacks *have* been cast in an inferior role. This is not questioned. White immorality (at least that of some whites) is expressed as liberal doubt. Continual reference is made throughout the documentary to "the destruction of the white man" and "the doomed white race." These phrases or "prophesies" are emphasized by the report representing racism as a phenomenon that can just as easily be perpetrated by blacks against whites. They also key into a sense of white weakness, that there is a section of whites who by the very nature of their personality structure, their tendency toward mental rigidity and hate, could precipitate an equally rigid black reaction, thus leading to the collapse of liberal America.

The construction of racism as a problem sets up liberalism as the antidote, but it is an intervention that bridges domestic and international concerns. Consider the following excerpt from the documentary as it shifts in focus to the relationship between the Middle East, Black Nationalism, and black racism. Mike Wallace continues:

> The leader of the United African Nationalist Movement is James R. Lawson, sometimes public relations man and black nationalist, a man who says he has authorisation to bring greetings from the United Arab Republic's president Nasser to black nationalist groups here in America. Newsbeat asked Mr Lawson to explain the nature of his organisation and its aims. As Lawson talks with reporter Lomax, you will see the strong pro-Arab feeling that pervades the teachings of the black racists.[12]

We present this quote because it places the construction of racism as a political problem within the international ascendency of American liberalism. The approach of the Eisenhower administration to Nasser is well known. US–UAR relations were particularly strained during the 1950s, specifically in light of the Soviet-Egyptian arms deal, the failed Anderson mission, and negotiations around the Aswan Dam. Eisenhower's Omega Policy aimed to reduce Nasser's prestige as a pan-Arab leader by cultivating a more suitable replacement in King Saud. Later rapprochement with Nasser failed to dissuade him from succumbing to further Soviet influence.[13] The documentary's inclusion of James R. Lawson therefore draws public attention to the significant threat that Black Nationalism, as an enemy within, is presumed to pose to American interests in the Middle East. The postwar construction of liberalism as oppositional to Soviet totalitarianism had significant domestic ramifications in the construction of black authoritarianism as an internal threat. The "hate that hate produced" is a cipher of circular logic, a clear representation of how racism was being constructed as a social and political problem in the postwar period, and it provided for an equally clear intervention by the "antiracist" liberal state.

This validation was encapsulated within the concept of "hate." For the elites, "hate" connoted a politically destabilizing force, but a force that could be controlled. The concept seemingly imparted predictive value. "Hate" provided the American establishment with a rational explanation of their possible downfall. But just as importantly, the logic of "antihate" also provided the elites with a response and a means of coercing, controlling, and eliminating any threats while remaining within the proscribed moral limits of the postwar political consensus.

While the enemy remained within the logic of "hate producing hate," enmity could be tolerated. Any attempt to move outside this boundary would throw the worldview of American elites into disarray. And this is precisely what Malcolm X as a symbol of Black Power came to represent. His subsequent trip to Mecca in 1964, from which he returned with a well-publicized "new consciousness" of human commonality indicated to the American establishment that prior demonization could not be accommodated within the ideological limits set by "Freedom versus Fascism." Malcolm X had moved beyond the binary of "hate producing hate"—from inversion to subversion. As historian Manning Marable has argued, the new preacher epitomized the worst fears of US elites: An American black radical of considerable influence made a connection between the second-class treatment of African Americans; the plight of Middle Eastern, African, and other colonially oppressed people's international revolutionary struggles; and a desire for socialism. The connection, personified by this "black messiah," could not be tolerated, specifically because such a connection represented a direct challenge to the ideological sustenance of US global capitalism. In short, for US elites, the existence of Malcolm X could no longer be rationalized within the logic of "hate producing hate." In the Cold War elite worldview, Malcolm X represented the potential ideological collapse of America.

The objective of postwar race relations policy was in effect the cultivation of a new anthropological liberal type in possession of a future sense who could counter psychocultural chaos and maintain America's moral ascendency against Soviet appeals to Third World nationalism. "Liberal type" was most aptly defined by John F. Kennedy as "someone who looks ahead and not behind, someone who welcomes new ideas without rigid reactions, someone who cares about the welfare of the people—their health, their housing, their schools, their jobs, their civil rights, and their civil liberties—someone who believes we can break through the stalemate and suspicions that grip us in our policies abroad. . . ."[14] Social progress was defined within the parameters set by Cold War alignments and competing visions of the good society from which the 1964 Civil Rights Act and 1965 Voting Rights Act were conceived. Social democracy capitalized on the opportunity that Left liberalism provided, but equality retained a limit point against which Black Power was able, at times, to push forward. It was such tenets that underpinned the new urgency on questions of race, but placed together, the two "anthropological species" of the postwar period—the authoritarian and the liberal—came to frame the construction of US race relations policy, and this dynamic of postwar racial ordering would take a similar but not identical trajectory on the other side of the Atlantic.

## A MYRDAL FOR BRITAIN?

Commenting on Britain's approach to race relations, the sociologist John Solomos makes the point that the latter followed the precepts of the American model.[15] There were indeed many crucial similarities between the US Civil Rights Act of 1964 and the British Race Relations Acts of 1965 and 1968,[16] but by 1951, only 50 percent of the British population had experienced any contact with blacks, most of which had been a result of overseas service in the armed forces.[17] The response of those sympathetic to colonial migrants remained at a voluntary level without government intervention until 1965, when the first Race Relations Act was introduced. This period, bereft of government intervention, has been categorized as a laissez-faire approach,[18] and in important respects, it was. But unlike the United States, Britain's postwar relationship to race was mediated by the fall of empire and the reception of "nonwhite" colonial migrants in possession of British passports—initially West Indians and later South Asians—who entered Britain as both students and labor recruits in response to postwar UK industrial demand. Although the entry right of colonial migrants remained unrestricted until 1962, their presence refashioned the colonial concerns of elites into domestic alarm. Authorities were initially keen to hush up any sign that white Britons held prejudicial views against black students whom the British elites considered potential future leaders and allies in the colonies to which they would return. The findings of a 1951 government survey that revealed negative white attitudes toward colonial students were kept confidential for fear of the impact it might have in the colonies.[19]

It is clear that the earlier seemingly more laissez-faire postwar approach to migration was already coupled by official unease. On the arrival of the SS *Empire Windrush* in 1948 carrying 492 West Indian migrants, Labour Party officials voiced concerns that large-scale migration might negatively impact limited welfare resources. This dovetailed with the earlier opinion that the culture of "nonwhite" migrants was antithetical to that of the British race.[20] Much of the official discourse around "nonwhite" migration remained secret and was not publicly voiced until the mid-1950s. It is clear, however, that a significant official momentum toward their control occurred and that this was predicated on a need to protect what the elite interpreted as the British public's racialized sense of national identity, of which the national welfare contract between capital and labor formed a significant bedrock.

Additionally, some key early postwar studies of race relations in Britain were directly influenced by AP. Commenting on academic studies carried out in Britain between 1948 and 1958, Michael Banton censured psychodynamic approaches, criticizing colleague Anthony Richmond for interpreting racism in psychologized terms. "Severe prejudice is a response to inner feelings of anxiety and insecurity," argued Richmond, "which have their origins deep in the unconscious mind and are often derived from early childhood experiences of deprivation or frustration."[21] This fatalism gave the impression that racism was practically unchallengeable, but AP was as much interested in prevention as it was with etiology, and, in keeping with Adlerian psychology, it included sociological explanation in its search for solutions.[22] Nevertheless, psychological explanations of race relations were readily available to the postwar liberal-welfare settlement premised as it was on the need for a post-Holocaust future-orientation untainted by the past, but it was a solution whose limit point was contextualized by the postwar economic boom. Situated historically within the Labour Party's commitment to the realization of a "community that relies for its driving power on the release of all the finer constructive impulses of man,"[23] and British Conservative prime minister Harold Macmillan's 1957 celebratory but cautionary reminder to the British people that they had "never had it so good,"[24] urban unrest (interpreted as "race riots") in 1958 precipitated by whites violently attacking West Indians in Notting Hill and Nottingham seemed to confirm the view that the presence of "nonwhite" migrants elicited a dangerous response.[25] Interracial chaos would have to be remedied through the control of colonial migrants. A series of immigration controls in 1962, 1968, and 1971 specifically targeted black migrants from the Commonwealth and set the tone for the institutionalization of racism by conferring second-class status on New Commonwealth ("nonwhite") migrants. British law signaled that it was legitimate to view "nonwhite" migrants as a threat. In effect, racism became respectable.[26]

One way of understanding this development is to situate it within the tenets of postwar liberalism. In 1945, the architect of the British welfare state, Sir William Beveridge, made a case for working-class incorporation:

> Liberty means more than freedom from the arbitrary power of Governments. It means freedom from economic servitude to Want and Squalor and other social evils; it means freedom from arbitrary power in any form. A starving man is not free, because till he is fed, he cannot have a thought for anything but how to meet his urgent physical needs; he is reduced from a man to an animal. A man who dare not resent what he feels to be an injustice from an employer or a foreman, lest they condemn him to chronic unemployment, is not free.[27]

The social democratic bargain was infused by the need to avoid conditions of poverty and unemployment, conditions generally thought to have contributed to the rise of fascism, but the bargain also assumed the right of protest for the working man, and it was an assumption that, as AP theorists would interpret it, appealed to rather than dislodged any putative economic function within the personality. Thus, political elites could justify the restriction of "nonwhite" migration on the basis of their supposed threat to the limited resources—housing, education, employment, health care—of the welfare state.[28] And it was a justification that obtained consensual support from the British Trade Union Movement.[29] The limitation of capitalism, its inherent irrationalization of equality, was reproduced and institutionalized via a distributive hierarchy in which whites came first. Viewed within this framework, the Race Relations Acts (RRA) of 1965 and 1968 can be understood as attempts to meritocratize in that they endeavored to alleviate discriminatory barriers to equal public access in the receipt of goods and services in the context of the postwar class settlement. Such legal codes operated within the social democratic consensus. Particularly important was a clause in the 1965 RRA outlawing incitement to racial hatred. Mark Bonham Carter, chairman of the Race Relations Board, also set up under the 1965 RRA, was uncomfortable with the inclusion of the clause due to its illiberalism:

> By introducing a provision of this kind, one runs the danger of providing special protection for a particular group, giving ammunition to the racialist opposition. Race

relations policy should seek to convince the public that a policy of equal treatment irrespective of race is in the interests of the whole of society, and that it is not designed for the benefit of particular groups.[30]

Hatred, argued Carter, could already be catered for under the 1936 Public Order Act. By making it race-specific, he believed, the risk of white backlash increased. But the incitement to racial hatred clause did not extend or significantly alter the centrality of proof of "intent" to any subsequent prosecution, and this had been used in successful prosecutions prior to the 1965 Act.

When the National Socialist Movement launched itself under the banner of "Free Britain from Jewish Control" in 1962 at a rally attended by 5,000 people in Trafalgar Square, the ensuing battles that took place between protestors and sympathizers led to the prosecution of the National Socialist's leader Colin Jordan for the *intention*, indicated by the choice of words used in his speech, to provoke a breach of the peace.[31] "Intent" is a cardinal mainstay of liberal prosecution. It summons forth the integrity of the individual as a willful knowing agent who executes his or her actions and behaviors restrained only by the potential of causing harm to others. It is the relinquishing of "restraint" that renders one personally liable to prosecution.

The hatred clause had been promoted by Left-Labour MPs such as Fenner Brockway, who between 1953 and 1964 made nine attempts to introduce antidiscrimination legislation without success.[32] Brockway's House of Commons arguments for legislation demarcate the problem and solution of discrimination, and reveal his cognizance and appreciation of the postwar liberal approach to racism:

There are under-currents of feeling, it may even be in the subconscious, which will respond under favourable conditions towards, or retreat under unfavourable conditions from, racial equality. . . . There is a minority which is causing ill will, with serious effects. . . . That minority is not only endangering the feelings of coloured people in this country towards the British people, but may have serious effects internationally as well.[33]

Racism emanates from an emotional source that eludes consciousness and that may manifest or be triggered under specific conditions. The problem is that a section of the white population willfully exploits this latent emotion among the general population of white Britons and in so doing incites the counteremotional response of blacks. Such racial polarization will damage Britain's moral authority internationally. The emotional is freed from restraint, leading to interracial disorder, but this does not lead Brockway to advocate for state intervention as a substitute for self-restraint. In the following, Brockway outlines the limitations of state intervention:

> I recognise that there must be a limitation of the powers of legislation. Often acts of discrimination are due to prejudice, to ignorance or to irrational repulsion, and those can be removed only by education or experience. More often they are due to social and economic conditions and fears: to housing overcrowding, concern about the under-cutting of standards if unemployment comes. Those can be removed only by social and economic solutions.[34]

State legislation is not a panacea. Indeed, the solution—that is, social progress—is determined by education and economics. As John Skrentny observes, in the United States, a shift in federal civil rights policy followed the 1965–1968 urban riots. The move from nondiscrimination to compensatory affirmative action, from equal to preferential treatment, was premised on an acceptance of the existence of institutionalized discrimination.[35] Keven Yuill, in his recent appraisal of affirmative action in the United States, argues convincingly that the Myrdalian consensus was opposed to positive measures toward discrimination. Concerned to promote equality through the *removal* of barriers, a sense of voluntarism based on the belief in educative amelioration and economic progress characterized the immediate postwar period in the United States. It was only once such approaches were seen to be failing, a point attested to by wide-scale urban rioting throughout the 1960s, that affirmative action emerged as a possible solution.[36] The Myrdalian consensus is reproduced in Brockway's antidiscrimination discourse:

> I also recognise that in seeking to establish the rights of coloured people in this country, we must not invade the personal rights of our own citizens. Probably the greatest effect of colour discrimination is where the private landlady refuses lodgings to a coloured person, but I would regard it as going beyond the legitimate sphere of legislation if we were to say that persons should not have the right to decide who should enter their own homes as lodgers.[37]

The state should not intervene in the private sphere even while the effect of discrimination there manifests in its most damaging form. This opposition to positive intervention is a clear invocation of the sanctity of individual rights, and it is next contextualized within the changing global position of Britain in respect of its colonies and beyond:

Sir, I urge that a legal declaration by this House against discrimination is necessary: first, to end the kind of cases to which I have referred; secondly, to prevent reaction in the Colonial Territories when migrants from those territories return to them, and where they often exert great influence; and, thirdly, to exert an influence in territories such as South Africa which now practice discrimination.[38]

Brockway was probably one of the most radical Labour MPs of the period. He saw antidiscrimination as integral to any project of human emancipation, and it was a project that, having many adversaries, generated the cardinal contradiction of the immediate postwar liberal hour:

Recognition that all persons are born equal in rights and dignity, whatever their race, colour or religion, is the fundamental condition of social justice, liberty and peace, and I hope that the House will give me permission to introduce the Bill.[39]

The House did not do so until 1965, but the logic of the Act deviated only slightly from what Brockway had advocated. It was only after "the problems" that he had previously alluded to became more "evident" that a significant proportion of MPs agreed to legislate for antidiscrimination, but this did not entail affirmative action as it did in the United States. Specifically, the incitement to racial hatred clause, and the centrality to it of "intent," sheds light on the postwar liberal consensus on race. The clause was not modified by the 1968 Act, nor was the subject addressed in any of the specific reports on race relations published between 1965 and 1968 such as the Political and Economic Planning Report, *Racial Discrimination* (1967), the *Report of the Race Relations Board for 1966–67*, or the *Street Report* (1967). The importance of the *Street Report* and the absence of any exploration of incitement to racial hatred lay in its remit as a survey of good race relations practice from abroad, particularly the United States. Coming as it did before the Kerner Report into the Watts Riots, and prior to the 1969 US Federal Hate Crime Law, Street and its recommendations still reflected the voluntarism and optimism of the Myrdalian consensus. Consequently, in Britain the subject of "intent" only became a significant question for political debate in 1976 amid the introduction of the Race Relations Bill of that year—a point to which we will later return—but "intent" was never relinquished. As in the United States (pre-1968), the British "race relations" approach posited solutions to discrimination based on social change through the freeing of rationally willed action. The ideal subject type of liberal welfare reformism prevailed but in a racialized form: "Nonwhite immigrants," dually constructed as a "race," were perceived to threaten both in their own right and in relation to the reaction their presence and protest may incite from the "white" population. But the state's view of the subject of racism—both target and perpetrator—was that causation had an irrational base that could be inflamed by the response of the oppressed to the discrimination their presence was deemed to elicit. The "diagnosis" was to have a significant effect on those on the receiving end of social democratic racial oppression.

As in the United States, where the rise of the civil rights movement coalesced with the emergence of black power groups critical of the liberal welfarist approach to race, there emerged radical constellations who were suspicious of what they saw as liberal apologia. Following the British government's definition/acceptance of the concept of "racial disadvantage," which underpinned the 1976 Race Relations Act, antiracist activist of the British Left and director of the Institute of Race Relations Ambalavaner Sivanandan objected to the connotation that "ethnic minorities" have "special needs" to be ameliorated through "positive action." This was akin, he argued, to "breaking my legs and giving me crutches" when "the point is not to break my legs in the first place."[40] Sivanandan's apprehension emanated from a black radical Marxism based on the black subject of historical change that carried over the legacy of US Fanon-inspired Panthers. As Panther George Jackson had earlier argued, "A mature fascism exists in this country, and it exists in disguise, and the disguise takes the form of all those idiotic, ridiculous statements about a welfare state."[41] Jackson inverted AP theory, using it against the authoritarian state. But what was key for Stokely Carmichael and Charles Hamilton was that:

> [Institutional racism] relies on the active and pervasive operation of anti-black attitudes and practices. A sense of superior group position prevails; whites are "better" than blacks; therefore blacks should be subordinated to whites. This is a racist

attitude and it permeates the society, on both the individual and the institutional level, covertly and overtly.

"Respectable" individuals can absolve themselves from individual blame: *they* would never plant a bomb in a church; they would never stone a black family. But they continue to support political officials and institutions that would and do perpetuate institutionally racist policies. The *acts* of overt, individual racism may not typify the society, but institutional racism does—with the support of covert, individual *attitudes* of racism.[42]

For Carmichael and Hamilton, writing on the back of the mid-1960s urban riots, institutional racism had another name—"colonialism"—and the colonists had no real interest in liberating the colonized. The existence of blacks as an internal colony of America reinforced by institutional racism held a mirror to the liberal Myrdalian approach to race relations; in fact, in condemnation of Myrdal, the Panthers protested, "There is no 'American Dilemma.'"[43] But the authors did not argue against "intent." In distinguishing between overt and covert racism, the point was to reveal hidden intent and its institutionalized—that is, "respectable"—racist form. However, in 1971, EEO law was significantly expanded by the Supreme Court decision in *Griggs v. Duke Power Company*. Under the ruling, plaintiffs could now sue employers not only for intentional discrimination but for the disparate impact or unintentional effect of employment practices.

The criticisms resonate with Yuill's examination of "affirmative action's surprising proponents." According to Yuill, the rise of affirmative action (AA) in the United States was not a consequence of demands or pressure activated by civil rights campaigners. Rather, conservative elites were at the forefront. Hard affirmative action as we know it was driven primarily by the Nixon administration. The seeming paradox between the rise of what is most commonly thought of as a Left-liberal policy and the promotion of that policy by a conservative US president, is explained by Yuill as a consequence of the state's legitimation crisis, part of the exhaustion of postwar liberalism. As noted previously, the immediate postwar Myrdalian liberal race relations paradigm espoused voluntarism and education as antidotes: Through educational effort, society would voluntarily facilitate the integration of blacks, especially in relation to employment. The central activating principle of early postwar liberalism rested on economic growth. As the economy grew, greater wealth would facilitate civil equality. However, the continuing degradation of blacks, the absence of real changes, and the devastating urban riots that took place as a result shook liberalism. Affirmative action represented two moves: the incorporation and dilution of African American radical consciousness catalyzed by the changing relationship between labor and the state, and the loss of liberal belief in the healing power of economic progress and human voluntarism. Key was the American public's cynicism toward those civic institutions held up by Myrdal as the catalyst to racial integration: trade unions, churches, businesses, but also the collapse of confidence in government itself. This change, argues Yuill, was indicative of a growing acceptance on the part of the establishment that economic growth could no longer continue indefinitely. Consequently, because "inequality" could not be conceptualized as economic imbalance, "equality" was redefined within the limit point set by social democratic capitalism. The move from a color-blind approach to one that concentrated on "effects" or "results" elevated the state, not human will, as the arbitrator in a diminishing economy.

As the alliance with labor dissipated, voluntarism was increasingly discredited as a means of fostering black employment. As recession hit business, government intervention was more readily welcomed. Being able to demonstrate compliance with AA allowed large firms to secure government contracts. The impact on unions was negative, precipitating white backlash, but a snowballing effect on the employment of minorities was catalyzed. Under the Nixon administration, penalties for noncompliance of antidiscrimination measures were extended to all parties in receipt of federal funds, including state and local government and higher-education authorities with their ever-increasing employment roles. Moreover, the federal government was itself opened up to positive action toward the recruitment, training, and employment of minorities. In addition, support for minority business enterprise satisfied conservatives who still believed in capitalism as the only way forward and liberals who sought action aimed at the ghetto. But in effect, the moves signaled the federal government's project of dividing blacks into "manageable pieces"—in short, the creation of a black middle class.[44] As a strategy, argues Yuill, it aimed to fracture African Americans as a protest block into smaller client groups forced to compete for a piece of the federal pie with an increasing list of minority "clients": Mexican Americans, Native American Indians, Puerto Ricans, and so on.

The criterion for inclusion was "disadvantage"; however, by far the most important constituency for Nixon, not included in AA, was the "silent majority": white, middle America, portrayed as victims of crime, the perpetrators of which included black rioters, anti-Vietnam protestors, and student radicals. In line with the tenets laid down by AP, Nixon feared that white alienation as a counter to black alienation could destabilize America. But in coaxing the silent majority, Nixon laid the basis for the future self-definition of whites as victims of the preferential treatment he had sponsored—a self-perpetuating dynamic that would maintain resentments and competing equality claims to be resolved by the state referee. The importance of Nixon's policy moves, as Yuill argues, lay in the creation of nonradical "ethnically disadvantaged" competing constituencies with which the state could orientate a connection in an era characterized by the failure of liberal institutions and the relinquishing of economic growth as the means of equality. Nixon's unrelenting anticommunism, his belief in capitalism as a superior system at a time when it was being most vociferously castigated, and the need to hold American society together amid the threat of radical black politics were key to the implementation of affirmative action. However, Nixon, persuaded as he was by the theory of racially inherent intelligence, also held the view that blacks could never really be equal. For Nixon, AA was not a policy of progress but a policy of equilibrium, not of racial integration but of black division, and the balance it created was to institutionalize not equal economic opportunity but competing claims predicated on "ethnic disadvantage."

What this tells us about postwar race relations policy is that the model of liberal progress, John F. Kennedy's anthropological "liberal type," the robust individual of strident capitalist competition as the antithesis of revolutionary socialism's collective "Man" could not be retained as a counter to so-called authoritarians. This represented a diminishing optimism in human exceptionality that manifested in the redefinition of the state's constituents vis-à-vis race. Economic progress was dislocated from the project of human emancipation, the fight against oppression reduced to interethnic competition for state recognition. The "winners" would be those who could demonstrate their entitlement as victims of authoritarianism, but their prize could no longer be that of freedom, for one group's advantage would always be another group's disadvantage—hopes reduced and imprisoned in a never-ending cycle of ethnicity claims. The absence of a solution to economic inequality was transformed into a virtue: equality irrationalized.

The similarities to and differences from Britain are telling. When the British Labour Party introduced the 1968 New Commonwealth Immigrants Act, then–Labour MP Richard Crossman wrote in his diaries, "We have become illiberal and lowered the quotas at a time when we have an acute shortage of labour." Though Crossman felt the Act was an "appalling violation of our deepest principles," he supported it because he was "an MP for a constituency in the Midlands, where racialism is a powerful force." But the Act, rushed through Parliament in three days and aimed specifically at controlling Asian migration from Kenya, did not deviate from the seminal logic of *integration through limitation* applied by the 1964 Labour government, which, while anti-assimilationist, stemmed from the presumption that black migration incites reaction affecting social integration. The 1968 Immigration Act dovetailed with right-wing Conservative MP Enoch Powell's infamous "rivers of blood speech," but while Powell was chastised for his prediction that black immigration would lead to race war, his was but a more pronounced version of the Labour Party's circular argument that racist immigration control had to be conceded in order to placate racist white constituents, This consensus, cemented by the Conservative Party's implementation of the 1971 Immigration Act, is key to the British social democratic context, and one to which we will shortly return. Where the Kerner Commission found racism to be prevalent in the United States, and an indictment of white society largely unaffected by anti-discrimination legislation, thus marking a turning point from Myrdal's liberal dilemma, by the early 1970s, the party political consensus in Britain was not a response to the insurrection of alienated blacks. Consequently, AA was not implemented in the United Kingdom. Indeed, the similarity and difference between the United Kingdom and the United States vis-à-vis the placation of alienated whites lay in the historical differences that existed between their respective black populations.

In the British context, class compromise and conflict with the state had a postimperial momentum that collided with the aspirations of postcolonial subjects. In a recent interview, Sivanandan reminds us that his early advocacy for black autonomy was ostensibly a mirror that he saw as demanding a much needed realization on the part of white British workers: that in order to solicit black membership in their struggle against capitalist exploitation, racism had to be reckoned with. Black politics were meant as a first or preliminary step toward the transcendence of capitalist exploitation. He adds the following comparative observation:

> The black that is created in this country is something that is unique to Britain. When I went to lecture in the U.S.A. in 1969 I went to see Bobby Seale when he was arrested in Oakland and I was in Harlem and Oakland and places like that. And they were surprised that here was this Asian who was talking black you see. And that is unique to Britain. Black became a political colour only in Britain. And this is some of the advantage of our common colonial history you see.[45]

In Britain—more specifically, England[46]—*black* was an umbrella term under which racially oppressed peoples gathered political momentum (although there were exceptions) around citizens' rights against an exclusionary class settlement, the force of which emanated from the British state's second-class treatment of postwar "New Commonwealth" migrants. In the United States, the Black Panthers moved between a nationalist stance and an intercommunalist power to the people position reaching out beyond Black Nationalism through Marxist internationalism. Despite cross-alliances with groups such as the Chicano Brown Berets, the Puerto Rican Young Lords, and the Young Patriots Organization, black remained but one color in a rainbow coalition, and it did not evoke a shared political identity for those oppressed by racism. Rather, for the Panthers, the black population—African Americans—constituted an internal colony. Though commonalities of oppression existed with other groups such as Native American Indians, "black" remained relationally distinct. Pertinent here is that even within the Panthers, the intercommunalists and black powerists clashed, the former accusing the latter of "black racism." While a coalition of color was mobilized, the key point is that the Nixon administration's recognition of other ethnic groups through affirmative action as a bid to divide the numerically larger and historically more overwhelming African American radical power base played on the political divisions that already existed among the various mobilizations of the oppressed.

Such political divisions had no comparable base in the United Kingdom at that time. Nor, however, was "black" as a political category deemed so threatening as to require a comparable state response in the United Kingdom. The simple historical fact of "black" being a political category that united *postwar* migrants from different colonial locations meant that blacks in Britain, at least in the 1970s, were numerically not as significant as in the United States. As a much younger population, alienated blacks—the so-called second generation—came to be viewed as a significant threat much later. The Notting Hill Carnival riots that broke out in 1976 gave a taste of things to come, and the construction of moral panic around the "black mugger" was symptomatic of an appeal to alienated British whites that resonated with Nixon's anticrime stance. However, the 1976 Race Relations Act that followed, although establishing the Commission for Racial Equality and adopting a distinction between direct and indirect discrimination, can in no way be compared with the development of affirmative action in the United States. Because the state's legislative response to postwar migration was to negatively signify all "nonwhites," their putative homogeneity as a "nonwhite" presence in Britain did not present the same basis for ethnic fracture. Moreover, there was simply not the same need to divide and recognize. This came much later as an instrument of the Thatcher government.

## MULTICULTURAL CAPITALISM

> If we went on as we are then by the end of the century there would be four million people of the new Commonwealth or Pakistan here. Now, that is an awful lot and I think it means that people are really rather afraid that this country might be rather swamped by people with a different culture and, you know, the British character has done so much for democracy, for law and done so much throughout the world that if there is any fear that it might be swamped people are going to react and be rather hostile to those coming in.[47]

In 1975, three years prior to her infamous speech on "cultural swamping," then leader of the opposition Margaret Thatcher laid out the Conservative Party's antisocialist vision of "inequality" as "respect for individual difference":

> We are all unequal. No one, thank heavens, is like anyone else, however much the Socialists may pretend otherwise. We believe that everyone has the right to be unequal but to us every human being is equally important. . . . Everyone must be allowed to develop the abilities he knows he has within him, and she knows she has within her, in the way they choose.[48]

The individualism being promoted here through an unashamed celebratory acquisition of the Christian Socialist R. H. Tawney's criticism of capitalist equality as "the equal right to be unequal" draws its force and its content from its purported superiority to socialism's collective subject. Although Thatcher presents her "individual" as timeless, the desired individual exists only as the antithesis of socialism's collective. This is not merely a discursive exercise. Within the subjective interpretation of elites, it is a real contest between the subject of capitalism as a superior economic system and the subject of socialism, the inferior being. However, the constructed individual of Thatcherism must include an inherent condition of economic inequality—that condition inherent to capitalism: its irrationalism. The key ideological move on the part of Thatcherism was the separation of economics from the notion of equality. In her speech, Thatcher does not deny universalism: "Every human being is equally important"; however, the celebration of inequality relates to inherent individual difference and the Conservative Party's pledge to facilitate the expression of these putative differences. In this move we see the redefinition of equality in that it is distanced from economic universalism. Shortly before this conference, the monetarist and leading advisor to the Conservative Party, Sir Keith Joseph, argued:

> Yet is there any substitute for the entrepreneur, from the one-man businessman to the tycoon? Someone has to create the wealth. State enterprise has yet to do so. Until now it has lived off the surplus created by the private sector. But as the state sector grows—and a new subsidised private sector with it, designed to perpetuate occupational population patterns inherited from the industrial revolution—the private sector is in danger of collapsing under the burden.[49]

The distancing from economic universalism lay in a distinction between productive and unproductive labor. The former was considered integral to wealth creation, the latter with the growing state sector and a drain on capital. The state was therefore in need of restraint. Ironically, the "unproductive state sector" would under Thatcher later become integral to the co-option of black militancy, but this also reflected the conceptualization of economy as lying outside the parameters of equality. Inequality was refashioned as a quality of culture: Difference would flourish within the cultural limits of British nationalism. A solution in the sphere of inequality (as defined under Thatcherism) validated the impossibility of economic equality, and this took on a revered significance amid the defeat of the "unproductive" collectivism of the labor movement.

On coming to power in 1979, the Conservative Party was confronted by what it interpreted as three key sources of instability: an uncontrollable trade union movement, rising black militancy and criminality, and the rise of the right-wing white supremacist political party, the National Front (NF). In the 1970s, the most militant of British trade unions was the National Union of Mineworkers (NUM). In 1972, the NUM took national industrial action for higher pay, forcing the conservative Heath government to introduce a state of emergency and a three-day workweek in a bid to save energy; the miners won. This was repeated in 1974, which forced a general election in which Heath lost. The NUM leadership was primarily Stalinist and so despite its militancy was tied to the British national framework. The British Communist Party's manifesto, *Britain's Road to Socialism*, had, with Stalin's endorsement, presented the SOIC case to British workers in 1951, and this was largely followed by Left trades unions within the social democratic framework. By the time of the "winter of discontent"—widespread trade union strikes from 1978 to 1979—the predominantly nationalist unions could not move to an internationalist position. SOIC also meant that few trades unions took the racial oppression of migrant workers seriously. British workers came first. The inferior working conditions of black workers went unchallenged. Informal color bars instituted a racial division of labor in which unions were complicit.[50] In a number of disputes involving unofficial strikes by black workers, the union supported management in employing "scab" labor to break the strikes. One of the first such instances was the 1965 revolt by black workers at Red Scar Mills in Preston, Lancashire, the strike broken by white workers and stewards of the Transport and General Workers Union.

In other cases, white workers went on strike against the employment of blacks. This alienation of black workers was reproduced across the United

Kingdom, leaving them in an isolated position in respect of the labor movement. However, the growing militancy of black workers and the rise of the NF threatened to destabilize the labor-capital contract of the social democratic order, especially as the NF generated support among the white working class. In 1975 at Imperial Typewriters in Leicester, 1,100 Asian workers (out of a total workforce of 1650) came out on strike against management for cheating on bonuses. They also demanded the right to elect their own shop stewards, which was against established union procedures. The NF organized strike-breaking activities among white workers; the strike was broken, and the factory was closed down. The privileged position of the union bureaucracy as a mechanism for absorbing working-class dissent was called into question.

From the early 1970s, NF successes in the 1974 general election and local elections demonstrated that its platform of white supremacy and advocated policy of forced deportation of black migrants had resonance in areas of high immigrant settlement among both Labour and Conservative supporters. In 1976, the NF polled almost 20 percent of the vote in Leicester. In 1977, they gained 109,060 votes in London council elections. The TUC's launch in 1975 of its Equal Rights Committee and its publication *Black Workers: A Charter for Equal Opportunity* was seen as superficial by black workers and dovetailed with the launch of the broad-church Anti-Nazi League. However, the anti-Nazi stance supported by the TUC fed into a sense of British chauvinism. All mainstream British political parties were anti-Nazi, a kernel of British nationalism, as was made clear by yearly Remembrance Day commemorations of the British war effort against Hitler. Anti-Nazism did not significantly take up the all-party consensus for immigration control that had made racism respectable.

While the Labour Party canvassed against Nazism and the NF, it competed with the Conservatives to allay the fears of whites. In 1976, the Labour MP Bob Mellish appealed to white alienation:

> I am not a racist, but I am not a humbug. This tiny island of ours is not much more than a dot on the map and the time has come to face the problem. It won't go away. . . . We're bulging with more than a million unemployed, there's shortage of housing, and every family in the land, just about, is battling to maintain standards. . . . My views are not really different than Labour's policy over the years. We instituted the voucher system and that, after all, is a system of entry control. I am opposed to

the floodgates being opened so that everyone can come crowding in, much as I sympathise with those who need help.[51]

Merlyn Rees adopts the Malthusian logic of overpopulation threat to depleting social democratic resources and makes a case for the white victim of black immigration. Later, as Home Secretary, Rees would boast of his party's record, "The exclusion figures speak for themselves. . . . Over 1100 deportations were made and nearly 500 illegal immigrants removed."[52] The appeal coalesced with the increasing criminalization of blacks, who after being corralled into inner-city ghettoes, forced to live in the worst housing and vastly overrepresented in the unemployment statistics were subjected on a daily basis to police harassment through stop-and-search practices and immigration and drug raids. Black defense against such police harassment, especially after the 1976 Notting Hill Carnival riots, was increasingly portrayed by the media as evidence of criminality, of the "black mugger" in need of control and tough policing.[53] "Labour's blustering," Paul Gilroy later argued "is no less saturated with racial connotations than the Conservative's. . . . The right and left converge at key points and share an understanding of what is involved in the politics of race."[54] In 1979, the Labour Party advocated compulsory virginity checks for Asian women entering Britain at Heathrow[55] and presented a Green paper that formed the basis of the 1981 British Nationality Act introduced by the Conservative government.

But the anti-immigration rationale for dealing with extremism and white victimization was put most forcibly by Thatcher before coming to power:

In my view, that is one thing that is driving some people to the National Front. They do not agree with the objectives of the National Front, but they say that at least they are talking about some of the problems. Now, we are a big political party. If we do not want people to go to extremes, and I do not, we ourselves must talk about this problem and we must show that we are prepared to deal with it. We are a British nation with British characteristics. Every country can take some small minorities and in many ways they add to the richness and variety of this country. The moment the minority threatens to become a big one, people get frightened.[56]

In this move Thatcher undercut the NF and the Labour Party, and on coming to power, the Conservative administration stepped up its policy of criminalizing blacks as the "enemy within." When rioting erupted in Brixton in 1981 against the Metropolitan Police's new *Swamp 81* stop-and-search policy that targeted "suspicious" blacks, the government response was co-option of "respectable" minorities. The newly appointed minister for race relations George Young summed up his party's response:

It helps if there are more black councillors, JPs, solicitors, accountants and other professionals. It is happening now, slightly faster with the Asian community than with the West Indians. It's not the whole answer of course. The middle class will never absorb two million people. We've got to back the good guys, the sensible, moderate, responsible leaders of ethnic groups. If they are seen to deliver, to get financial support from central government for urban projects, then that reinforces their standing and credibility in the community. If they don't deliver people will turn to the militants.[57]

The emergence of a black middle class was to be enhanced through state funding of urban projects targeted toward *ethnic* groups. The implication that the economy could not expand to include all migrants, even if it was accommodating some Asians, presented an argument not only for the division and recognition of *different ethnic groups* by the state as a means of diluting the protest of working-class blacks but an understanding that equality lay outside the orbit of economics. This was reflected in the terms set by the government-sponsored Rampton and Scarman inquiries.[58] The former concluded that racism was a psychological problem, the result of individual prejudice that could be absolved through the promotion of multicultural education.[59] Scarman advocated giving black people a stake in the system so as to ensure "social stability."[60] The government responded through the allocation of its 270 million Inner-City Partnership Funds, which were dispersed through the Department of the Environment to local authorities and implemented at first mostly by Labour-controlled local councils such as the Greater London Council but also through Conservative local administrations such as Bradford City Council. A grant system was established through which black defense groups were brought into the state, recognized, and co-opted into an emerging multicultural framework that broke the demand for economic and political solutions to inequality.

But the limits to economic solutions really became clear when the conservatives crushed the miner's strike of 1984–1985. With the defeat of the most militant section of the working class, the Left consolidated its position through a turning away from the proletarian subject of history and toward new social movements, particularly those of ethnic minorities. The move dovetailed with Left disaffection amid the support garnered among its traditional constituency by the NF and other right-wing groups. Moreover, the Left's attachment to the state as a site of resistance undermined its capacity to take on the primary arm of domestic state repression: the police. The culmination of these factors gave validity to the Conservative government's reinforcement of the criminalization of incitement to racial hatred. When in 1985 rioting broke out again in Brixton after police shot Dorothy Groce during a raid, and in Broadwater Farm where the police officer Keith Blakestock was killed, the government introduced the 1986 Public Order Act, adding new offenses in relation to riots, violence, and harassment, and reinforcing *intentionality* as a factor in "racial hatred." By doing so, the state was elevated as arbitrator of interethnic disputes where race relations were transformed into ethnic relationships between groups whose alienation as manifested in riots was understood to be driven by negative emotions.

In his seminal paper *The End of Anti-Racism*, Paul Gilroy cautioned activists who interpreted state funding and support for antiracism through the prism of progressive politics. Gilroy was wary of "the emergence of a proto–middle class grouping narrowly constituted around the toeholds which some blacks have been able to acquire in the professions, mostly those related directly to the welfare state itself—social work, teaching, and now antiracist bureaucracies."[61] Although for Gilroy the state was an important site of contestation, such incorporation was "obviously an uncomfortable contradictory position—squeezed between the expectations of the bureaucracies on which it relies and its political affiliation to the struggles of the mass of blacks which it is called upon to mediate, translate and sometimes police."[62] A key component of official antiracism with which Gilroy took issue was "the extent of the antiracists conceptual trading with the racists and the results of embracing their culturalist assumptions."[63] Nowhere was this clearer, asserted Gilroy, than in their acceptance of blacks as "the problem and the victim," for "suffering confers no virtue on the victim."[64] But although Gilroy was most certainly correct, his analysis suffered from a lack of self-reflexivity and therefore missed the extent to which the cultural turn in which he was instrumental distanced economics and class as integral to human emancipation—a point to which we will return in Chapter 5.

The rise of what Martin Barker called "new" or "cultural" racism only makes sense when we take economy out of the equation, and this is precisely what the Thatcher government achieved.[65] A redefinition of racism accompanied the changing trajectory of political action and the state's response to such throughout the post–World War II era. While antiracist activists in 1960s and 1970s Britain mobilized on the basis of the demand for political equality against police brutality, discriminatory immigration laws, and racist attacks, the incorporation of antiracists into the machinery of the state and the promotion of cultural identity claims within the local state since the 1980s reflect a redefinition of racism premised on a move from a denial of the right to be equal to a denial of the right to be different. And it is a redefinition that shared key conceptual roots with the trajectory of emancipation claims under the Reagan administration, to which we will now turn.

## RACENOMICS

> Let us be aware that while they [Soviet Communists] preach the supremacy of the state, declare its omnipotence over individual man, and predict its eventual domination over all the peoples of the earth, they are the focus of evil in the modern world. . . . I urge you to beware the temptation . . . , to ignore the facts of history and the aggressive impulses of any evil empire, to simply call the arms race a giant misunderstanding and thereby remove yourself from the struggle between right and wrong, good and evil.[66]

It was Reagan's anticommunism that cohered his American vitriol vis-à-vis rugged individualism as the cornerstone of capitalism, a superior economic system. But while Reagan proclaimed optimistically that there were "no great limits to growth because there are no limits of human intelligence, imagination, and wonder," his policies reflected a diminishing economic universalism.

Under one of the most popular US presidents of the postwar period, treasury secretary Paul Volcker's monetary policies plunged the country into the worst recession since the Great Depression and disciplined wage demands such that the purchasing power of working people declined during the 1980s.[67] In 1982, social spending was reduced by $27 billion per year, while in 1986, the tax rate for the highest income bracket decreased from 70 percent to 28 percent.[68]

In 1960, approximately 39.5 million (22 percent) people lived in poverty. By 1973, this had decreased to a record 11.1 percent, but starting in 1978, the rate of poverty increased, reaching a peak of 15.2 percent in 1983 due to the 1981–1982 recession. At the end of the Reagan administration in 1989, the poverty rate was 12.8 percent. As one commentator noted, the 1983–1990 figures for economic growth were as impressive as the immovability of the poverty rate was depressing.[69] But what is seldom noted is that capitalist economic growth expanded relative to the reversal of working-class gains. Growth under Reagan was slower not only than that of the 1960s but of the postwar 3.6 percent annual growth average. In 1972, the elite industrialists' Club of Rome published its infamous report *The Limits to Growth*, which predicted that economic growth could not continue indefinitely due to natural resource depletion. The significance of the report lay not just in the massive public interest it generated but in the way its antiprogress logic could be used by governments and capitalists as justification for cutting mass consumption and working-class wages, and thus maintaining profits as growth slowed down.

In Britain, resource depletion was used against the bargaining power of the National Union of Miners in the 1970s, a necessity balanced by appeals to anti-immigration sentiment, while, in the United States, Nixon's appeal to the white "silent majority" coincided with plans to decrease population growth through "constructive actions to lower fertility."[70] As bizarre as this may sound now, the depth of reactionary miserablism that swept Western elites in the 1970s was formidable, made even more cataclysmic by the OPEC oil embargo of 1973 and the "crisis of confidence" that followed.[71] As Sean Wilentz notes, Jimmy Carter's second State of the Union Address was symptomatic, "federal resources were limited. . . . Government cannot eliminate poverty or provide a bountiful economy or reduce inflation or save our cities or cure illiteracy or provide energy."[72] Amid the general "malaise" that Carter bemoaned, the Democrats, according to Wilentz, held "a certain contempt for the intelligence of the average American." Although the Republicans were by no means pro-masses, Reagan's optimism countered Carter's pessimism: "[The Democrats] say that the United States has had its days in the sun, that our nation has passed its zenith. . . . My fellow citizens, I utterly reject that view."[73] But it was an optimism that took its force from the existence of the communist other.

Reagan keyed into Americans' alienation from the state while attempting through massive restructuring to restore capitalist class confidence. The glue that held this dual strategy together was anticommunism. Prior administrations, by admitting futility in the face of economic decline, laid open the possibility of capitalist bankruptcy, creating a political vacuum. In elevating a posited ideological relationship between American statism and Soviet communism, the Republicans were able to present themselves as an alternative to both and individualism as a superior subject to the collective. Capitalism was simply a better economic system that had been bankrupted by statism, and this could be reversed. By appealing to the masses' sense of alienation, the state legitimized itself as a vehicle for introducing policies that undercut the postwar social compact. Reagan launched his first election campaign in Neshoba County with the declaration that he supported "states' rights"—the state in question being where three civil rights activists were murdered in 1964 while promoting black voting rights. Reagan's choice of Neshoba and the slogan are to this day cited as evidence of his avowed commitment to reverse federally imposed civil rights and undo the Great Society, and, as history testifies, the ideological appeal to "white backlash" underpinned the rise of conservatism in the United States. As Cornel West and others noted at the time, Reaganomic attacks against the urban poor and welfare had a disproportionate impact on blacks:

> Those most adversely affected by these policies have been blue collar industrial workers and the poor, particularly women and children. Thus Reagan's policies, which are often supported by the coded racist language of the religious right and secular neoconservatives, are racist in consequence. Poor women and children are disproportionately people of color, and jobs in the "rust belt" industries of auto and steel played a major role in black social mobility in the postwar period.[74]

The race card, however, must be contextualized by the employers' offensive against the organized working class set off by Reagan's crushing of the PATCO air controllers' strike in 1981. In particular, the replacement of the strikers with permanent workers marked a significant shift from previous labor-conflict management strategies. Despite the availability to employers of this form of worker discipline since it was made lawful by the 1935 National Labor Relations Act, it was not widely utilized until after PATCO. In addition to creating widespread insecurity among unionized labor, the strengthening of management's bargaining position catalyzed by PATCO contributed to the negative impact on union wage growth—and consequently the average wage levels of unionized workers—and significantly reduced the total wage bill paid by management between 1982 and 1990.[75] As noted in our previous discussion of Nixon, disaffection with traditional civic forms of organization had already begun to set in since the 1960s, and trade union membership was in decline throughout the 1970s. However, rather than being interpreted as a vindication of capitalism, such disaffection triggered a state legitimation crisis and its pursuit of new forms of appeal to an increasingly alienated and non-unionized (if not anti-union) public. When the Reagan administration took power, its perspective on social democratic forms of civic organization was that they were outdated relics. Reagan's defeat of the PATCO workers gave license to capital—an onslaught against labor that ousted its historical place as a movement of the "general interest . . . of all human kind."[76] On a more everyday level, labor-management relations were transformed by the removal of one of the key historical sources of conflict. This implicit elision in the era of capital-labor restructuring is the space within which we must interpret the Reagan administration's approach to affirmative action.

Writing in 1991, Robert Detlefsen made the point that despite a publicly professed opposition to unresponsive big government's race-conscious quotas and busing policies and its efforts at reform, "no sweeping changes" that could be taken to represent a reinstitution of a liberal color-blind approach to equality "occurred during Reagan's two terms in office."[77] Although some changes were made, Reagan resolutely failed to implement merit-based non-discrimination against group-orientated civil rights policies. Detlefsen puts this seeming paradox down to two factors. First, there was an "inconsistency of purpose" between federal agencies with responsibility for civil rights. One example among many was disagreement between the Justice Department's Civil Rights Division and the EEOC over the issue of quotas. The EEOC rejected the Civil Rights Division's internal affirmative action program because it did not include goals and timetables. Under Executive Order 11246, federal contractors who failed to fully utilize minority and female workers had been required to adopt goals and timetables for positive action. Internal clashes due to the absence of administrative consensus significantly limited a reversal of policy. Second, there existed immense opposition to the Justice Department's reform initiatives, not by the public but by the intelligentsia, including judges, academics, journalists, and the civil rights community. Detlefsen invokes the idea of a "constitutional culture" in which key actors and interest groups are able to exert judicial influence. Because reform in the sphere of civil rights is generally enacted through the courts, a pro–civil rights constitutional culture effectively blocked the Reagan administration's reforms. Detlefsen's findings are largely supported by Nicholas Laham's 1998 study, adding that many Republicans, including a significant proportion of the cabinet, sided with Democrats in opposing AA retrenchment. Thus, Reagan backed down on reforms in a bid to avoid a Republican split. The later vantage point of Laham's analysis enables him to draw the conclusion that while Reagan was not able to reverse AA during his tenure, the administration exacted a significant legacy beyond its eight years, even on the years that Bill Clinton, who shared no ideological allegiance, was in office. We will return to this point in Chapter 4, but the point is echoed by Hugh Davis Graham, who argues that Reagan's counter-offensive against AA brought mixed results due to three key developments: (1) the expansion of public law litigation: a form of policymaking championed by the NAACP whereby private and public interest groups bypass elected public officials by suing government agencies on behalf of class-action clients in order to force policy change; (2) patterns of policy replication: existing policies were applied to new client groups; and (3) clientele capture whereby advocacy groups had formed close ties with the government departments responsible for civil rights enforcement. In short, because these three factors in effect bypassed the political process, it was difficult for conservatives to attack AA through "populist appeals to voter resentment."[78] However, two key policy arenas reveal that the politics of race developed distinctively under the Reagan administration: business and criminal justice.

In the move from soft to hard affirmative action programs under Nixon, the focus had been primarily on the claims of African Americans, but, as has already been discussed, recognition was gradually extended to other groups, particularly in light of new and expanding migration patterns to the United States.[79] This was distinctively so under the Small Business Administration's (SBA) section 8(a) program, which offered benefits such as subsidized loans and surety bonds to minority entrepreneurs. The Civil Rights Act Title VI on contract compliance gave agencies the authority to draw up regulations for the enforcement of benefit redistribution to minorities. Under the Carter presidency minority set-asides, which included federal procurement programs, were authorized by Congress, and this was upheld by the Supreme Court in 1980. Set-aside programs, by which a proportion of all government contracts are to be allocated to minority businesses, were implemented by both city and state governments and amounted to over 230 by 1990. In 1977, 10 percent of the $4 billion Public Works Bill was set aside for minority businesses. Under the Reagan administration, set-asides were extended to the substantial federal budgets for transportation and defense. In 1973, blacks, American Indians, Spanish Americans, Asian Americans, and Puerto Ricans were recognized by the SBA. By 1979, recognition was extended to Cambodia, China, Guam, Japan, Korea, Laos, Northern Marianas, the Philippines, Samoa, Taiwan, the US Trust Territory of the Pacific, and Vietnam. Under Reagan, recognition was further extended to India in 1982, Tonga in 1986, Sri Lanka in 1988, and Indonesia, Nepal, and Bhutan in 1989.[80] The cultivation of middle-class minorities was of strategic importance, accompanying as it did a wholesale attack against the working class in which minorities were also overrepresented. The support for multicultural capitalism split minority constituencies into ethnic competitors, but it also divided ethnic groups along class lines, such that economic equality was diminished as an emancipatory universal goal.

In 1985, it became publicly known that the Reagan administration was considering an executive order that would relieve companies under federal government contract from the requirement to set numerical goals and timetables for the hiring and promotion of minorities and women. Guidelines drawn up by the OFCCP in 1968 affected all firms with contracts worth $50 million or more, which by 1986 corresponded to 15,000 companies, 23 million workers at 73,000 installations. The paradox is that while opposition to the proposed reform was expected from civil rights groups, big business joined them. In a survey carried out by *Fortune* magazine, 90 percent of company CEOs declared they would continue their AA programs even without the need for compliance. Moreover, the National Association of Manufacturers, which represented some of the largest US firms, launched a major campaign against the administration's proposal. Detlefsen gives two reasons for this turn of events. First, government compliance had effectively been a defense against claims of reverse discrimination. As long as company AA procedures were seen to be in compliance with the law, successful litigation by aggrieved whites could be avoided. This was linked to the problem of what would be seen as reversing AA procedures. Having institutionalized AA bureaucracies within their corporate infrastructures, the prospect of firing personnel responsible for tackling racial discrimination, their jobs being redundant, would have created a public relations disaster, precipitating public protests and consumer boycotts. Second, the need for federal compliance gave larger companies a competitive edge over smaller firms for which in-house AA infrastructures were too costly.[81] At a corporate level, AA procedures had become synonymous with gaining lucrative government contracts. Relinquishing compliance would have opened large firms, which had invested in AA infrastructures, to a wider field of competitive tendering. In such a scenario, one can imagine that the pressure to shed AA personnel would have increased, thus precipitating the aforementioned public relations catastrophe.

Pro-business opposition to Reaganite AA reform reveals that unlike the tenets of monetarism, capitalism and profit making increasingly depended on the state not only for contracts but in order to assuage capitalist competition. Right-wing antistatism had not fully appreciated this on either side of the Atlantic. Capitalist survival requires the aid of legislation, legal mechanisms, and ideology. But capitalism is not rendered unstable by intercapitalist class competition alone, it is beset by the source of wealth and the value of labor: the working class. While the Reagan administration voiced the ideological celebration of rugged individualism against communism and statism, the politics of race represented a deeper crisis related to economic growth. It has been demonstrated that in-house EEO policies were favored by employers not only because they avoided litigation but also as a more efficient form of dispute resolution than unionized grievance procedures.[82] In-house AA programs represented a substitute for unionized labor relations. This becomes clearer when we examine the transformation of corporate Equal Employment Opportunity (EEO) and AA into "diversity management." The transformation of EEO/AA in-house specialists through the prism of human resources (HR) into diversity managers developed exponentially during the Reagan administration.[83] It is during this time that the corporate discourse—a diverse workforce is better for business—was galvanized. The cynical mantra that employees recruited through diversity drives are more efficient is summed up in the *Harvard Busi-*

*ness Review* by corporate diversity guru R. Roosevelt Thomas' address to companies who had not yet gotten with the program:

Several years ago, an industrial plant in Atlanta with a highly diverse workforce was threatened with closing unless productivity improved. To save their jobs everybody put their shoulders to the wheel and achieved the results they needed to stay open. The senior operating manager was amazed. . . .

When the threat of closure energized this whole group of people into a level of performance he had not imagined possible, he got one fleeting glimpse of people working up to their capacity. . . . Now, as he put it himself, he had been up to the mountain top. He knew that what he was getting from minorities and women was nowhere near what they were capable of giving. And he wanted it, crisis or no crisis, all the time.[84]

Although a convincing explanation for why this should be the case is rare, apparently a more diverse workforce is more efficient in a crisis—that is, when they feel their jobs are threatened. Of course, the obvious addition to Thomas' advice would be "keep them in a state of crisis; that way you will continuously get the best from them." But an answer to "Why?" may lie in two factors. Union grievances are typically based on economic demands for higher pay, better working conditions, entitlements, and so forth. They take their strength and bargaining position from a collective understanding that each individual in the union can act in concert as economic beings, despite other noneconomic differences, to effect a better standard of living. The historical weakness of trade unions has been that the "economic beings" who make up their membership have been collectively racialized, and to an extent this explains their discriminatory form. Nevertheless, employees who are either recruited on the basis of their ethnicity or who work in an ethnically diverse environment and are trained to see and respect ethnic differences are encouraged to view their employment status as ethnically based. A collective economic demand is placed out of reach. This is made more probable if we consider that HR is primarily an individualistic management philosophy. A word from its sponsor:

In my view, the image to hold in your own imagination and to try to communicate to all your managers and employees is an image of fully tapping the human resource potential of every member of the work force. This vision sidesteps the issue of equality, ignores the tensions of coexistence, plays down the uncomfortable realities of difference, and focuses instead on individual enablement.[85]

HR employee-management relations are not secured by collective power. Under diversity management, the employee is not an individual devoid of group; he or she is an ethnic individual upwardly classed but without collective power—the product of a vision that sidesteps the issue of equality. But what of the ethnic individual who is downwardly classed?

If, as Gilroy contends, suffering confers no virtue on the victim, the introduction of the Hate Crime Statistics Bill (HCSB) in 1985, according to James Jacobs and Kimberly Potter, dismantles that claim.[86] Grounded in the politics of identity, they argue, the criminalization of hate makes a virtue out of an identity of victimhood that the victim must retain if recognition is to be conferred. Initial lobbyists of the bill included the Anti-Defamation League, the Anti-Klan Network, the Institute for the Prevention and Control of Violence and Extremism, and the International Network for Jewish Holocaust Survivors. Their aim was to require the Department of Justice to collect and publish statistics on the nature and number of crimes motivated by racial, religious, and ethnic prejudice. Lobbying by gay and lesbian groups succeeded in gaining the inclusion of sexual orientation in the bill as a target of hate, and the Hate Crime Statistics Act (HCSA) was signed into law by Republican president George H. W. Bush in 1990. To political elites, argue Jacobs and Potter, antiprejudice/bigotry provided symbolic currency: through "message sending" to lobbyists their allegiance and, by extension, that of the voting population was enlisted. Antihate symbolizes a "prejudice-free character" that "asserts a moral claim to your support."[87] However, the genealogy of hate crime legislation cannot be understood as a consequence of identity lobbying alone. The legislation needs to be further contextualized within the wider parameters of criminalization and victims' rights—two centerpieces of the Reagan administration.

In 1981, Reagan launched Victims' Rights Week with this statement:

> We need a renewed emphasis on, and an enhanced sensitivity to, the rights of victims. These rights should be a central concern of those who participate in the criminal justice system, and it is time all of us paid greater heed to the plight of victims.[88]

In addition to launching this annual recognition of victims' rights, Reagan initiated the President's Task Force on Victims of Crime, which published a report of 62 recommendations in 1982. Under Reagan, the Office for Victims of Crime within the Department of Justice was created in 1983, and the federal Crime Victims Fund established by the US Congress was created in 1984. By the time the HCSB was introduced in 1985, Reagan had already established a political movement within government for the recognition of victims of crime. However, this needs to be situated within a wider appeal to white alienation and black criminalization. If we extend Nixon's appeal to the "silent majority" into the Reagan era and pair it with the popular perception of the black or ethnic criminal of the urban ghetto, then advocacy for the criminalization of hate by identity groups must surely backfire. For when the politics of race is reduced to interethnic competition that threatens to become unrestrained due to an invisible emotional determinant—hate—then logically hate crime can just as easily be perpetrated by ethnic minorities against whites. The main difference between the Republicans' endorsement of hate crime legislation in the 1980s and the passing of the initial federal Hate Crime Law in 1969 is that "the hate that hate produced" no longer applied to the conflict between white extremists and black militants amid capitalist competition with communism but to ethnically determined subjects of identity in competition not only for a share of an ever-shrinking economic settlement but for recognition of their suffering conferred by a nation-state in which the Right won the political battle and the Left won the culture war. By the end of the 1980s, the contest between liberalism, socialism, and conservatism had transformed social democratic "race relations" into multicultural capitalism.

CHAPTER FOUR

# OTHER THAN MEXICANS

In Chapter 3 we demonstrated how the postwar politics of "race relations" in the West were initially cohered around a posited need to liberate the forward-looking free-willing individual of liberalism from the prewar authoritarian order. An emancipatory condition of the Wilson-Lenin post–World War I settlement underpinned the right to self-determination of colonially oppressed peoples, and was carried forward in the call for universal rights increasingly demanded by those living second-class lives in the domestic spheres of the West. The political right to self-determine entailed both political and economic equality as universal preconditions to be attained, and the post–World War II state response to this demand revealed the limit point of social democratic capitalism. The gradual omission of *Homo economicus* in "race relations" theory and policy was set within the contest between two mutually reinforcing anthropological species: liberal man and authoritarian man; their contestation exposed the limits of universal equality. Contest was emphasized by collective action both domestically in the United States around the civil rights movement and to a more limited extent in the United Kingdom by the political and industrial action of migrants from the ex-colonies, but the trajectory of these movements was cohered within the wider ideological contest of Left and Right in which the Soviet Union provided the key organizing principle (both for those who were pro and those who were anti), but the liberal-conservative diffusion of radicalism in the United Kingdom and the United States underpinned the changing state response to "race relations." By the end of the Reagan-Thatcher era, the collapse of the Soviet Union and the political Left in the West revealed itself in the diminishing possibility of economic equality.

In this chapter we explore how the redefinition of universal equality into the recognition of ethnic identity-claims unfolded in the post–Cold War era. We will demonstrate how the defensive multiculturalism of a politically defeated Left fused with the cultural defeat of the politically victorious Right. Multicultural capitalism—the realignment of universalism—entailed the establishment of a new limit point to equality: the "interethnic" anti–*Homo economicus* national compact between the "included" and the "socially excluded" of the Third Way. Unlike the racial politics of the social democratic bargain, the "socially excluded" had no political or organized form. The very designation of groups whose economic integration was now deemed "impossible" reflected the void of purpose among the political classes of the post–Cold War era. In the absence of any future-orientated organizing principle with which to cohere itself, the new political classes of the Third Way pursued social inclusion as a postracial interethnic settlement devoid of economics, within which those who did not "fit" were to be regulated. The conceptualization of "lack of fit" drew its boundaries against the Left-Right political matrix and respective ideological allegiances. Strict adherence to ideology was in itself rebranded as a relic of the past—a rigid authoritarianism that manifested in "hate."

For the Third Way political classes, whose very existence was premised on holding the present together in the absence of an alternative to capitalism, any form of rigid adherence heightened the potential for disorder. Concomitantly, all forms of disorder came to be understood as the result of rigid adherence. From this perspective, multiculturalism was a problem if it reinforced rigid adherence to ethnic identity. In their search for a vision with which to hold the present together and on which to found their legitimacy, the political classes of the post–Cold War era positioned themselves against the "rigidity of hate producing hate." The pursuit of cosmopolitan national unity emerged as the framework through which social relations were to be regulated. Cosmopolitan nationalism reflected the elites' perception of social relations as being constituted by volatile ethnic emotional allegiances. The complete dislocation of economics from equality provided the foundation on which the relationships among migrants, minorities, and white majorities were to be understood. Consequently, the need to maintain and respect cosmopolitan identities that do not give rise to hate has emerged as a hegemonic organizing principle of the mental economy. The emergence and institutionalization of the economy of mind provides a narrative that links the demise of social democratic race relations under Reagan-Thatcher to the maintenance of postracial order under Barack Obama.

## MONGOLIAN EYES IN THE NEIGHBORHOOD

He half-tripped, was half-pushed to the floor. The policeman nearest to me had the black automatic pistol in his left hand, he held it down to the guy and unloaded five shots into him.

He looked like a Pakistani but he had a baseball cap on, and quite a thickish coat. It was a coat like you would wear in winter, a sort of padded jacket. It looked out of place in the weather we've been having.[1]

On July 22, 2005, 15 days after four British Muslims took their own lives and those of 57 commuters by detonating suicide bombs on the London transport system, 27-year-old electrician Jean Charles de Menezes, a Brazilian migrant who lived and worked in London, was "cornered like a fox" and shot dead by British Metropolitan police (Met) while boarding a train at Stockwell Street underground station. Surveillance officers had misidentified de Menezes as Ethiopian-born British citizen Osman Hussain, wanted in connection with attempted bombings that had failed to detonate on the transport system the previous day. The Met's shoot-to-kill policy, *Operation Kratos*, gave high-ranked officers the authority to shoot suspected suicide bombers without warning. Though de Menezes had no connection with terrorism and was completely innocent, police suspicions were "confirmed" by the observation that he, like Hussain, "had Mongolian eyes." In fact, once "identified," de Menezes' subsequent behavior and demeanor (while objectively without irregularity) were interpreted as those of a terrorist on a mission. The Met, one of the most powerful and well-resourced police forces in the world and staffed with highly trained personnel using sophisticated intelligence and surveillance techniques, acted lethally on the basis that the physical characteristics of an innocent man were, in the eyes of the surveillance team, those of a suicide bomber. Physical characteristics easily signified suspicion such that the migrant de Menezes was associated with terror, deemed a public threat, and therefore a legitimate target for extermination. In the imagination of the police officers an indisputable thread connected two disparate individuals. Merged with Hussain in the signification of threat, de Menezes' objective connection to the suspect (i.e., that they were both migrants) assumed a subjective meaning that obliterated all reason. The police decision to execute reveals that when it comes to migrants, "suspicion" is not objective. Rather, it is the objective process through which certain biological characteristics are paired with threat that provides validity to the irrationalist subjective form that the contemporary policing of migration takes. The process is instrumentalized by the state, formalized through law, and practiced on both sides of the Atlantic.

On April 23, 2010, the state of Arizona enacted the Support Our Law Enforcement and Safe Neighborhoods Act, SB1070. The law, which aimed to strengthen the control of illegal immigration across the Mexico-Arizona border, drew unprecedented reaction and protest. The most controversial part of the law required that "a reasonable attempt . . . be made to determine the immigration status of a person during any legitimate contact made by an official or agency of the state or a county, city, town or political subdivision if reasonable suspicion exists that the person is an alien who is unlawfully present in the U.S." The clause evidently paves the way to racial profiling. On what basis would a police officer *reasonably* suspect that a person is an immigrant whose legal status should be verified? It is doubtful that a "white" person in a southern border town would be asked to verify his or her legal status. "Reasonable suspicion" of unlawful presence is most likely to be aroused by persons of Mexican and other "nonwhite" ethnic origins. Moreover, people who are wrongly identified as belonging to such groups will also be "reasonably suspected." As in the United Kingdom, there is no objective basis for the suspicion subjectively aroused other than the process through which the irrationalist signification of threat is legitimized by law.

Oppressive police practices toward racialized groups in the United States have been well documented, coming to light most famously in the brutalization of Rodney King by officers of the Los Angeles Police Department (LAPD).[2]

However, what sometimes goes unnoticed is that the treatment of internal minorities has a reciprocal effect on that of *migrants* and vice versa. Viewed in historical context, recent legislative measures like Arizona Law SB1070 can be interpreted, in effect, as an attempt to legalize common law enforcement practices that can adversely affect "nonwhite" minorities as a whole and not just in Arizona. A 2004 report by Amnesty International USA revealed that "racial profiling is so pervasive that it has impacted nearly 32 million people in the United States," including Native Americans, Asian Americans, Hispanic Americans, African Americans, Arab Americans, Persian Americans, American Muslims, and, in some instances, white Americans. Moreover, profiling of citizens and visitors of Middle Eastern and South Asian descent, and others who are identified as originating from these areas, has substantially increased since 9/11.[3] As Leo Chavez makes abundantly clear, the threat to national security posed by Mexican and other Latin American migration is "a powerful theme in the post-9/11 political debate over security."[4] But the idiom of threat has extended across ethnic groups such that racial profiling in police, immigration, and airport security procedures has expanded. For example, the very title of the Border Protection, Anti-Terrorism, and Illegal Immigration Control Act of 2005 (H.R. 4437) clearly represents the process through which terror and immigration are at once paired in the signification of threats to the US public. The bill sought to address "border security vulnerabilities . . . related to the prevention of the entry of terrorists, other unlawful aliens, narcotics, and other contraband."[5] The apparent ease with which lawmakers move between terrorism and unlawful aliens reflects to an extent that "today the two seminal considerations regarding the Americanization of matters racial have to do with the twin towers of immigration and terrorism."[6] The bill was introduced after then deputy secretary of the US Department of Homeland Security Admiral James Loy testified before the 109th Congress:

> Entrenched human smuggling networks and corruption in areas beyond our borders can be exploited by terrorist organizations. . . . emerging threat streams strongly suggest[s] that al-Qaida has considered using the Southwest Border to infiltrate the United States. Several al-Qaida leaders believe operatives can pay their way into the country through Mexico and also believe illegal entry is more advantageous than legal entry for operational security reasons. However, there is currently no evidence

that al-Qaida operatives have made successful penetrations into the United States via this method.[7]

The negative representation of migrants extends the boundaries of lawful suspicion. Loy's testimony provides a basis for viewing Mexican migrants as potential carriers of terrorist exploitation. Indeed, a report published in 2005 by the Congressional Research Service (CRS)[8] clarifies that the US Border Patrol (USBP) categorizes unauthorized aliens as "Mexican" or "Other Than Mexican" (OTM). On one level the distinction is purely administrative. Unlike Mexicans, OTMs cannot be immediately deported back across the Mexican border because they must be returned either to their country of origin or to a willing third country; Mexico will not accept them. However, the OTM category includes a subclassification that refers to those migrants who originate from a "special interest country" considered to harbor terrorists or foment terrorism. But what are the criteria by which an OTM is to be identified? In a climate of suspicion, misidentification, as was the case in the United Kingdom with Jean Charles de Menezes, can take on lethal proportions, and the person in the street is no less likely than the London Met, LAPD, or Arizona state police to misidentify. It is the "special interest OTMs" who are thought to constitute the most significant migratory threat to US security, and it is their signified physical connection with other migrants and US citizens that underpins the state's regulative framework. Thus, while it is important to draw out the continuities between the race policies of both past and present US–UK administrations, there are significant differences applicable to the contemporary context that warrant further attention.

What is disconcerting about the OTM category is the simultaneous (in)visibility it identifies as suspicious. Although OTM includes a subcategory that refers to migrants from "special interest countries," it can also refer to all groups. The category of people who are not Mexican includes everyone on the planet except Mexicans. Does this then mean that Mexicans are beyond suspicion? The answer is no, but it does mean that we are all potentially under suspicion. The importance of the OTM lies in its applicability in targeting the negative object—the common link among all OTMs—of risk. It is the degree of risk that an individual comes to represent that identifies his or her presence as a threat.

## SAFETY CONSCIOUSNESS

In terms of the contemporary domestic law and order framework through which migration is linked to internal minorities and the wider public, a key discourse, if not the dominant interpretative paradigm, is that of "safety." The discourse of safety links Jean Charles de Menezes and Arizona Law SB1070. There can be little doubt that the police officer who shot de Menezes did so with the intention to kill, yet he could not be prosecuted for acting under orders issued by the Met's operations commander. The Met *was* held liable, not for unlawful killing but under the Health and Safety at Work Act 1974 for "failing to provide for the health, safety and welfare of Jean Charles de Menezes."[9] "Safety" was the key word surrounding the entire prosecution. During the case, Met deputy assistant commissioner and operations commander Cressida Dick refuted claims that she missed the "one safe opportunity" to stop de Menezes.[10] But a wider case for safety was being made: that in tracking and killing a potential suicide bomber (even if the wrong man was killed), the Met was attempting to protect the greater public to ensure public safety. Given that the Met had shot and killed the wrong man in a city renowned for its mix of different ethnic communities who travel on the London Underground every day, few would be reassured by the Met's defense. Later, former Met deputy assistant commissioner Brian Paddick attempted, unsuccessfully, to key into the London public's insecurity when he stood for the position of mayor with the campaign pitch that he "knows how to make Londoners feel safe."[11]

Obvious parallels can be seen with Arizona's Support Our Law Enforcement and Safe Neighborhoods Act, SB1070. At the signing of SB1070, Governor Jan Brewer explained her rationale for doing so:

> There is no higher priority than protecting the citizens of Arizona. We cannot sacrifice our safety to the murderous greed of drug cartels. We cannot stand idly by as drop houses, kidnappings and violence compromise our quality of life.
>
> While protecting our citizens is paramount, it cannot come at the expense of the diversity that has made Arizona so great. Nor can safety mean a compromise of freedom for some, while we, the many, turn a blind eye.
>
> We must use this new tool wisely, and fight for our safety with the honor Arizona deserves.[12]

Safety is put forward as a justification for increasing police border protection powers and simultaneously as a protection of diversity, of minorities. Brewer is mindful that state repression has often been justified at the expense of some groups in society, and she seeks to reassure that this will not be the case with SB1070 because the primary goal is that of protecting an ethnically diverse community from the effects of border harms. Immigration regulation is justified through an appeal to the *equal right to be safe*. The logic disarms opponents who work within the safety framework, but not completely. Dan Pochoda, legal director of Arizona ACLU, had on the previous day issued a statement that "forcing local police to demand people's papers and arrest those who can't immediately prove their status will do nothing to make us safer," but rather, "what it will do is divert scarce police resources to address false threats and force officers to prioritize immigration enforcement over all other public safety responsibilities."[13] The Act will heighten sensitivity to immigration; misplaced hypervigilance will drain police resources and result in neglect of other community safety threats. Pochoda is mindful that law can legitimize anti-immigrant sentiment with the effect that nonimmigrant minorities will be targeted, ultimately undermining the equal right to be safe. Both Brewer and Pochoda are advocates for community safety; for Brewer, uncontrolled immigration makes communities unsafe, and for Pochoda, immigrants and communities are made unsafe by Arizona Law SB1070. For President Barack Obama, however, both uncontrolled immigration and SB1070 threatened safety. The law, he argued, would, "undermine basic notions of fairness that we cherish as Americans, as well as the trust between police and our communities that is so crucial to keeping us safe."[14] At a meeting with Brewer at the White House on June 4, 2010, Obama pledged to assuage safety fears by sending 1,200 National Guard troops to the United States–Mexico border, most of which were to be positioned on the Arizona-Mexico border.[15]

Despite the nuanced pro- versus anti-Arizona debate, it is a mistake to view it as representative of an old-school Left versus Right contest. The consensus discourse that appeals to safety is no more an endorsement of Reagan's "rugged individualism" than it is of Thatcher's pro-enterprise dictum that "there is no such thing as society, only individuals. . . ." There is little in the adventurist myths of the cowboy rancher or business entrepreneur that appeals to a putative need to feel safe; in fact, it is quite the opposite. Nor is Obama an internationalist antiborder, anti–ruling class Bolshevik.[16] Rather, Obama's inclusion of community-police "trust" within the paradigm of safety is telling in that it situates immigration within a wider concern to uphold the legitimacy of state institutions, and the legitimacy deficit has a history that predates the current administration. It is an observation reinforced by champion of the Third Way Amitai Etzioni: "Trust is a key element of ends-based relationships; while general social trust among the general public has been diminishing, trust in public leaders and institutions is particularly vulnerable."[17] The idea of mistrust played a key role in the defeat of President George W. Bush's Immigration Reform Act in 2007. Touted as one of the biggest shake-ups of immigration law since Reagan's 1986 Immigration Act, the Bush proposals were slammed by so-called GOPs for not going far enough to instill trust. "The general consensus," charged Republican senator Bob Corker, "is that at the end of the day, the American people do not trust Congress and do not trust the administration to carry out the things that are in the bill." Speaking of their alternative bill for what they saw as a stronger border security enforcement proposal, Republican senators Saxby Chambliss and Johnny Isakson added, "We believe the way to build greater support for immigration reform in the United States Senate and among the American public is to regain the trust in the ability of the federal government to responsibly administer immigration programs and enforce immigration laws."[18] The ensuing debate and crushing of the bill reveal deeper issues about Republican unity to which we will return later, but what is clear is that there was no disunity on the need to instill trust. In short, the Bush proposals were rejected because, it was argued, they did not make Americans feel safe enough. Speaking toward the end of his tenure as president, Bush reflected on the impact of the defeated bill:

> No question the American people expect us to enforce our borders. And I understand it and agree with that. But there's a humane way to do it and the approach I laid out was logical, humane and upheld our values. And has there been a political consequence to the Republican Party? Evidently. But that doesn't mean we can't regain the trust of the Latino vote. It's just that I'm not going to be out there regaining the trust of the Latino vote because I'm retired—in 12 days.[19]

The complexity of gaining trust by making people feel safe is, for the political classes, intensified by the presence of what is presented in the United

States as substantial ethnic minority populations—in this case, "Latinos"—but the need for an "interethnic safety-trust" compact runs deeper than what some have interpreted as an opportunist bid to enlist voting constituencies, although that is certainly part of it. What contemporary immigration debate in the United States reveals is that there is competition between groups ethnically conceived, not for economic gain or welfare (the dislocation of economic welfare from equality was achieved in the Reagan-Thatcher era), but for recognition of victimization. The so-called "immigration threat" is one medium ("terrorist threat" is another) through which some "whites" perceive themselves to be victims, and they want this recognized. This takes the form of demanding that the "state keep us safe, as is our right." White recognition, if it is granted, then becomes the medium through which some "minorities"—in this case, anyone who can be mistaken for constituting an immigration or terrorist "threat"—protest in the name of victimization. Again, the demand is that the "state keep us safe, as is our right." The state responds to its "victim constituencies" by conferring recognition, but it is a balancing act that in itself threatens to victimize, for recognizing one group's victimization requires that a *high-risk perpetrator* be identified who cannot claim that the label is itself evidence of victimization. As the case of Jean Charles de Menezes reveals, such identification is fraught with difficulties. Without a credible perpetrator, the process must collapse through inertia, of which the inability to reach political agreement on immigration control is a testament. In fact, victim recognition is self-perpetuating: it is devoid of any possible resolution. More problematically, it has a genealogy that began with Nixon's recognition of the "silent majority" and Reagan's elevation of "victim's rights." Today, the absence of a solution to inequality is resolved through the virtue of victim recognition that takes on a particular set of characteristics in relation to the politics of race and immigration, and it is not unique to the United States.

In 2002, New Labour's home secretary David Blunkett laid out the United Kingdom Home Office's rationale underpinning British migration and asylum policy:

> Confidence, security and trust make all the difference in enabling a safe haven to be offered to those coming to the UK. To enable integration to take place, and to value the diversity it brings, we need to be secure within our sense of belonging and

identity and therefore to be able to reach out and to embrace those who come to the UK.[20]

Britain needs to be made safe for migrants. There is lack of confidence, and there is insecurity and a sense of distrust among the British population, an identity crisis that cannot cope with the demand that the integration of diverse identities brings vis-à-vis migration. The safety of migrants is tied to the safety of the host population. This is extended as follows:

> Having a clear, workable and robust nationality and asylum system is the pre-requisite to building the security and trust that is needed. Without it, we cannot defeat those who would seek to stir up hate, intolerance and prejudice. The Government, and those agencies and organisations delivering nationality, immigration and asylum services, need to demonstrate that they know what they are doing, and that they are doing it well.[21]

The perpetrator that makes both migrant and host populations unsafe is "hate." If the population does not trust the government agencies that are responsible for immigration, "hate" intervenes, a dangerous emotion is stirred, and safety is threatened. Government intervention is legitimized as a means of circumventing "interethnic hate," the fear of which is appealed to as a means of fostering social stability and interethnic harmony. Indentifying with the government on the basis of its ability to pacify "interethnic hate" makes us feel safe, which in turn is the prerequisite for national cohesion: the avoidance of postracial disorder. How did we get here? The basic tenets of current government policy on race and immigration can be summed up in what we call "Third Way antiracism."[22]

## THIRD WAY ANTIRACISM

The political theorist Bhikhu Parekh broadly demarcates three distinct ways in which "modern states conceptualize their identity": liberal, communitarian, and ethnic or national, alerting us to the notion that immigration policy reflects "a state's conception of who should be its members," which is dependent on "the kind of polity it thinks it is and how it believes itself to be constituted and held together."[23] Government's perception of the national interest is shaped by the view it holds of the relationship between the individual and state institutions. In short, governing the polity requires an understanding of the nature of the individuals to be governed and the political context in which those individuals act. Parekh's point has salience when we consider that the problems to which Third Way governance professes to orientate itself are anchored between the twin pillars of risk and trust,[24] leading to what has been conceptualized as the "institutionalisation of caution"—a loosely defined "communitarian consensus" on the purported need to combat the causal-effects of globalization, social breakdown and unrestrained egoism.[25] The latter is generally considered to be a consequence of free-market liberal individualist policies established during the Reagan-Thatcher era, and while the most celebrated political proponents of the Third Way were President Bill Clinton and Prime Minister Tony Blair, the concerns underpinning their policies have outlived their respective administrations.

James Heartfield notes a basic flaw in the Third Way. It is taken as axiomatic by its proponents and by its critics that the ideological defense of individualism in the 1980s succeeded in letting loose Thomas Hobbes' unrestrained perpetrator of "war of all against all." The post–Cold War political classes initially celebrated both Thatcher's "There Is No Alternative" (TINA) to the free market and Fukuyama's End of History victory of liberal individualism, but as the victorious Right—John Major's Conservative Party and George Bush's Republicans—collapsed into the vacuum of a defeated Left, the capitalist state had to contend with a widespread crisis of purpose. The Third Way became the means by which the state attempted to relegitimize itself in a world without alternatives to the capitalist system. But what the neoconservative-libertarian coalition of the Thatcher-Reagan administrations misunderstood was that in attacking the social-democratic base of individual action, they also undermined the social base of their own attack: Both antisocialism and anticommunism were supported by a shared social base. The human individual can only express his or her individuality as a social actor, whether the individual's social base takes the form of a political party or a trade union. Autonomy is not the same animal as individualism. Autonomy requires a shared social understanding of the basis of freedom. Cut off the social base of collective power and the individual does not gain strength but crumbles. This should not be taken as an argument on our part for a defense of social democracy against neoliberalism; rather, the analysis reveals both what it is that the Third Way was trying to do—appeal to while simultaneously restraining the dangerous ego-driven individual—and why it was flawed. The robust individual was not released by neoconservative libertarianism; rather, Thatcher and Reagan all but destroyed the foundation of "Big P" Politics—the humanist pursuit of autonomy, freedom, the meaning of Hope.

In the absence of emancipatory Politics, the state-society relationship is recast within multicultural capitalism's inability to deliver economic equality. The irrationalization of equality reveals itself in the state's attempt to legitimize itself through the postracial lens of making the present "world without meaning" bearable to its interethnic subjects. As Heartfield notes, "Third Way" politics is *therapolitics*, appealing to emotion as a means of restraining its effect on dangerous willful action.[26] For example, in holding the Conservative-Libertarian era responsible for increased criminality, the therapolitics of the Clinton-Blair administrations attempted to tap into a disinterested public on the basis of fear, thus legitimizing state through the governance of emotion. Working on different sides of the Atlantic, sociologists James Nolan and Frank Furedi have each drawn attention to the therapeutic turn in social policy and to a pessimistic view of human subjectivity that underpins the current policy approach of the "therapeutic state."[27] For Nolan, the "postmodern" US state has turned to psychological explanations and interventions in order to provide meaning. Faced by a growing legitimacy deficit, a key characteristic of the Clinton administration was its "crisis of meaning," which prompted a search for new sources of symbolic justification.[28] Connecting with the "emotional vulnerability" of victims provided a means through which the state-subject relationship was recast. For Nolan, the move represents a shift from ideals fused around classical Republicanism, Lockean Liberalism, and Protestant Christianity—three sources that collectively legitimated the American State. Their fusion previously acted as a shared source of justification for policy on the basis of soliciting the allegiance of the free-willing individual. In comparison, cultural codes that justify therapeutic policy are not based on a belief in the superiority of willful action; rather, current policy seeks to connect with factors that lie beyond the will: emotions.

*Therapolitics* helps us to situate the Clinton administration's approach to race. Less than a year after the Los Angeles riots, in his first inaugural speech,

Clinton asked us to join the Democrats in "celebrating the mystery of" and issuing a call for "America's renewal":

> Americans deserve better, and in this city today, there are people who want to do better. And so I say to all of us here, let us resolve to reform our politics, so that power and privilege no longer shout down the voice of the people. Let us put aside personal advantage so that we can feel the pain and see the promise of America.[29]

Clinton's invocation, "feeling America's pain" to release the "promise," is summoned in opposition to the personal greed and callousness of individualism. Democrats are healers who will set free the nation's anti-Reaganite primal scream, giving "voice" to and recognizing the people's "pain" suffered in silence under the oppressive, domineering, unrestrained egoism of corporate greed. Even before President George H. W. Bush was ousted, Clinton's postriot visit called for the healing of divisions—both the cause and the effect of LA's downtown ethnic disorder.[30] And later, conviction of two police officers involved in Rodney King's assault facilitated the healing of pain.[31] Lest we take the "feeling and healing of pain" as purely metaphorical, in Clinton's second inaugural speech, ethnic therapolitics assumed a higher intensity, and this was with particular reference to community bonds versus national fragmentation and its cause, "hate":

> Our greatest responsibility is to embrace a new spirit of community for a new century. For any one of us to succeed, we must succeed as one America. . . . The challenge of our past remains the challenge of our future: Will we be one nation, one people, with one common destiny—or not? Will we all come together, or come apart? . . . The divide of race has been America's constant curse. Each new wave of immigrants gives new targets to old prejudices. Prejudice and contempt, cloaked in the pretense of religious or political conviction, are no different. They have nearly destroyed us in the past. They plague us still. They fuel the fanaticism of terror. They torment the lives of millions in fractured nations around the world. . . . These obsessions cripple both those who are hated and of course those who hate. Robbing both of what they might become. . . . We cannot—we will not—succumb to the dark impulses that lurk in the far regions of the soul, everywhere. We shall overcome them, and we shall replace them with the generous spirit of a people who feel at home with one another. . . . Our rich texture of racial, religious and political

diversity will be a godsend in the 21st century. Great rewards will come to those who can live together, learn together, work together, forge new ties that bind together.[32]

We will return to the Third Way's posited relationship between migration, hate, and national cohesion for the insight it sheds on the response of later administrations to migration and terrorism. But it is important to note Clinton's inclusion of the formulation that "obsessions cripple both those who are hated and of course those who hate." It is taken as self-evident that racism has a psychological etiology that victimizes not only those on the receiving end—the targets—but *also* the perpetrators. The distinction between target and perpetrator, between cause and effect, is blurred. To the blurring of the target/perpetrator is added a new distinction that emerges within the relationship between "the pretense of religious or political conviction" and hate. Though obviously developed in response to the 1993 World Trade Center and 1995 Oklahoma bombings, the distinction represents a departure. Few US presidents, including Clinton, would publicly problematize religious or political conviction; what, after all, does it mean to be "one nation under God," but in demarcating the "pretense" of conviction, Clinton makes a qualitative distinction between genuine and false religious and political allegiances. The depiction of hate as a force manifesting through false *conviction* signals that the latter is considered to be a cover for dangerous emotional drives that catalyze community fragmentation and national incohesion. Genuine religious conviction has the opposite effect. As Etzioni elaborates, religion can provide an important postsocial democratic source of meaning through which communities are established and social ills tackled:

Communities, data shows, can play a major role in providing preventive and acute care, reducing the need for publicly funded social services as divergent as child care, grief counselling and professional drug and alcohol abuse treatment, as well as assisting in curtailing juvenile delinquency.

The strongest evidence for these statements is found in religious communities that meet my definition of shared affective bonds and a moral culture. Practically all kinds of anti-social behavior are relatively low among Mormon communities in Utah, Orthodox Jewish communities in New York, and Black Muslim groups. They are also lower, on average, in villages and small-town America as compared to large cities, where communities are less prevalent.[33]

The virtue of religion lies in the "preventive" nature of "affective bonds" that not only help to foster social cohesion by containing antisocial impulses but reduce the need for publicly funded social services. The distinction between good (real) and bad (false) religion provides a rationale for cuts in public spending. It was shortly after his second inaugural speech that Clinton launched One America in the 21st Century: The President's Initiative on Race. Claire Jean Kim argues that One America reversed both Myrdal's color-blind approach and the Kerner Commission's emphasis on white racism.[34] Rather, One America was strongly pro-multiculturalist, pinpointing the existence of culturally diverse points of view, beliefs, and practices and emphasizing dialogue as a means of promoting racial reconciliation. Government could facilitate this, but the problem was not of a kind that could be solved by spending. Kim characterizes One America as a conservative-liberal move of historical precedent. In one sense this is correct, but Furedi implicates what he calls "permissive therapeutics" in the *collapse* of Left-Right political ideologies through which previous social webs of meaning influenced subjective identifications and social allegiances.

Current psychologization is neither an instrumental right-wing individualist ethos nor a left-wing liberatory advance. While a therapeutic cultural impulse has been tracked in the past, today the "cure" is missing. Medicalization and psychologization of social and cultural phenomena have a history in which the "sick role" and the absence of responsibility implicated in "ill health" were temporary conditions contrasted with "health." In this sense, psychologization previously included a transformative future orientation, albeit within limits. Current therapeutics erode abnormal/normal distinctions, adding permanence to psychological conditions that in turn promote no external orientation of transformation beyond the self. It is the fusion of what seems like multiculturalism and therapeutics in One America that is hailed as a virtuous solution, not to an American Dilemma but to an American crisis of identity. But the "multiculturalism" located by Kim is in need of deeper analysis, for strict adherence to ethnic identity is called into question by the "pretense of religious or political conviction." Thus, Etzioni's "Good Society" calls for a "community of communities" that promotes "diversity *within* unity" and promotes mental health against the isolating impact of unrestrained individualism.[35] It is toward this goal that ethnic identities should be committed. The collapse of a transcendent orientation once provided by competing political ideologies of Left and Right creates a vacuum that is filled by the psychologization of everyday life, incorporating a solution to the very problem it delineates: to sensitize and not invigorate the dark impulses that lurk deep in troubled souls. This has serious implications for the politics of race.

The therapeutic turn takes its most profound form in the work of one of the most celebrated proponents of the Third Way, sociologist and advisor to the United Kingdom's previous New Labour government, Anthony Giddens. In an article titled "The Third Way Can Beat the Far Right," Giddens makes this point:

> Among the emphases of Third Way thinking are two prime elements: reform of labour markets and welfare systems, to place an emphasis on job creation; and the need to address issues traditionally dominated by the right, such as crime and immigration.[36]

This should not be confused with a call to move right; rather, it is an inversion of what Giddens sees as the role of the traditional Left *and* Right. Traditional meanings of social concepts are reinvented not within an individualist paradigm but beyond the reach of a Left or Right framework. The approach is shared by Clinton's triangulation and Blair's "beyond the conservatism of Left or Right"—for example, as Giddens states, "Welfare is not in essence an economic concept but a psychic one, concerning as it does well-being"; thus, "welfare institutions must be concerned with fostering psychological as well as economic benefits."[37] Any remaining link between economic progress and human welfare is practically severed, material incapacitation eclipsed by psychic healing.

Nor does racism (either pro or anti) figure prominently in Giddens' work; it is the existence of "xenophobic ethnicities or nationalisms" amid the need to encourage cosmopolitan nationalism—a national identity that embraces diversity—that troubles him.[38] His concern stems from the holy trinity of globalization, ontological security, and violence that hinge apparently on the question of migration. When you have manufactured (manmade) risk intensified by globalizing tendencies, it becomes necessary to regulate migration. According to Giddens, this is because "immigration has long been fertile breeding ground for racism"[39] and although migration has an "energizing effect upon the society at large, . . . cultural differences . . . may *cause* resentment or hatred" (italics added).[40] The assumption that cultural differences can provoke hatred leads to the conclusion that migrants from different cultures potentially disrupt cosmopolitan national unity. The problem for Giddens, and for the Third Way generally, is that cosmopolitanism contrasts favorably with multiculturalism in the degree of rigid adherence that individuals feel toward their respective ethnic groups. People who are too tightly bound to an ethnicity are likely to run into trouble, so while ethnic diversity is to be embraced, it should not override the cosmopolitan community bond. Giddens asks, "Under what conditions are the members of different ethnic groups or cultural communities able to live alongside one another and in what circumstances are the relations between them likely to collapse into violence?"[41] This is the question that principally undergirds Clinton's One America. Again, the conceptualization is neither Left nor Right, for while "difference . . . can become a medium of hostility . . . it can also be a medium of creating mutual understanding and sympathy."[42] And how do we guarantee the latter? Giddens assures us that *dialogue* expressed within a unity of moral purpose ensures that "difference" will not beget "a degenerate spiral of communication . . . where antipathy feeds on antipathy, hate upon hate."[43] There is little divergence between this formulation and that of One America where dialogue is presumed to play a positive role not only in facilitating a community of diversity but in disarming hate. But it also helps to contextualize the Clinton administration's thinking behind the Hate Crimes Sentencing Enhancement Act of 1994 and the Church Arson Prevention Act of 1996, especially when we consider the flesh that Giddens puts on the bones. Hate producing hate is most likely to occur "wherever fundamentalism takes hold, whether it be religious, ethnic, nationalist, or gender fundamentalism."[44]

The crucial step in Giddens' theory is the merging of the concept of fundamentalism with the theory of the Authoritarian Personality as an oppositional figure to cosmopolitanism. This is very different from the two anthropological species—authoritarian racist versus liberal individual—of the Kennedy era, which were grounded in the attainment of a new society through the establishment of economic growth, education, and political rights. For Giddens, fundamentalism is not essentially tagged to lack of economic growth, ethnicity, or any specific group because its etiology is, to a large extent, emotional. Anxiety is an essential state of humanness requiring the acquisition and maintenance of a protective cocoon that develops through relationships of basic trust in early parent-child interaction. But anxiety does have a sociocultural form. In posttraditional societies such as those in the West, where submission to a given authority is replaced by radical doubt and the proliferation of authorities, "the dilemma of authority versus doubt"—that is, the source of anxiety—"is ordinarily resolved through a mixture of routine and commitment to a certain form of lifestyle, plus the vesting of trust in a given series of abstract systems."[45] What Giddens means is that the contemporary worldview of an individual needs to be flexible enough to accommodate and integrate other belief systems, points of view, and lifestyle choices that will increasingly be brought into an individual's proximity as a consequence of globalizing tendencies such as migration from putatively more "traditional cultures." The valued "posttraditional" individual, whether migrant or host, minority or majority, needs a regulative governing framework that he or she can trust to deliver cosmopolitan community relations that do not challenge or harm the very essential compromise of worldviews entailed by such relations. The threat to this harmonious picture is rigidity of belief. "Compromise" can "disintegrate under pressure," especially where "individuals find it psychologically difficult or impossible to accept the existence of diverse, mutually conflicting authorities."[46] Such individuals have a predilection for *dogmatic authoritarianism*, which Giddens distinguishes from *faith*, because where the latter "rests on trust," the former represents an abrogation of trust through the "slavish adherence" to "overarching systems of authority."[47] The propensity for intolerance of "conflicting" abstract systems is the character trait of the dogmatic authoritarian, not of those who have faith. The distinction between "slavish adherence" and "trust" fits with Clinton's distinction between genuine and false conviction.

It also dovetails with the Blair administration's establishment of the UK Home Office Faith Communities Unit, whose goal is to "assist faith communities to develop their individuals and organizations in order to reach their full potential. The positive effects of this work will include an increased ability for faith community members to motivate and improve their own community as well as strengthening their links with the wider community."[48] The key difference between Giddens', Etzioni's, Clinton's, or the Blair government's fundamentalist-faith distinction and the authoritarian-liberal distinction of the Kennedy era is that the former do not posit the attainment of a Great Society superior both to that which currently exists and to the communist alternative in terms of its ability to spur greater economic and social progress for humanity. Rather, they stress the Good Society as making the present more livable by tackling the affects of the past. They fuse moral and psychological equality, not political and economic transformation. Thus, Giddens replenishes the Authoritarian Personality thesis, demonstrating how immigration presents obstacles to the fruition of cosmopolitanism—a national fusion of horizons that most befits the transition from multicultural to cosmopolitan capitalism. A policy focus on "faith groups" helps to build trust and, crucially, cosmopolitan community cohesion and allegiance. Yet, because anxiety "is a generalised state of the emotion of the individual" and fear is "apprehension that has an externally constituted object," migrants and ethnic groups can become the target and perpetrator of fear that heightens the generalized state of anxiety in the society they enter.[49] The stirring of dangerous emotion caused by immigration creates a space in which dogmatic authoritarianism grips via the promotion of hate. Anything that may penetrate the protective cocoon needs to be regulated. Consequently, "the Home Office welcomes all projects and organisations which encourage dialogue and co-operation between the different faith communities of the UK."[50] Dialogue between those who have the capacity to trust is central to circumventing degenerative spirals of communication, which can precipitate interethnic cycles of violence. For Giddens, emotional governance is a requisite for what he sees as an essential human requirement for ontological security. In a historical period of high modernity where experience of risk is bolstered by globalizing tendencies that precipitate migration, the potential for penetration of the protective cocoon is heightened and hate is more likely. Consequently, Giddens develops a theoretical approach to immigration regulation via an appeal to an emotionalized subjective state that gives government the authority to intervene as an antihate protector of the cosmopolitan order. The emotional subject underpins both Giddens' social theory and his prescription for governance—emotional governance. And it more or less ties into the current state regulative framework on both sides of the Atlantic.

The aims of the theorist and those of the politician and state are not equivalent. We are not here arguing that Giddens' or Etzioni's social theory was or is adopted by politicians and implemented as policy. Not only are there key differences between the way in which communitarian theory was developed in the United States and in the United Kingdom—Etzioni and Giddens are not identical—but the policy arenas in which Third Way ideas may have been taken up in relation to race are not historically equivalent, as we have demonstrated in Chapters 2 and 3. Nevertheless, just as it was possible to draw out key areas of historical overlap vis-à-vis racial ordering, there are convergences in the epoch of postracial disordering. Specific and significant tenets are shared by communitarian theory and policy formation because they are of the same historical moment and speak to the problem of legitimacy in the post–Cold War juncture. As Giddens himself admitted:

> I should stress that the Third Way is just a label for how you continue the revival of social democratic politics. The European democrats found themselves back in power without a coherent philosophy and the Third Way is simply a label for what that philosophy might involve and it's only some way along in its evolution.[51]

But lest we assume that Giddens' or Etzioni's analysis is only applicable to grasping the philosophical underpinnings of Tony Blair's New Labour and Clinton's New Democrats, salience to post–Cold War context becomes apparent when we consider post-9/11 debates around "Islamofascism" and the distinction between faith and fundamentalism that took off under what is usually hailed as a right-wing Republican Bush administration.

## FROM MALCOLM X TO THE "MUSLIM FASCIST"

> Many white religious leaders have also gone on record against the Black Muslims. . . . a Catholic priest described you as "a fascist-minded hate group." Do you consider this to be true?[52]

> The recent arrests that our fellow citizens are now learning about are a stark reminder that this nation is at war with Islamic fascists who will use any means to destroy those of us who love freedom, to hurt our nation. . . . This country is safer than it was prior to 9/11. We've taken a lot of measures to protect the American people. But obviously we're still not completely safe, because there are people that still plot and people who want to harm us for what we believe in. It is a mistake to believe there is no threat to the United States of America.[53]

Writing in 1981, Palestinian author Edward Said argued that American political culture presents caricatures of the Arab and Muslim worlds to the American public. Such caricatures legitimize American and Western interventions in the Middle East, providing ideological cover for imperialist expansion. What passes for objective knowledge about Arabs and Islam is in fact the West's understanding of itself cast through the lens of "the Muslim" or "the Arab" as representation. Jack Shaheen, a professor of mass communication at Southern Illinois University and world authority on media images of Arabs and Muslims concurs:

> For more than a century Hollywood . . . has used repetition as a teaching tool. Tutoring movie audiences by repeating over and over, in film after film, insidious images of the Arab people, . . . these slanderous stereotypes have affected honest discourse and public policy.[54]

At the level of a purely discursive analysis, President George W. Bush's appraisal of events repeated a familiar theme drawn from the demonizing rhetorical orbit of post–World War II American racial iconography. Yet, it is a mistake to draw too brisk a line of continuity. What is most intriguing about the term "Islamic fascist" is the reaction that followed Bush's use of it. Validating Said and Shaheen, Stephen J. Wayne, a professor of government at Georgetown University, characterized the Republican's approach as follows: "Most people are against fascists of whatever form. By definition, fascists are bad. If you're going to demonize, you might as well use the toughest words you can."[55] The *Washington Post* responded, "Conservative commentators have long talked about 'Islamo-fascism,' and Bush's phrase was a slightly toned-down variation on that theme."[56] Nihad Awad, executive director of the Council on American-Islamic Relations, cautioned, "It is counterproductive to associate Islam or Muslims with fascism,"[57] while Muslim activist Mohamed Elibiary thought it likely that "the president's use of language is going to ratchet up the hate meter."[58] *Nation* columnist Katha Pollitt agreed: "'Islamo-fascism' looks like an analytic term, but really it's an emotional one, intended to get us to think less and fear more. It presents the bewildering politics of the Muslim world as a simple matter of Us versus Them, with war to the end the only answer, as with Hitler."[59] Concern emerged around the possibility that Islam and terror are paired as moral equivalents and that the measure of that equivalence is provided by totalitarianism and its effect: the Holocaust. Implicit in this interpretation is the belief that negatively stereotyping an ethnic or religious group as fascist provides a spurious moral legitimacy for acts of racist exclusion or, more specifically, "racial hate"—a dangerous ethnic emotion.

But what Pollitt does not recognize is that appealing to emotion in a bid to connect with the public had already become standard practice under Clinton. As stated earlier, juggling appeals to victimization is a precarious balance to strike, and when it is seen not to work, as in the case of the foiled bomb plot to which the Bush quotation at the beginning of this section responds, the feelings of victimization escalate on both sides—thus Bush's recognition of "safety fears." But as Furedi notes, "The advocacy of safety" correlates with "the rejection of risk-taking," and this "has implications for the future. If experimentation is discredited, society effectively acknowledges its inability to tackle—never mind to solve—the problems which confront it."[60] When we situate the response to Bush's use of "Islamic fascist" in wider critiques of the Bush administration, it becomes apparent that critics are concerned about how stigma may escalate risk. One of the key critical themes leveled at Bush was that he himself undermined safety due to his Authoritarian disposition:

> This is why George W. Bush is so clear-eyed about Al Qaeda and the Islamic fundamentalist enemy. He believes you have to kill them all. They can't be persuaded that they're extremists, driven by a dark vision. He understands them, because he's just like them. . . . This is why he dispenses with people who confront him with inconvenient facts. . . . He truly believes he's on a mission from God.[61]

This Third Way critique came from "Republican Libertarian" Bruce Bartlett, a domestic policy adviser to Ronald Reagan and a treasury official under George H. W. Bush, but it is an appeal to a consensus view. In their 2004 analysis of American foreign policy, *Imperial Overstretch: George W. Bush and the Hubris of Empire*, Roger Burbach and Jim Tarbell ask, "Who is this man?" A "great salesman," "arrogant," with a "dominant personality" stemming from problematic "id-control," Bush has sold us "questionable schemes" that were "not what he portrayed." Apparently, this Willy Loman of US foreign policy pushed America into a spurious war because he had a troubled childhood, which explains his alcoholism, domineering personality, and consequent policy choices. The authors present an array of expert witnesses, including White

House speechwriters, academics, and psychologists in order to explain that George W. Bush lived in the shadow of his overbearing father:

> The outcome of [his] childhood was what psychologists call an authoritarian personality [which] imposes the strictest possible discipline on themselves and others [and] is organized around rabid hostility to "legitimate targets," often ones nominated by their parents' prejudices. Intensely moralistic, they direct it towards despised social groups. As people, they avoid introspection or loving displays, preferring toughness and cynicism. They regard others with suspicion, attributing ulterior motives to the most innocent behavior. They are liable to be superstitious. . . . Perhaps the group [Bush] reserves the strongest contempt for are those who have adopted the values of the 60s. He says he loathes "people who felt guilty about their lot in life because others were suffering."[62]

But if Bush suffers from an abnormal psychological condition that conned us, on what basis can he or those who elected him be held politically accountable? The critique leveled at Bush turns out not to be a political attack after all but one that ascribes victim status to his actions. Such a status is, of course, amenable to Bush, who went to war ostensibly to avenge the victimization of America. Far from undermining government policy actions, the critique plays by the same rules—and it backfires. The image of Bush as mentally aberrant coalesces with that of Clinton, who (after much "coaxing") openly "confessed" his foibles—vis-à-vis Monica Lewinsky—and in a bid to exonerate his "lapses of judgment," publicly embraced introspection.[63] Regardless, reducing the actions of the US political administration to the (functional or dysfunctional) personality of the president is as wrongheaded as the AP interpretation once used to assail the struggle for black freedom and as mystifying as the modified Third Way anti–public spending apologia for the problems of Los Angeles' urban black and Latino youth. Speaking in 1963 at Western Michigan University, Martin Luther King lashed out against the stifling suffocation perpetrated by "enlightened" psychological explanations:

> There are certain technical words within every academic discipline that soon become stereotypes and cliches. Modern psychology has a word that is probably used more than any other word in modern psychology. It is the word "maladjusted." This word is the ringing cry to modern child psychology. Certainly, we all want to avoid the maladjusted life. . . .

But I say to you . . . there are certain things in our nation and in the world which I am proud to be maladjusted and which I hope all men of good-will will be maladjusted until the good societies realize. I say very honestly that I never intend to become adjusted to segregation and discrimination. I never intend to become adjusted to religious bigotry. I never intend to adjust myself to economic conditions that will take necessities from the many to give luxuries to the few. I never intend to adjust myself to the madness of militarism, to self-defeating effects of physical violence. . . .[64]

King's polemic recognizes the psychocultural entrapment that writes off black emancipation. Explaining acts of anti-oppression as an effect of psychosis placed limits on the possible. The virtue of King's insight was that it was grounded in the pursuit of a better society, free from segregation and discrimination, and he *intended* to do something about it. The oppressed recognized their victimization in order to go beyond the allocation of second-class status. King took on bigotry not as an end to itself but as a means of overturning the economy of white privilege. There could be no separation between economic and political emancipation because his dream was grounded in the essential regard that he bestowed upon the possibility of human overcoming. When Martin Luther King spoke out against "returning hate, for hate multiplies hate," there was no question of targeting "hate" being in itself the endpoint, nor was "hate" devoid of intent. The movement for freedom *intended* to alter the limitations *intentionally* structured by the anti-egalitarian movement. Such was the power, he believed, of human will on either side of the political war for freedom.

It is no secret that King had many differences with Malcolm X and the Black Power movement; it hardly needs to be restated:

I totally disagree with many of his political and philosophical views—at least insofar as I understand where he now stands. I don't want to seem to sound self-righteous, or absolutist, or that I think I have the only truth, the only way. Maybe he does have some of the answer. I don't know how he feels now, but I know that I have often wished that he would talk less of violence, because violence is not going to solve our problem. And in his litany of articulating the despair of the Negro without offering any positive, creative alternative, I feel that Malcolm has done himself and our people a great disservice. Fiery, demagogic oratory in the black ghettos, urging Negroes to arm themselves and prepare to engage in violence, as he has done, can reap nothing but grief.[65]

Strategies and philosophies differed, but what *needs* to be said is that on one position there was full agreement:

> On some positions, Cowardice asks the question, "Is it safe?" Expediency asks the question, "Is it politic?" And Vanity comes along and asks the question, "Is it popular?" But Conscience asks the question, "Is it right?" And there comes a time when one must take a position that is neither safe, nor politic, nor popular, but he must do it because Conscience tells him it is right. I believe today that there is a need for all people of good will to come together with a massive act of conscience and say in the words of the old Negro spiritual, "We ain't goin' study war no more." This is the challenge facing modern man.[66]

Differences on the virtue of violent or military solutions were important when considering the right course of action, but neither Martin Luther King nor Malcolm X questioned the rightfulness of putting freedom before safety, politics, or populism. For in the absence of emancipation, no human was safe. Today, the philosophy of "modern man" is reversed.

As Furedi notes, the "celebration of safety alongside the continuous warning about risks constitutes a profoundly anti-human intellectual and ideological regime. It continuously invites society and its individual members to constrain their aspirations and to limit their actions."[67] Marking a distinction between Islam as faith (a trust concept) and Islam as fascism (rigid authoritarian adherence) has become, for many commentators, key to the deployment of the latter because they think it is both the right and the safe thing to do. American historian and Middle East analyst Daniel Pipes, who has been at the forefront of popularizing the association between Islamic terrorism and fascism, is "careful" to cite "Islamism" rather than Islam as the threat. Asked in an interview if he equated "Islam with fascism," his response was "No. I equate Islamism with fascism. . . . Islamism is a totalitarian ideology. An Islamist is a danger in the same way a fascist is a danger."[68] A distinction is made between the practice of Islam as faith and rigid ideology—a distinction echoed by the "authoritarian" George W. Bush:

> Islamic terrorist attacks serve a clear and focused ideology, a set of beliefs and goals that are evil, but not insane. Some call this evil Islamic radicalism; others, militant Jihadism; still others, Islamo-fascism. Whatever it's called, this ideology is very different from the religion of Islam. This form of radicalism exploits Islam to serve a

violent, political vision: the establishment, by terrorism and subversion and insurgency, of a totalitarian empire that denies all political and religious freedom.[69]

The term "Islamofascist" is used to designate a form of intolerance—the dogmatic imposition inherent to totalitarian projects—a disrespect for conflicting beliefs or worldviews. Fascism as authoritarian imposition is to be carefully disentangled from the Muslim religion. Islamofascism threatens safety, whereas Islam does not. For Bush, faith was distinguishable from totalitarianism. But why even bother to make such a distinction? Whether we agree or disagree, could it be that Bush thought it right to do so? Burbach and Tarbell do not question that Bush acted intentionally, nor do they insinuate that he acted against his own judgment when it came to military action in Iraq. Rather, they argue that intention was *guided by dangerous emotional traits.* Bush's authoritarian co-conspirators—his aides Karl Rove, Karen Hughes, and Joe Allbaugh—we are told, formed an "iron triangle" around Bush that ensured his "id was captured, shackled and manacled and locked away" at all times, insulating the public from the "real agenda."[70] Consequently, in 2002, "Bush's aggressive authoritarian personality guaranteed that unilateral preemptive war would become a reality."[71] Burbach and Tarbell's anti-authoritarian analysis is unhelpful. When George H. W. Bush made his 1990 pre–Gulf War proclamation of a new world order with America at the helm, this coupled Francis Fukuyama's end of history thesis, and it seemed to signal that an era of unstoppable American capitalism was on the cards amid continuing military conflicts between, in Fukuyama's words, "the pre-Historical (third) and post-Historical (first) worlds."[72] This was in step with Samuel Huntington's prediction of civilizational clash[73]—"sino-Islamic connection" versus the West—and appeared to some commentators to expose a hidden ethno-imperialist rational behind US foreign policy: no longer a cold, but a hot, war on the make, a new right on the take. Both pros and antis incorrectly assumed that capitalism and the state could be self-sufficient—that, in the words of Noam Chomsky, "The pretext is gone [but] the policies remain the same."[74] As we demonstrated in Chapters 2 and 3, neither capitalism nor the modern state has ever existed without the radically subjective that both held it to account and against which the conservative subjective could justify itself. Collapse the contest made possible by the pursuit of human exceptionalism, and the basis for any forward movement dissipates into inertia. Neither Fukuyama nor Huntington foresaw this.

Just a few years prior to George W. Bush's faith/fundamentalism distinction, Hishaam Aidi made the point that "commentators are advancing theories warning of a dangerous epidemic spreading through our inner cities today, infecting misguided, disaffected minority youth and turning them into anti-American terrorists." Aidi notes, "The pathogen is Islam, more specifically, an insidious mix of radical Islam and black militancy."[75] Certainly the prospect of alienated minority American youth turning to radical Islam and black militancy is a problem for the state, but a deeper more profound problem arises if minority American youth *believe* they are being unjustly labeled as evil perpetrators of terror and nonminority Americans actually believe that minority youth *are* evil perpetrators of terror. By appealing to the faith/fundamentalism distinction, state officials think they offer alienated minority youth a way out of "hate," a means of circumventing any identification with what is interpreted as authoritarian currents. Islamic faith is presented as a victim of rigid fundamentalism that is "not insane" but that attempts to key into and move dangerous emotion. The faith/fundamentalism distinction gives nonminority Americans a point of contact and commonality with the potentially alienated. The state bestows psychological, not economic, welfare on the American public. For the current political classes, an appeal to faith promotes cosmopolitan tolerance as an answer to the prospect of millions of potential ethnically volatile individuals (from whichever ethnic group) who just might *find it psychologically difficult or impossible to accept the existence of diverse, mutually conflicting authorities.* It is a script that could have been written by Giddens or Etzioni. There is no real reason to believe that Bush did not think such a course of action was correct, unless of course we agree with critics across the political spectrum that he was "untrustworthy," but we are yet to see any alternative course of action being offered. If American capitalism was that powerful, it would not need the state to sustain it, and if the United States was that invincible, it would not need to placate angry minority youth through the fostering of faith networks and appeals to fear. Bush's pronouncements were symptomatic of a political class concerned with holding the present together but with no political vision of a future beyond what currently exists. Equality, like peace, is placed beyond human intervention, located within the mystical realm of emotion—the new capitalist limit point—beyond "the conservatism of either Left or Right."

## "LITTLE EICHMANNS" AND THE COSMOPOLITAN COMMUNITY

Although rhetorically oriented toward the United States, Bush's various pronouncements on Islamic terrorism share key ideological underpinnings with Tony Blair's Third Way prescription. In the West, the archetypal iconic demons of Left/Right conservatism are Stalin and Hitler. Bush interprets Islamic fascism as a descendant of totalitarian ideologies of the past:

> you have seen this kind of enemy before. They're successors to Fascists, to Nazis, to Communists, and other totalitarians of the 20th century. And history shows what the outcome will be: This war will be difficult; this war will be long; and this war will end in the defeat of the terrorists and totalitarians.[76]

The potential for polarization that this rhetoric advances is particularly stark when groups see themselves as the victims of the conservatism of either Left or Right. The potential chaos precipitated by conflicting victimization claims surfaced in October 2007, when the David Horowitz Freedom Center launched "Islamofascism Awareness Week" across 114 US college and university campuses, with the stated aim of "highlighting the threat from the Islamic Jihad and the oppression of Muslim women." Criticism of the campaign was denounced by Horowitz:

> Anti-American leftists and organizations supporting the Islamic *jihad* organized a national campaign of vitriol and hate. . . . Speakers for the events and students organizing them were attacked as religious bigots and anti-Muslim "racists" and "fascists." Attacks were spear-headed by the misnamed American Arab Anti-Discrimination Committee. . . . Under the Orwellian banner of defending tolerance, Abourezk's group sent letters to the presidents of all the colleges hosting events, in an attempt to get administrators to shut them down and silence their speakers in advance. . . . Cliopatria blogger Ralph Luker described our events as "Hate Your Neighbor Week," which was accurate only if your neighbor were Osama bin Laden, Ayman Zawahiri or Mahmoud Ahmadinejad.[77]

Horowitz doth protest too much. But there is a wider point to be taken from this exchange. Today, "anti-fascist hate" boomerangs. There can be little doubt that the image of fascism carries an implicit accusation of "racist" and that it has popular salience; no semiotic analysis need be conducted to prove the self-evident. For those opposed to the term "Islamofascist," distinguishing between Muslims and Islamists does not overcome its inherent flaw. Vilifying Islamists promotes suspicion in toto of Muslims. A climate of intolerant totalitarianism that those who deploy the term wish to counter is seen by those who oppose the term as inherent to its very deployment. On the other hand, opposition to the term is portrayed as Orwellian double-think; their cultural pluralism is seemingly "uncovered" as fake—a mystifying carrier of totalitarian thought-control that aids and abets terror.

Somewhat mind-boggling to the casual observer is that the act of pairing Islam with fascism can be portrayed as racist, while defending Islam can also be "exposed" as an act of defending fascism and, thus, racism. The Islamofascist "debate" triggers wider disengagement from the politics of equality threatening to escalate suspicion and fear across the social spectrum. On this, Pollitt is correct. But the point of Bush's usage of the term is that the attempt to key into the "fear-safety" couplet not only reveals a need on the part of the state to connect emotionally with the private fears of the public but a presumed need to harness that emotion by anchoring it in the present against the past *and* the future. Today, no matter how vigorously one launches the "antifascist" boomerang, its forward trajectory is but a momentary eclipse of its inevitable return, which may disorientate when it smacks the unsuspecting, laying the field open to a myriad of eager and more skilled players, but neither pitcher nor catcher moves any further forward. The "Islamofascist" card is symbolic of a political class that has no vision.

Much of the confusion and incoherence stems from the designation and acceptance of "hate" as the central protagonist of inequality. The *Oxford English Dictionary* defines *hate* as a noun, "An emotion of extreme dislike or aversion; detestation, abhorrence, hatred," and as a verb, "To hold in very strong dislike; to detest; to bear malice to." Following Norman Fairclough, the former can be conceptualized as a condition, and the latter as a process.[78] The latter has both subject and object predicates: The subject (perpetrator) of hate holds the object of hate (target) in contempt. The condition has neither subject nor object. The subjectlessness of the condition inheres in its definition as an emotion, and this takes on extreme proportions when emotion is given a heightened significance in the constitution of the human subject and/or specific individuals/groups can be characterized as more or less emotionally destructive. But the crucial point about the elevation of hate to the status of "autonomy" is that it transforms the idea of equality between two persons into the equality of emotion. The state regulative response moves accordingly. This became very apparent in the United Kingdom under the Blair administration. The timing of the Blair government (1997–2007) in relation to both the Thatcher-Reagan era and the Clinton administration in many ways made the New Labour government the prime mover of Third Way politics, specifically in relation to criminal justice.

Paul Iganski has explored the development of the concept of "hate crime" in relation to racially aggravated offences, and legislative measures instituted against such, in New Labour's 1998 Crime and Disorder Act.[79] The underlying principle is that racial attacks are "socially divisive and morally repugnant.... We believe that if racism is allowed to grow unchecked it will begin to corrode the fabric of our open and tolerant society."[80] The idea of social corrosion underpinned the 1997 Crime and Disorder Bill, and, as Iganski suggests, the severity of racist expression is "perhaps" related to "the common-sense assumption that hate speech leads to, or provokes, violence and discrimination against the groups concerned."[81] The severity of racial hate crime—that is, the expression of racialized emotion—is predicated on its relationship to interracial violence and the consequences of such for social breakdown. Thus, hate crime is placed high on the scale of governmental priorities, and because expressions can be reflective of hate, racist expressions are reflective of dangerous emotion. The logic lends itself to the conclusion that emotions should be governed as a means of circumventing degenerate spirals of communication.

While the criminalization of incitement to racial hatred was reinforced by the Thatcher government,[82] and the 1994 House of Commons Committee on Crime and Disorder was an initiative of the Major government, the 1998 Crime and Disorder Act, which reinforced the idea of incitement to racial hatred, fell into place within New Labour's policy rationale: "Tough on crime, tough on the causes of crime" ("toctocc"). However, when the problem of racialized emotion is framed by the rationale underpinning the control of immigration to a "cosmopolitan nation," it is recontextualized with renewed significance, for, as Giddens concludes, "toctocc" should require the government to be "tough on immigration, but tough on the causes of hostility to immigrants."[83] What causes hostility toward migrants? As noted above, Giddens begins from an assumption that "cultural differences . . . may cause resentment or hatred." The logic of "toctocc" when applied to hate crime is that because hatred can lead to crime, a tough response to hatred is required. However, the ability to stir up hate is predicated on the availability of anxiety, which the presence of some migrants is deemed to heighten, especially among certain groups:

> It is in those communities least likely to have benefited from added value economic activity and entrepreneurship where the biggest challenge lies. For even at a time of high levels of economic activity and buoyant employment, the low skill or no skill groupings are likely to be most fearful of the low skill, no skill entrant into the local economy.[84]

The putative economic function, as AP theorists would have once argued, is not the prime mover in these migrant-host relations. There is something else about the "low skill or no skill groupings" that makes them more fearful of migrants. As increased anxiety is perceived to be a potential consequence of the presence of migrants who may threaten jobs, and anxiety is preyed upon by perpetrators of hate, the "wrong type" of migration is a potential cause of hate crime, and thus social polarization. Government needs to "manage migration" in order to stem the tide of hate crime and, thus, the spiral of interethnic violence that may follow. Ironically (or not), tough controls are tied to the need to protect those migrants whom the government designates as "legitimate victims" from the hatred that their presence may incite. Such is the demand of "an ethics of care." In the words of Stanley Cohen, "Crime may be presented as part of the wider discourse of risk."[85] And from the above, we can deduce that migration has become a medium through which crime and globalization are seen to be linked. In a cosmopolitan society, hatred toward the cosmopolitan other becomes a crime. This leads to the posited need to control immigration in order to alleviate public anxieties so that those who wish to spread racial hatred have no influence. The aversion of such risk and the building of trust are imperative to fulfilling government's requirement for legitimacy. The "inefficient management of migration" erodes people's sense of belonging and affinity with government. Consequently, the presence of migrants deemed most likely to stir anxieties must be regulated. The common denominator is that the socioeconomic and/or character traits of certain migrant groups can elicit anxiety upon which dogmatic authoritarianism can prey.

Matters are made more complex when the government is confronted by the claims of British-born minorities against British institutions. When Sir William Macpherson's investigation into the murder of black teenager Stephen Lawrence and the subsequent verdict that the Metropolitan Police had mishandled the investigation were labeled institutionally racist, it was hailed as an antiracist victory.[86] Closer scrutiny both of the inquiry's terms of reference and of the report's findings reveals two salient points. Given that the Lawrence campaign and its charge of racism held a mirror to the immorality of the British police force and the government's concern with the ability of British institutions to command legitimate authority (i.e., trust) among the British populace, the government agreed to the inquiry because of the purported impact that the campaign could have on the legitimacy of British institutions more widely. Consequently, advice submitted to the inquiry, which stressed the concern to establish trust, was highly significant. As Macpherson states:

> As Dr. Oakely points out, the disease cannot be attacked by the organisation involved in isolation. If such racism infests the police its elimination can only be achieved by means of a fully developed partnership approach in which the police service works jointly with the minority ethnic communities. How else can mutual confidence and trust be reached?[87]

The subsequent definition of institutional racism reflected the need to be responsive to the campaigners' demands, and therefore to facilitate trust, but this requirement also necessitated that the police as an institution not be undermined in its capacity to confer trust. Consequently, the concept of "unwittingness" provided the required bridge over the public inquiry's contradictory terms of reference. Following Lord Scarman's report[88] into the Brixton riots of 1981, which "accepted the existence of what he termed 'unwitting' or 'unconscious' racism," Macpherson's criticism rested not only on "unwittingness" not being given "equal weight" with intentional racism, but on the fact that "unwittingness" had not previously been sufficient to warrant the charge of institutional racism. On day three of the Macpherson inquiry, the commissioner of the Metropolitan Police Service (MPS) raised the following concerns:

> If this Inquiry labels my service as institutionally racist, the average police officer, the average member of the public will assume the normal meaning of those words.

They will assume a finding of conscious, wilful or deliberate action or inaction to the detriment of ethnic minority Londoners. . . . I actually think that use of those two words in a way that would take on a new meaning to most people in society would actually undermine many of the endeavours to identify and respond to the issues of racism which challenge all institutions and particularly the police because of their privileged and powerful position.[89]

Macpherson responded:

We hope and believe that the average police officer and average member of the public will accept that we do not suggest that all police officers are racist and will both understand and accept the distinction we draw between overt individual racism and the pernicious and persistent institutional racism which we have described.[90]

Moreover:

Nor do we say that in its policies the MPS is racist. Nor do we share the fear of those who say that in our finding of institutional racism, in the manner in which we have used that concept, there may be a risk that the moral authority of the MPS may be undermined.[91]

The concern of the MPS commissioner and Macpherson revolved around the idea of willful intent. The pairing of institutional racism with willful intent would undermine the institution. Consequently, post-Macpherson, an accusation of institutional racism easily translates into *not of the will of the perpetrator.* Moreover, "Without recognition and action to eliminate such racism it can prevail as part of the ethos or culture of the organisation. It is a corrosive disease."[92] The unwitting perpetrator of racism becomes a victim of his or her own thought processes, which are shaped by external forces that enter the individual's head and make that person act against his or her own free will. In addition to the "unknowing" element, the *Oxford English Dictionary Online* defines *unwitting* as "unsoundness of mind; insanity." The only way an individual agent can be held responsible is to treat him or her via thought reprogramming so that he or she is no longer the victim of diseased thoughts. By this definition, neither perpetrator nor institution can be held responsible under liberal law, unless greater weight is given to the emotional constitution of the human subject. This would require a redefinition of the human subject, such that agent autonomy (and thus responsibility) is diminished. Perpetrators of actions who claim that they were compelled to them by external or informal forces beyond their control must be conferred a diminished capacity to act and, consequently, a diminished responsibility for said actions. A similar point is made by Furedi, who argues that "the key word" in the Macpherson definition of institutional racism is "'unwitting': an unconscious response driven by unregulated and untamed emotions," Macpherson "helped codify feelings and emotions into law."[93] The overall outcome is to redefine racism as the symptom of a sick society and the perpetrator as a psychologically aberrant victim. Consequently, Macpherson's preferred "cure" was that of "race-awareness training"—therapy for "unwitting racists" as a means of promoting self-reflexivity. More specifically, Macpherson laid the groundwork for the institutionalization of emotional governance in the form of antiracism: Third Way antiracism.

The inquiry led directly to the Race Relations Act (2000 Amendment). The Act became a tool for generating community cohesion. The aims and objectives of the Home Office Community Cohesion Unit mirror that of tackling issues raised by the reports of Denham, Cantle, Clarke, and Ritchie following urban uprisings in the summer of 2001 in the towns of Burnley, Oldham, and Bradford.[94] All the reports on the events stressed the need to reunite polarized communities by building a sense of security through alleviating the "anxiety" that "race relations" can bring in the absence of "sensitive" management. The government's Connecting with Communities program reflects an understanding that cultural attachments are deemed to be important as a means of fostering psychological attachment both within and between communities. The state is invited to recognize the multiple victimizations that have led to and that create ethnic antipathy. The subsequent diagnosis of "parallel lives" as a cause of social breakdown creates a space for psycho-cultural intervention.

Despite some disagreement between then CRE chairman Gurbux Singh and Ted Cantle,[95] the community cohesion agenda laid forth by the government set a standard adopted by the CRE:[96]

> We will identify and work with key players nationally, regionally and locally to take forward the community cohesion agenda. We want to particularly focus on cross-community activities and models that will enable functional, cohesive communities across Britain.

> The Race Relations (Amendment) Act 2000 provides an opportunity for public bodies to promote community cohesion. Particularly in relation to the third aspect of the general duty: promoting good relations between different racial groups.[97]

The "race relations" problematic is incorporated under the dominant framework of the community cohesion narrative. The main body previously charged by the government with ensuring the maintenance of a racialized civil order, the CRE, and the Third Way position of the government mutually reinforce and reinterpret the construction of the racially risk-averse human subject, placing both the government and the CRE in the position of managing relations between risk-prone communities. Antiracism is constructed as a therapeutic intervention into the thought processes of unwitting individuals in order to circumvent the potential for a degenerating cycle of anticosmopolitan ethnic violence. The logic upon which such intervention rests is that unregulated anxiety leads to social breakdown, especially when "culturally distinct communities," threatened by "globalizing processes," interact in an area of high social deprivation. Additionally, institutions must not perpetuate such a cycle. As government attempts to appeal to emotion through tapping into fear, it is confronted by the consequence of legitimizing its authority through an appeal to the perceived victimization of the unwitting perpetrator. Where the perpetrator acts wittingly, Third Way antiracism provides a causal story that takes its cue from the relationship between authoritarianism and hate crime. Both require the psychological intervention of the state: the former through "awareness training," and the latter through criminalization.

The Other Than Mexican category with which we began this chapter should now fit into place. The dual (in)visibility of the threat it poses lies in its quality as a cipher of *dangerous emotion* that can potentially infect us all. The OTM, we are told, is carried by it and therefore carries it in the neighborhood, shopping malls, movie houses, restaurants, and cafes; across borders; on foot; and on airplanes, buses, trains, ships, and the subway. The Brazilian migrant Jean Charles de Menezes was killed for it, Governor Brewer introduced SB1070 to stop it, President Clinton launched One America to heal it, Prime Minister Blair introduced the Crime and Disorder Act to police it, and President George W. Bush sent terror suspects to Guantánamo to torture it. It is also the reason President Obama stood against Arizona SB1070 while pledging 1,200 extra National Guard to monitor the United States–Mexico border. But the set piece of the Obama administration's race intervention was the signing into law of the Matthew Shepard and James Byrd Jr. Hate Crimes Prevention Act (Public Law No. 111-84) in 2009. The law, which prohibits acts of violence perpetrated against an individual because of his or her actual or perceived race, color, religion, national origin, gender, sexual orientation, gender identity, or disability, was included in the $680 billion National Defense Authorization Act for Fiscal Year 2010. Coming nearly a decade after President George H. W. Bush signed the Hate Crime Statistics Act into law, and following in the footsteps of President Clinton's Campus Hate Crimes Right to Know Act of 1997, *PL111-84* represents a move in the definition of equality, which is highly, but more than, symbolic. Critics argued that there was no relationship between hate crime and military defense and that the law created a special class of victim. The OTM category alerts us to why both criticisms are misplaced. Justification for the law is laid out in the "findings" section of the written document. The first and second findings are as follows:

1. The incidence of violence motivated by the actual or perceived race, color, religion, national origin, gender, sexual orientation, gender identity, or disability of the victim poses a serious national problem.
2. Such violence disrupts the tranquility and safety of communities and is deeply divisive.

Section 4712 of the Act also includes a "prohibition on attacks on United States Servicemen on Account of Service." The policing of, and military defense against, dangerous emotion rests on a blurred distinction between victim and perpetrator, especially when military spending aids, as it does, overseas actions and domestic defense against the suspects of terror. Anti–hate crime legislation does not drop "intent." The perpetrator is he or she who *intends* to act against the target. But the explicit inclusion of hate as the driving force behind intent provides an escape clause. The perpetrator who admits to hating automatically summons the deeper question as to the etiology of the dangerous emotion. The most readily available answer—that he is himself a victim of authoritarianism—not only provides an explanation for "evil" but undermines the enforcement of civil rights. The pursuit of equality is placed beyond human hands. The criminalization of dangerous emotion does not locate the cause of oppression within the social structure, the institutions of "White Power," nor does it admit to the contradiction between universal rights and the inability of the capitalist system to deliver those rights. Oppression is redefined when the cause of inequality is located in "hate," but such is the current demand for cosmopolitan national unity. The move signals no pessimism of the intellect but pessimism of the will: an economy of mind. The state requests our trust in its endeavor to keep us safe from the possibility that our discontent may lead us astray like "Little Eichmanns" driven by factors that lie beyond our will to the postracial disorder.[98] But there are still those of us who believe in the human will, in the power of universal freedom, and in the superiority of "Big P" Politics over the politics of fear, and we subscribe to the view, today so anachronistic, that we have nothing to fear but fear itself. In the following chapter we critically examine the possibility for "Big P" Politics today.

CHAPTER FIVE

# WHAT MAY I HOPE?

> Black radicals forced the white Left to see and hear differently, and they and a few white rebels heard in the sounds and movements and writings the birth of a utopian future rising out of the abyss of racism and oppression
>
> *Robin D. G. Kelley,* Freedom Dreams[1]

## MASTERS AND SLAVES

In 1971, American linguist Noam Chomsky and French philosopher Michel Foucault engaged in the now infamous Chomsky-Foucault debate, where each presented and defended their respective approaches to questions of human nature and politics.[2] Chomsky sought to liberate what he saw as the essential human need for creative work repressed by the structures of multinational corporate capitalism. Emancipatory politics required an ideal human subject upon which notions of justice could be founded. Foucault differed. Critique that invokes an ethical vision must acknowledge its own internality to power. Ethical vision based on transcending the present social condition can never represent more than a claim conceived within the power relations in which it emerges and therefore cannot bring about the fundamental overthrow of that society. Notions of justice grounded on a foundational subject, whether that subject be liberalism's individual or Marxism's collective, were implausible emancipatory tropes historically derived in the culturally specific project of Enlightenment: the age of reason.

Chomsky-Foucault reflected a post-1968 world gripped by aftershock, instability, and lament and captured an embryonic but crucial schism. Despite the specifics of anarcho-syndicalism, Chomsky's retention of a human ethical foundation was at that time dominant, reflecting post-Holocaust Enlightenment unity underlying the antagonistic projects of liberalism and socialism. Their mutual commitment to human advancement based on competing visions of "Man" as individual or social was held in-check, at least in the West, by social democratic reformism. Foucault's position, by contrast, was emergent. A disaffected ex-member of the French Communist Party, Foucault derided Marxism's revolutionary vanguard, its elevation of the working class as historical agent of social advance. For Foucault the modernist orientation of proletarian theory was underpinned by a bankrupt humanism that it shared with liberalism. And this was a view held by many on the French Left.

Louis Althusser erased humanism from Marxism; what he saw as a break between the "early" Hegelian and "later" scientific Marx underpinned his theory of the human subject as ideological effect. Through the Ideological State Apparatus, "*the individual is interpellated as a (free) subject in order that he shall submit freely to the commandments of the Subject, i.e. in order that he shall (freely) accept his subjection*, i.e. in order that he shall make the gestures and actions of his subjection 'all by himself.'"[3] This attack against human centeredness presented a seductive challenge to foundational determinism—no one factor such as the economy or class could be held as a foundational determinant of all other phenomena. This would prove to be attractive to Marxists who lost faith in the industrial working class, creating a space for their later privileging of new social movements. But the move enabled a decentering of economic determinism that did not dismantle any positivist concept of class, much to E. P. Thompson's consternation.[4] In deprivileging a determining human foundation, Althusser relativized class but left the Stalinist conception of class intact, thereby enabling him to remain in the French Communist Party.

Humanism's theoretical obliteration was not arbitrary; it had ideological roots in the legitimization of reaction against social transformation. The key can be discerned in relation to the Stalinist reading of Hegelian dialectics. The "negation of the negation" had entailed an intrinsically open-ended conceptualization of social transformation. Within the capitalist epoch, human beings are presented with the means by which the obstacles to (negation of) human advancement can be overcome (negated), but only once they have attained consciousness of said obstacles. Under the capitalist system of exchange and exploitative extraction of surplus, human beings are alienated from their ideal human condition. Free will, the expression of which can only truly be realized through the individual's dealienated social constitution, is suppressed (negated) by the narrow individualism of competitive capitalism. As a historical subject, only the proletarian class as a human-determining class can negate this negation. The formulation was dropped from Marxist theory by Joseph Stalin. As Christopher Arthur has noted, Stalin relinquished this crucial element in Marxist dialectics because it "characterizes a certain structure of self-determination."[5] To present a rationale for the USSR, Stalin theorized that the Soviet working class did not present a negation of "socialism in one country"—the favored endpoint exported via Moscow-backed communist parties internationally. For Stalin, the realization of Soviet communism (and his own place within it) meant the proletarian subject of history was surplus to requirements. Althusser argued that the proletarian negation of the negation was an idealist leftover from Hegel's master-slave dialectic, divorced from Marx's later works, and he said of Stalin's position:

> One further word on the negation of the negation. Today it is official convention to reproach Stalin with having suppressed the "laws of the dialectic," and more generally with having turned away from Hegel, the better to establish his dogmatism. . . . It seems to me that it would be simpler to recognise that the expulsion of the "negation of the negation" from the domain of the Marxist dialectic might be evidence of the real theoretical perspicacity of its author.[6]

Stalin's theoretical maneuvering provided justification for the quashing of all opposition to his iron fist, but it had far-reaching effects, especially in Western Europe where the working class had failed to deliver. One effect was that Althusser backed the idea that consciousness and its raising were not crucial or central components of social change. Any theoretical approach to history must now be one premised on history without a subject.

It is within this climate that we need to situate Foucault. The working classes had supported the National Socialists in Germany; were complicit in the racist treatment of minorities in France; were nationalist rather than internationalist or anti-imperialist; were sexist and homophobic; and represented the inherent limitation of collective emancipation projects based on the liberation of an ideal human. Additionally, the "human" centrality of the collective subject of revolutionary progress complimented the so-called rational-subject of liberal capitalism—the individual—such that radicalism could not help but appeal to the very currents that colluded in its own hegemonic suffocation. Foucault moved antisubjectivism beyond ideological interpellation through a reconceptualization of power:

> Individuals are the vehicles of power, not its points of application. . . . It is already one of the prime effects of power that certain bodies, certain gestures, certain discourses, certain desires, come to be identified and constituted as individuals. The individual, that is, is not the *vis-à-vis* of power; it is, I believe, one of its prime effects. . . .[7]

On this formulation, "radicalism" must be aware of its own immanence to the power relations in which it operates. Because radicalism could only function as immanent critique, Foucault redefined "liberation" as the radical shifting of all-pervasive power from within. The historical subject, being imbued with a sense of overcoming historical forms of domination through the raising of consciousness, was a degenerate project. Despite various nuances of position, the contemporary disavowal of human subjectivity came to exert a seminal influence on the theorization of "race."

Postwar Left liberation politics were underpinned by the rise of anticolonial self-determination movements. Symptomatic was the French Left's ambivalent reaction to black subjectivity, captured by the Fanon-Sartre Negritude debate. In *Black Orpheus*, Sartre celebrated Negritude as the authentic antithesis of Western rationalism but as a "weak stage" in the dialectical overcoming of a racist class society.[8] In *Black Skin, White Masks*, Fanon vented at Sartre's dialectical assimilation of the Negro: a subject robbed of history, of past and future. The Negro existed solely as negation in an abstract Eurocentric class question.[9] Azzedine Haddour notes that there are three available readings of the Fanon-Sartre debate: Fanon's celebration of Negritude was transitional, rejected by the *Wretched of the Earth*; Fanon is read through Sartre's interpretation; and Fanon increasingly adopted Negritude as an ideological position. Haddour suggests Fanon came to accept Sartre's dialectical view, but that a distinction should be made between what Fanon calls Negroism as a cultural movement and Negritude as race consciousness. Though Fanon retained a concern with race consciousness, this was not an ideological endorsement.[10]

Haddour's distinction is helpful, but it does not tell us the whole story. For Fanon, the politico-economic domination of the colonized West Indian broke the pretension of a shared African mythical past to which Negritude appealed, because "what is often called the black soul is a white man's artifact."[11] But this was a necessary difference with whites in the movement of the colonized to the appropriation of a new humanism, and it could not be captured in Sartre's class dialectic. The European was ill-equipped to spontaneously countenance the dynamic of the colonial encounter. Colonized man was neither black nor white man: "Black is not a man. . . . There is a zone of non-being, an extraordinarily sterile and arid region, an utterly naked declivity where an authentic upheaval can be born."[12] In searching for self through a unified Negro cultural past, the West Indian is confronted by nonexistence (absent a unified Negro past): the naked truth that he is a colonized being in a postcolonized body. He is neither black nor white and must make himself anew from the knowledge of his nothingness, thus precipitating a new history of "Man." Sartre's dialectic blocks this move.

Sartre himself was ambivalent toward Western humanism; it is, after all, this ambivalence that allowed for celebration of Negritude as a challenge to white domination:

> [It is] the strip-tease of our humanism. There you can see it, quite naked, and it's not a pretty sight. It was nothing but an ideology of lies, a perfect justification for pillage; its honeyed words, its affectation of sensibility were only alibis for our aggressions.[13]

The rise of the colonial subject as a radical figure for the Western Left can only be understood through this ambivalence. The French Left did make a space for nonclass subjects, but on *their* terms. Sartre is genuinely thought of as a humanist—as sharing, some might argue, an antihumanist humanism with Fanon.[14] But in conceptualizing Sartre's dialectical position as humanist, we are forced either to fit Fanon into the formulation or exclude the anticolonial subject from humanism in toto. Fanon's position lies neither outside of dialectics nor inside Sartre's "humanist" position. The characterization of Sartre or Fanon as antihumanist humanist is a misapprehension both of how Sartre formulates the master-slave dialectic and how this affects Fanon.

Pivotal was Alexandre Kojève's reading of Hegel, delivered in a series of lectures in France in the 1930s. James Heartfield notes, Kojève read Hegel's master-slave dialectic through a humanist lens more in keeping with contemporary suspicions of spirit and religiosity.[15] In Kojève's reading of Hegel, antagonistic social positions as they appeared in capitalist society, conceptualized as master (self) and slave (other), were immanent to the unfolding of that society. Kojève *sociologized* master-slave so that *society* was thought of as a relational self-other form. By "humanizing" Hegel, Kojève extinguished the underlying essence—that is, the spirit—of subjectivity and thus its historical development from partial to fully self-conscious agent (the movement of consciousness). The transcendent quality of consciousness, the basis for overcoming divergent social positions vanished in theory and was substituted with a sociology where individual (self) was realized through, but separate from, society (other). Incommensurable self/other categories took the place of emergent consciousness, leaving no theoretical basis for the abolition of the entire capitalist social space. To paraphrase Žižek, "Freedom of choice *within* the coordinates of existing power relations" was left in tact, while precluding "an intervention which undermines those very coordinates."[16] Theoretically, in the absence of consciousness, the transcendent moment had been replaced by immanent critique. Through Kojève, Hegel dispirited had a monumental impact on French thought and beyond, and categories of self and other were established as absolutes. For Simone de Beauvoir, the sexes were irreconcilable, and for Sartre, it was the colonized and the colonizer. What is missing from interpretations of Fanon-Sartre is that the white Western working-classes, by virtue of their racialized whiteness and barbaric superiority over "nonwhites" were not human beings, but an anthropological being devoid of the humanness denied to blacks. The latter point was never clearly developed, and therefore it remains unarticulated as a potential movement maker or breaker. The dialectical abyss spanning Fanon and Sartre could not be crossed by a theoretical bridge built on the diminished subjectivities of colonized and colonizer, and their incommensurable forms are clearly evident in the Left's theoretical appropriation of Black Power, to which we now turn our attention.

## P.O.W.(ER)

Just four years prior to Chomsky-Foucault, C. L. R. James spoke in London on Black Power, a resounding endorsement of the movement and of the then leading role played within it by Stokely Carmichael.[17] As James saw it, Black

Power was the new socialist vanguard, and he drew on Lenin's insights into the Russian Revolution of 1905 and the Irish Rebellion of 1916 in order to eradicate workerist and positivist conceptions of class struggle. For Lenin, argued James, to be proletarian was a constant coming-into-consciousness of the barriers that stood in the way of transcending capitalism, not by standing outside and wishing for an inevitable outcome but by engaging with the present so as to move forward to a new, albeit unknown, future. Being "working class" in the positivist sense adopted within the industrial workers and Stalinist movements was not the essence of radical subjectivity. Proletarianization invoked the coming-into-consciousness of an internationalist vogue that could connect oppression and the exploitative capitalist relation. For James, proletarianization made Black Power a banner for the universal emancipation of humanity, and for this reason he applauded the following statement by Carmichael:

> We do not seek to create communities where, in place of white rulers, black rulers control the lives of black masses and where black money goes into a few black pockets: we want to see it go into the communal pocket. The society we seek to build among black people is not an oppressive capitalist society—for capitalism by its very nature cannot create structures free from exploitation. We are fighting for the redistribution of wealth and for the end of private property inside the United States.[18]

The invigorated radicalism of the postwar era was premised on while reaffirming a renewed intellectual validation; they drew mutual strength against a climate of postwar pessimism. But in the four years between C. L. R. James' speech and Chomsky-Foucault, Black Power was all but decimated as a political force. Nixon's incorporation tactics[19] were bitter icing on the cake of J. Edgar Hoover's COINTELPRO all-out assault on the New Left. As Ward Churchill and Jim Vander Wall note:

> [By 1971], "the chilling effect" on political dissent had been demonstrably achieved: the movement for social change, loosely described as the "New Left" had been shattered, its elements fragmented and factionalized, its goals and methods hugely distorted in the public mind, scores of its leaders and members slain, hundreds more languishing in penal institutions as the result of convictions in cases which remain suspect, to say the least.[20]

The state's move on the New Left, particularly the Black Panther Party (BPP), was nowhere more evident than against the US prison population, where

George Jackson, imprisoned from 1960 until his death in 1971, and Angela Davis (imprisoned from 1970 to 1972) connected incarceration with political oppression. Both figures were instrumental in drawing links between the internment of political prisoners and detention of the black poor; their critique of capitalism centered imprisonment as a function of colonial oppression that gave birth to a new revolutionary vanguard. But in a crucial respect, the assassination of George Jackson in San Quentin and the prison riots that followed at Attica State in which 179 were killed and 1,289 tortured, signaled not only the extent to which the state could go in its attempt to forcibly obliterate opposition but its "success" in doing so, and both events drew worldwide attention.

Brady Thomas Heiner[21] argues convincingly that the BPP had a significant influence on Foucault. While Nietzsche's weight, via Heidegger, is unquestioned, Heiner unravels "the philosophies and struggles of the Black Panthers [which] led Foucault both to Nietzsche and to genealogy as a method of historico-political critique,"[22] marking a theoretical shift between 1970 and 1976, including a move toward the power-knowledge couplet: biopolitics and genealogical method. Heiner locates Foucault's "radicalization" with the establishment in February 1971 of *Le Groupe d'Information sur les Prisons* (GIP), a prison activist group of which Foucault was a founding member. Through his close acquaintanceship with co-GIP activist Jean Genet; the Panthers' struggle and, more specifically, the plight of imprisoned Panthers; the place of race in the American class system; and the perpetuation of racism in the American penal system were brought into Foucault's theoretical orbit. Heiner documents Foucault's appropriation specifically of George Jackson and Angela Davis. In a series of GIP publications throughout 1971–1972, the activists covered conditions in the French prison system, in particular focusing on prisoners' suicides and their predominance among incarcerated immigrants and young people, and also on the life, work, and prison assassination of George Jackson. For the GIP, the prison system and, in particular, the antiracist struggles permeating incarceration in the United States had opened a new radical front.

Two points of significance must be drawn out. First, Heiner argues that the influence of the Panthers has been erased both by Foucault and by those who have unpacked his methods. Heiner's aim is "to enable them [the BPP] to oppose and struggle against the coercion of Foucault's appropriation of them."[23] Second, we contend that the "erasure" is due to a *reversal* of the Panther's transcendent claim. Foucault did not share the basic tenets of

Marcuse's Great Refusal—the essence of Angela Davis' politics of liberation—emancipation beyond capitalism founded on a liberatory subject denied. For to do so requires acknowledgment of an idealized universal subject that Foucault rejects despite his later pronouncement that "we must not conclude that everything which has ever been linked with humanism is to be rejected, but that the humanistic thematic is in itself too supple, too diverse, too inconsistent to serve as an axis for reflection."[24] The death of a liberatory Enlightenment subject is a constant in Foucault's work, and it is for this reason that, to quote Heiner, "Foucault symptomatically denies the actually existing race struggle that in fact motivated his method to begin with."[25] The will to truth: An institutionalized regulating system of constraint that excludes by its epistemic reproduction of what may legitimately be said or thought within a given social formation—in effect, that which ordains the immanence of all critique—may have been developed in the period from 1970 to 1976, but it can only be said to partially reflect the Panther's struggle. The revolutionary impetus for Davis and Jackson was the centrality of the black vanguard as a new universal subject of the abolition of capitalism as a system of oppression. The Panthers did not deny universal truth; rather, they were the objects of its denial and a movement of its making. Black incarceration had a politicizing and radicalizing effect. Attacking the US prison system was a political act aimed at the metabolic overthrow of the entire capitalist system. It is the defeat of this vanguard that comes to influence Foucault's theoretical development. The GIP's concern with prisoner self-annihilation in France fuses with the liquidation of George Jackson and the Attica repression: the smashing of the black revolutionary vanguard. The fusion comes through in Foucault's conceptualization of power without a subject. It is the extinguished radical subject that speaks (without voice) through Foucault.

Foucault conceptualizes power as *rapports de force*: "a form of power which makes individuals subjects . . . subject to someone else by control and dependence; and tied to his own identity by a conscience or self-knowledge. Both meanings suggest a form of power which subjugates and makes subject to."[26] Power relations are those in which force is exercised, but power also includes the process by which force relations are stabilized or overturned to the formation of patterns that occur via connecting force relations and to the particular strategy that renders these patterns functional. Endemic changes within force relations produce shifts in the patterns of power—shifts that are resistible only inasmuch as sets of force relations can be amassed in opposition. "The main objective of these struggles is to attack not so much 'such or such' an institution of power, or group, or elite, or class but rather a technique, a form of power."[27] Configurations that appear as a central power (the sovereign state) are purely the overall effect of force relations. Law and domination are merely forms that all-pervasive power takes in a given society, but there is no possibility of a society *without* power. Power's all-pervasiveness emanates from the power/knowledge couplet. Standard conceptualizations of power as repressive, which Foucault *rejects*, presuppose the possibility of social relations *not marked by power*, and Foucault denies this possibility most vehemently with regards to "truth":

> We are subjected to the production of truth through power and we cannot exercise power except through the production of truth. . . . true discourses . . . are the bearers of the specific effects of power.[28]

Strategies of force are discursively ordered via the production of truth discourses. Power relations cannot be deduced from a mode of production as in the "Old Left" formulation; they are the effects that occur in, for example, economic, sexual, and knowledge relations as "the internal conditions of these differentiations."[29] Nor are individuals the originating actors, for resistance requires discursively ordered *intent*. The subject is an effect of power and intentionality discursive, not individual or social in the classical sense attributable to an anthropological essence. Only in discourse are power relations "both intentional and non-subjective."[30] Individualist accounts of agency and the assumption of class domination are disgarded. It is not possible to conceive of subjects outside of discourse. Foucault's denial of determining effects such as that of the economic structure provides no possibility for alternative action based on appeals to objective interests. Without objective interests, repression is reconceptualized as a "juridical-disciplinary notion" whose "two-fold . . . reference . . . to sovereignty on the one hand and to normalisation on the other" both "vitiate[s] and nullifie[s] from the outset" any "critical application of the notion of repression."[31] Resistance is inscribed in relations of power as an irreducible opposite: Power comes from neither above nor below.

In an early perceptive critique, Mark Philp[32] noted significant problems with such a conception. If the discursively determined subject carries its opposite within its discursive constitution:

1. Is the "other" of discourse automatically resistant, that is, *is* otherness resistance?
2. While the shape of the "other" is discursively determined, the shape of the resistant "other" is a function of force relations, but Foucault does not offer an account of force apart from specifying the determining existence of force relations.
3. On what basis would the "other" be welcomed as a liberator by the dominated subject? How would he/she recognise himself as dominated if no pre-discursive subject exists? And how would he/she know if the "other" was preferable?

The automatic inscription of otherness in discourse can neither offer a satisfactory explanation for resistance nor justify it. As Philp observes, Foucault could argue that B's resistance occurs because of the conflicting demands that A makes on B's discursively constituted identity and interests. But because Foucault "believe[s] that power is not built up out of 'wills' (individual or collective) nor is it derivable from interests," this would not seem possible.[33] Nor can it be justifiably claimed that a discursively constituted will could resist discourse. The will is *incarcerated* in discourse. If relations of force arise in relations of inequality, then we could argue that the subject will resist inequality on the basis that it is unjust: The subject has an interest in equality because the right to equality is self-evident. But Foucault provides no basis for such self-evidence. It may be true that coercion or those congealed power/knowledge artifacts that dominate, once made visible, can precipitate instability and that by building a network of resistance, we can surmount patterns of strategic domination, but such resistance would require at least a *justificatory* impulse on which the coerced can formulate a sense of interests. For Foucault, power does not arise out of interests or wills. Rather, inequalities are produced and maintained by force. This leaves Foucault's account of resistance wanting.

The other option is that force and counterforce are essential ahistorical and universal human attributes. Politics would simply be a means through which this ahistorical force moves. Not only would this undermine the relative stance underpinning Foucault's defiance of historically specific normative claims, but it could not "provide the basis for a justification of resistance—like Hobbes' war of all against all, the account is completely naturalistic."[34] Thus, Foucault inverts the Clausewitzian formula—politics is merely war by another name. We are left fighting within our own reified nature in the face of which we must submit to our inherent limitations. Foucault's anti-universalist discursive position places willful intent/action beyond "Man," introducing self-other interplay at a microlevel. The radical move is symptomatic of theory without a liberatory subject or alternative course than to make the present livable. The idea that Man is a discursive technology of power in itself places social change beyond the capacity of meaningful human action. The adoption of such a position is surely problematic for theorists who seek to understand racism, and it was anathema to Black Power.

## RACE REFACED

If, as Heiner suggests, Foucault appropriated BPP struggles Eurocentrically, silencing their influence on his work on power and resistance, and if, as we have argued, by doing so Foucault reconceptualized emancipatory politics, appropriating liberation to an immanent framework that fitted with Western European intellectuals' experience of radical limitation, then how are we to consider the contemporary reappropriation of Foucault by theorists of "race"?

David Theo Goldberg's Foucauldian treatment of "race" locates its origination with "liberal modernity."[35] The discourse of race has force imbued with the presumption of reason, and it is through the rationalist scientific gaze that the inner and outer worlds of human beings are first conceptualized and then homologized and homogenized, the capacity for reason itself being a signifier of civilizational accomplishment. Race developed as a technology for exercising the scientific gaze—a technology of power. We have no disagreement with the view that "race" became an empirical demarcation upon which human worth was evaluated. Our objection lies in the positing of an identity between internal and external worlds that extinguishes the value of *transcendent* critique; the existence of consciousness and the possibility of its raising beyond the present disappear if we are to take the identity between inner and outer worlds as given. Goldberg does not challenge this identification and therefore reproduces the substantive theoretical moment in which the conscious human subject is extinguished. This in turn has an impact on how state racism is conceptualized. Race is considered to be "irreducibly a political category."[36] But the use of the "political" here equates to the all-pervasiveness of power, not of its overcoming by individual or collective action. Goldberg is therefore unable to conceptualize a project of freedom as a radically subjective dimension of social action that distinguishes itself from the conservative statal application of repression. Rather, "autonomy" under Goldberg's schema must be a form of modern repression that only gives the *appearance* of an external oppressive regime *imposed* on an *essential subject* of freedom. "The racial state . . . strive[s] . . . for a racial subjection . . . usually perceived as externally imposed upon subjects," turning "imposition into self-assumption, assertive charge into autonomous, self-imposed choice, harness into hegemony." Indeed, "there is no clear-cut contrast between state and individual, between asserted institutional power and capillary governmentality."[37] Racialized exclusion is institutionalized via presumptive criteria that delineate "the beneficiaries of the entitlement (those who would enjoy the fruits of the endowment) from those to be restricted in their enjoyment or denied their rights, goods, and services."[38] It is the unity that racialized discourse acquires in positioning the location of bodies in the body politic that "highlights the material force at racism's heart."[39]

Just as Foucault argued that the discourses of the human sciences brought Man into being, so Goldberg argues that "racial man" is a product of the same because "authority is established and exercised only by being vested with the force of discrimination, exclusion, and enforcement."[40] Because "*interpellation* is the process by which individuals are hailed or called to subjectivity by others," which "presupposes mutual recognition by individuals," and "individuals are interpellated as subjects in and by means of language,"[41] discourses of race, as constituted in the modern age, are technologies of power that locate racialized bodies in time and space. Race is "a new technology for defining identity and otherness, for determining inclusion, and establishing entitlements."[42] The use of machine metaphors underlies the theorization of the social as an autonomous powerhouse with no subject for its driver. Power is complicit in the formation of the racialized subject as "the drive to exercise authorial power—whether out of the pure pleasure of the act or as a means to further ends—clothes itself in the theoretical fashions of rationality."[43] Means and ends, as inherent to rationalism, are implicated in racial subjection.

For Goldberg, modern culture interpellates modern subjects as rational. Modern culture's "preconceptual sets" embody "race" and therefore interpellate racist subjects, implicating all subjectification that is not antimodernist within a racist project. Herein lies a contradiction that is clear when he makes his conception of racism explicit:

> Racisms involve promoting exclusions, or the actual exclusions of people in virtue of their being deemed members of different racial groups, however racial groups are taken to be constituted. It follows that in some instances expressions may be racist on grounds of their effects. The mark of racism in these cases will be whether the discriminatory racial exclusion reflects a persistent pattern or could reasonably have been avoided.[44]

How can racial exclusion be reasonably avoided if reason is the hallmark of racial subjection? According to Cornelius Castoriadis, it would seem that Goldberg has adopted "a discourse . . . which has *already presupposed* the equality of human beings as reasonable beings," while denying that presupposition as an example of racist culture.[45] The main problem with a "critical multiculturalism" that "pursues the interdisciplinary interpellation of (or calling to) subjectivity from within while transgressively challenging the confinements, the borders, of institutional structures, subjects and subjectivities, and imposed disciplinary forms" is that the "transgressive challenge" implicitly relies on a *justification* underpinned by a notion of universal political equality predicated on the existence of an essentially and therefore transcendent rational being, which is historically antithetical to the conclusion reached by a theory of subjective interpellation.[46] To paraphrase Žižek's critique of Judith Butler, we could say that Goldberg "ends up in a position of allowing precisely for marginal 'reconfigurations' of the predominant discourse—who remains constrained to a position of 'inherent transgression,' which needs as a point of reference the Other in the guise of a predominant discourse that can be only marginally displaced or transgressed."[47]

There is a deeper problem shared both by Foucauldians and those who attempt to move beyond Foucault's limitations. Linda Alcoff provides probably the most relevant and currently influential defense of difference. She argues,

"When I refuse to listen to how you are different from me, I am refusing to know who you are. But without understanding fully who you are, I will never be able to appreciate precisely how we are more alike than I might have originally supposed."[48] There is nothing inherently wrong with difference, nor for us does denial of difference entail some political virtue. The question of most relevance to our thesis is not so much centered on your readiness to hear about my difference, but rather that today, little compels you to even begin listening to me (or I to you) in the first place, difference or not. There is currently no foundation for moral equivalence. In such a historical context, marginal transgression is reconceptualized as radical political action.

Similarly, Goldberg recognizes that "universalisms offer the virtues of principles generally acknowledging the injustices of broadly construed racist expressions," but considers that "they hide within their claims to universal values the inherent limitations of their lack of specificity, and they deny the value in culturally construed particularities inconsistent with the putatively universal principle."[49] He therefore advocates "moral indeterminacy as a necessary feature of social praxis."[50] One can read "moral indeterminacy" to mean "we" *should not* take a moral stance. A more generous reading implies that any moral position must recognize its inherent partiality and the relative limit of truth claims so as to render our positions revisable in the light of other truth claims. The latter is in keeping with Alcoff's relativization of horizons: "Social identities are part of our interpretive horizon and have an effect on what we perceive or notice, but it is incoherent to propose that horizons be 'overcome.'"[51] Either way we are left with the question of arbitration. Who or what is to decide what the limits of a moral position may be, and on what grounds? How can we assess the fairness of such claims? Alcoff must surely accept that the validity of the political position she eloquently defends philosophically must appeal to some sense of Truth, or why should we accept it over any other? More worryingly, perhaps, Alcoff leaves us with a sense in which "overcoming" a bourgeois interpretative horizon is invalidated:

> In stratified societies, differently identified individuals do not have the same access to points of view or perceptual planes of observation or the same embodied knowledge. The queen may freely walk in the servants quarters, but she will not view them in the same way as the servants do. Two individuals may participate in the same event, but different aspects of that event will be perceptible to different people.[52]

This is all well and good, but on what grounds should we and could we build the Republic? If the queen refuses the guillotine as oppressive, do we forfeit our plebiscitarian contract, or did we not really want this anyway? Alcoff's call to situate our understanding of the subject within unequal capitalist relations is somewhat undermined.

For Goldberg, the subject would have to undermine the normative premise of the modernist project, but, since both racism and the rational subject are discursively ordered modern inventions, then it is only because of modernity that we have the ability to view racism as wrong, for according to Foucault, the discourse (and force) of antiracism must be the other of the discourse (and force) of racism. Citing Frantz Fanon, Goldberg informs us that:

> The post-racial state would not be a state in which black (or white) people necessarily would *not* be recognized as black (or white), nor one in which the norms of regulation and governance were set by and in terms of black interests, whatever they might amount to. Rather such a state would be one in which people of color in general, like white people generally, would be recognized as fully human.[53]

What is the "fully human," and what is the basis of its attainment, the standard by which all can expect to be treated? Goldberg does not provide a serious answer, nor can he. Fanon's rejection of the limitations of Western humanism did not entail a rejection of humanism in toto; his pursuit of "a new history of Man" holds a mirror to current thought.[54] Goldberg's near silence is symptomatic of a theoretical void in contemporary social analysis, premised on a wider and anachronistic disaffection with humanism, and it fully represents the dilemma facing advocates of postraciality in a world disordered by the "victory" of capitalism. As detailed, nuanced, and sophisticated as Goldberg's position is, we are left with little to which we can appeal in order to fight inequality today. The true humanness he aspires to in justification of antiracism is undermined by the antihumanist precept from which he embarks.

As our discussion of Goldberg and Alcoff reveals, the problem does not simply hail from Foucault's theory; rather, the curtailment of radical subjectivity is related to the experience of politics as primarily a repetitive concern that does not bring progressive change (the logic of defeat). Liberation, as Franz Neumann once derided, is reduced to "an indifferent repetition of the endless struggle of 'in groups' versus 'out groups'" without resolution.[55] Endless repetition is exemplified in Omi and Winant's[56] thesis that "the state is composed of *institutions*, the *policies* they carry out, the *conditions and rules* which support and justify them, and the *social relations* in which they are embedded"; they add that "every state institution is a racial institution," signaling that the state operates derivatively on the basis of a racialized social order contested by groups who mobilize, either through "war of position" or "war of maneuver," to alter the negative meaning of "race." While Omi and Winant retain the crucial element of justification, "race" is here posited as a universal structuring, and structured by, human action, either negatively or positively endowed, that moves from a point of "*unstable equilibrium1*" to "*unstable equilibrium2*." Each new point represents a reinstitutionalization of the racial order.[57] There is no escape. The more we search for an emancipatory space, the more apparent it becomes that a virtue is being made out of the absence of solution. Similarly, while Stuart Hall seemingly made a place for a nonclass bound subject, "conscious subjects" were redefined as incarcerated identities:

> Identities are points of temporary attachment to the subject positions which discursive practices construct for us. They are the result of a successful articulation or "chaining" of the subject into the flow of discourse.[58]

Identity refers to multiple intersections between ethnicity, class, gender, and so on. Intersections denote a relationship between past and present identities: "Identities are the names we give to the different ways we are positioned by, and position ourselves within, the narratives of the past,"[59] thus breaking any essentialized notion of identity, which was the folly of Enlightenment humanism. Hall finds virtue in "chaining." The "new identity" is created in this intersection between the constant creation of self-histories in relation to whichever current context we are in. The "new identity" can again change in response to how it is shaped in its current position (which is again relative to "new present" intersection with the "new past"). Thus, new identities constantly move to past identities in relation to the "new present." The "movement" is conceptualized as social change, but the movement is identity change that remains immanent to constant shaping, "identity as a 'production' which is never complete, always in process, and always constituted within, not outside, representation."[60] It may sound radical, but the theory of representational self-other interplay posits no external transformation beyond self-other representation.

> Identity is not only a story, a narrative which we tell ourselves about ourselves, it is stories which change with historical circumstances. And identity shifts with the way in which we think and hear them and experience them. Far from only coming from the still small point of truth inside us, identities actually come from outside, they are the way in which we are recognized and then come to step into the place of the recognitions which others give us. Without the others there is no self, there is no self-recognition.[61]

What is the basis of us being able to position ourselves? We can merely position ourselves into narratives of the past; the future is reconceptualized as constant change within the present social formation. Hall's self-ascriber moves from identification to identification, a constant war of position(s), in the reversed Clausewitzian redefinition alluded to by Foucault, moving us from disequilibria to disequilibria. Following Foucault's relational conception of power, retention of *significant affecting* directs us to the minutiae that make up the fabric of daily life—the *microphysics* of power. We are destined to stand inside the terms as they appear in constant repetition of the oppressive moment; oppression in and of itself can be shifted but not eradicated. It is the eradication of interests and values that exposes two serious weaknesses inherent in current conceptualization and critique of racism. The question that remains unanswered is, on what basis would/could/should one resist racism without the affirmation of a transcendent universal human subject denied? Ultimately, for all their talk of agency and desilencing, theorists of the "cultural turn" are unable to successfully challenge this fatalistic development; immanent critique is all that remains available to us, but if this theoretical development played itself out in the United States vis-à-vis the assault on Black Power, then in the United Kingdom, a similar intellectual path has been worn in relation to the defeat of the labor movement. It is within their commonality that we can begin to discern the collapse of emancipatory politics, in theory and in practice.

## ECONOMIC WITH THE TRUTHS

The problematization of an emancipatory working class subject weighed heavily on the British New Left, but it took its most developed form vis-à-vis "race" in Paul Gilroy's mid-1980s critique. Building on US Black Power criticism of Old

Left racial myopia and liberal color blindness, Gilroy set out to demonstrate that the negative attribution of blackness had been countered and represented as positive articulation. His focus was on "racial meanings . . . as a salient feature in a general process whereby culture mediates the world of agents and the structures which are created by their social praxis."[62] Where the British Right celebrated the lack of "black in the Union Jack," the cultural left identified a space of resistance through which hegemonic symbolic practices of whiteness were being countered in urban Britain. Writing at a time when the British labor movement was under intense government attack—a class war that eventually dismantled the postwar welfare consensus—Gilroy's premise was that a theory of class in racism analysis should be deprioritized, shifting the analytical focus to the politicization of race. Highlighting the impact on "industrial class politics" of "crisis and technological change" that "combines with a related loss of ability to identify with work among those who remain employed," Gilroy intuited Stuart Hall's and the Communist Party's later concern to delineate a subject of New Times. We will discuss this later, but for now the crucial point is Gilroy's critique of the Marxist class subject and his targeting of a theorist he perceived as its most representative advocate: Robert Miles.

According to Gilroy, Miles' theoretical and political failing was his silencing of black subjectivity in favor of "the apparently unlimited potential of an ideal category of workers."[63] His proclivity to "dissolve 'race' into class," delegitimized black mobilization, which Gilroy understood as emancipatory in that "race" could energize oppressed communities. Gilroy argued that "the construction of the Black Community as a complex and inclusive collectivity with a distinctive political language" undermined Miles' critique, which did not allow for the black subject's transformation of the meaning of "race."[64] Gilroy's target was "the idealist residues of Hegelianism concentrated in Marx's analysis of the proletariat," which he took from André Gorz's reading of Marx to signal "rather than being confined to Marx's early writings, metaphysical, ontological views of the origin and mission of the proletariat pervade Marx's mature work"; that is, rather than finding a definite break between early Historical idealist and later Scientific materialist Marx, as Althusser did and in whose footsteps Hall tread, Gilroy was critical of a continuity of proletarian universalism in toto. Gorz's suggestion, with which Gilroy had "considerable sympathy" was "that the Hegelian philosophy which constructs the proletariat as a universal class has encouraged a 'mythologised proletarian ideal' which can never be matched by the composite, fractured and heterogeneous actions of the empirical working class." It was such "outmoded criteria" that theorists such as Miles used "to measure the activities of the new social movements and find them wanting."[65] Therein lay Gilroy's dual critique. The idealized proletarian subject denied validity to groups not mobilizing around class politics, but the failure of the proletarian subject to realize its prophesized destiny—to emancipate the human race—created the political possibility and necessity of "progressive" race politics. It was the presumed failure and reactionary nature of class politics that underpinned the political and theoretical catalyst for a progressive new subject of history.

In one sense, Gilroy's critique of Miles is correct. By attempting to "outflank from the Left" Miles held onto proletarianization as a unique form of social transformation and did not take the Althusserian step of de-Hegelianizing Marx by positing a break between early and later "scientific" writings; that is, he did not see history as a process without a subject.[66] So, on attributing the Hegelian idealization of a proletarian subject to Miles, Gilroy is quite right. Miles' Hegelian versus Kantian[67] analysis did initially draw from Nicos Poulantzas and C. Wright Mills, but differed in that classes as agents were *not* conceptualized in the Poulantzasian form of technical relations onto which are constructed social class relationships of distribution, ownership, and appropriation.[68] It has become quite common, particularly within sociology, to situate Miles at one end of the structure-agency or structuralist-culturalist debate and Gilroy at the other.[69] But where Gilroy's work moved from that of the CCCS and Hall's Althusserian bent, Miles' *never* reproduced the antisubject position of Althusserian Marxism. This is represented in their respective approaches to ideology:

> Ideological statements are made by individuals; but ideologies are not the product of individual consciousness or intention. Rather we formulate our intentions within ideologies.[70]

> An ideology cannot, in itself, have any effect, but is the means by which people evaluate or stimulate an outcome or event (although the outcome may not be the one that the actors intended). The active agent is, therefore, not the ideology but the person or group generating and articulating the ideology.[71]

Nevertheless, stating that a position is Hegelian tells us little, as Fanon-Sartre reveals. Rather, it is the theory of reification that Miles derives from Georg Lukács that distinguishes Miles from Hall's Althusserian Marxism. Miles also differed from Theodor Adorno in his use of Lukács by retaining the proletarian subject of history. In adopting a Lukácsian insistence on the process of reification, Miles makes explicit the Hegelian edge implicit in his work. The addition is an important one because, as Miles made clear, his analysis, "shares certain core assumptions and concepts" with that offered by Hall and colleagues in *Policing the Crisis*, "but differs in one fundamental respect, its reification of 'race.'"[72]

At the risk of crude oversimplification, Lukács' theory of reification holds that capitalist contradiction is naturalized—*appears* as normal, unchangeable, and beyond human agency. For Miles, the generality of ideology lies in the mistaken perception that the products of human actors are the products of "a power independent of human beings," which are, in turn, "represented as . . . determinant[s] of social relations."[73] For Lukács, only proletarian consciousness could break reification. For Miles, racialized human beings "white" or "black" are designated as naturally bound to remain in reified social relations—outside of History. Specific ideologies such as racism, nationalism, and sexism share general characteristics in common, which enable elements of each to be expressed in combination:

> The central shared characteristic is the mistaken postulation of natural divisions within the human species which are defined as inherent and universal. These divisions are therefore presented as inevitable determinants of social organisation.[74]

"Natural divisions" do not refer to physical stuff located materially outside human society, but the form taken by day-to-day activity. The sensual appropriation of life solidifies and becomes rigid such that experience in a capitalist society is taken as a natural form of existence beyond question or conscious change. Consequently, all ideologies must be adequate to the task of making sense of phenomenal relations.[75] Miles uses the concept of "race" as reification to designate the continuance of an erroneous belief that "race" naturally determines. Race consciousness embodies the belief that human beings cannot progress to a truly human equality and is therefore an obstacle to transcendence. The existence or determining role of racialized consciousness in social relations is not denied. Because racialization can determine social position, consciousness should be raised, via transcendent critique, beyond race toward something better. Unlike Hall, "Ideologies have effects only because they are constructed by human actors in order to give meaning to and to structure human activity"; and in direct contrast to Althusser, "The active agent is . . . the person or the group generating and articulating the ideology," not the ideology itself.[76] Put another way, the theory of the death of the subject entails the continuance of reification unchallenged.

Miles implicitly allows for a position of nothingness. His retention of a distinction between essence and appearance and of a class-based anticapitalist *consciousness* attempts to preserve the Hegelian dialectic of master and slave, and a theoretical critique that transcends appearance by first occupying the space between it and essence. Though the essential relations of *capitalist* social organization are class relations, this does not stop us from acting on the reifying and fractionalizing stimulus of racist, nationalist, and sexist ideologies. Nor does it stop us from acting on the appearance or meaning of "race." For Miles, "although human beings have the capacity to act in ways which transform the material world . . . the scope for such transformative activity is always constrained by the character of the particular material circumstances in which they live"—in this case, capitalist.[77] The key term is *constraint*. Human consciousness can be raised such that the constraint of capitalist exploitation is overcome. This is of course the purpose of Miles' intervention: to raise consciousness beyond mere appearance in order to locate an underlying objective basis for human oppression. The distinction presupposes repressive forms of political relations. Consequently, despite appearances to the contrary, under capitalist social relations, "the state is . . . an essential relation of production, regulating *all* those relations which sustain the commodification and exploitation of labour power."[78] Bourgeois politics are conceptualized as antihuman and therefore repressive. One cannot theoretically sustain the view that the state is a relation of production comprised of conscious human subjects if one does not first privilege human consciousness.[79] "Race" as configured in the statal regulation of conscious human actors obscures the *possibility* of human commonality. This is the premise for a renunciation of race as reification. The conscious human subject drives the liberation logic of Miles' radically subjective stance and is the implicit theoretical target of the cultural turn, which brings us back to Gilroy.

Gilroy accuses Miles of attributing radical progressive spontaneity to the working class. However, if "the form of class consciousness, which Miles identifies as non-ideological, emerges only in this narrow conception of production relations," then what purpose or utility would there be in critiquing racialization and racism? Gilroy does not identify where Miles outlines the apparent "narrow conception." Nevertheless, having being attributed this theoretical stance, Miles is consigned to the dustbin of Eurocentric economism:

> Black political action has often been articulated through what appears to be a utopian political language. The distance from economism which has characterised it has baffled critics who would measure it by Eurocentric yardsticks and are consequently unable to perceive the sophisticated critique of capitalism which informs the social movement of blacks in the overdeveloped countries.[80]

Gilroy plays Fanon's anti-Sartre and US Black Power cards, but in this case both are anachronistic. It is true that Miles criticizes "the possibility that either the political and cultural life of 'races' or their experiences of racial subordination can become unifying factors enabling groups to act across formal lines of class. . . ." But if one sees human emancipation as inextricably aligned with proletarian revolution, and racialization through racial separation as divisive, as Miles did, then it becomes incumbent on Gilroy, who at that time purported to be working within "historical materialism,"[81] to demonstrate in what way Black communities in mid-1980s Britain furthered the realization of human emancipation through the cause of proletarian revolution. Since Gilroy opposed "the 'black and white unite and fight' variety"[82] of mobilization, which he also attributed to Miles, on what basis could a unified black collectivity further the cause of proletarian revolution, when, as Gilroy correctly contended, white workers saw and experienced themselves as having both national and racial interests in common as white Britons? The possibility of an internationalist subject founded by self-determination collapses. It is difficult for Gilroy to reconcile his interest in forms of consciousness; in raising consciousness toward the realization of History, while he gives up on the racialized "white" working class. Moreover, as Miles argued, the most significant omission in the approaches of Gilroy and others was their "silence on the question of the class divisions within the 'black masses' and on the ideological and political continuities, as well as divergences, in the consciousness and practice of various 'fractions' of the British working class." Gilroy overestimated the degree of political homogeneity in the black community and the degree to which the celebration of black cultural difference would be shared, for example, by Indian and Pakistani communities. There is at least a desire for proletarian unity in Miles' approach that is missing from Gilroy, but by the time *Ain't No Black* was published, the Thatcher government had destroyed the British trade union movement and was funding left-wing local government multicultural policy through its urban program. Gilroy's radicalism kicked at an open door despite later protestations.[83]

## LOST IN RACE

Criticism of the class subject is not only pertinent to the United Kingdom. It took its most devastating form with the turn to Foucault paralleling the Reagan administration's assault on the (predominantly black) US working class. Snatching at the coattails of Gilroy's "victory," Goldberg offered a "corrective" to structural Marxist approaches to racism because of the tendency to conceptualize racism as an epiphenomenon of more stable elements in the social structure such as politics or the economy. Into the latter category he situated Miles, who he saw as "the most recent defendant of this approach":[84]

> [Miles] accordingly casts the issue far too narrowly in concluding that "patterns and structures of material inequality between populations [racially] differentiated are created in the context of class differentiation." Clearly, racial creation and racially defined inequalities have often served the ends of class exploitation. But three counter-considerations militate against class reductionism. First, such exploitation has at times simply been a contingent by-product of racialized expression; second, racial management has occasionally been pursued at the expense of class differentiation; and third, explanations of various and widespread exclusions enabled by racial expression are not nearly exhausted by class determined or economically functionalist constraints.[85]

Goldberg misreads Miles. "Class exploitation" does not appear in the sentence quoted. At no time has Miles argued that "class exploitation" is an end realized by racialization (as Goldberg does in the above quote). The class reductionism Goldberg attributes to Miles does not hold. One could merely read

Miles' explicit statement and definition of "exploitation" in the *Dictionary of Race and Ethnic Relations*.[86] For Miles "economic" is placed in inverted commas to denote that exploitation cannot be conceived within the parameters of bourgeois political economy as a separate sphere of social relations based on the acquisition and distribution of financial rewards. Class is not "economic" in the sense that Goldberg conceives it, but it is an objective relation premised on the extraction of surplus through and on which human beings exist—the form of social organization that human existence takes under the rubric of such an exploitative relation, premised as it is on "free" wage labor. Exploitation so defined is an essential relationship *only* of capitalist society and cannot be equated with what Goldberg refers to as "economically functionalist constraints": Class is not a simple "economic" category in the functionalist sense. A "context of class differentiation" refers to structures of meaning attributed to human beings within capitalist relations of exploitation; "racial differentiation" refers to additional meanings that are weaved throughout the exploitative relation. The difference between them is that a discourse of human, not "race," emancipation projected via consciousness of alienated labor—capitalist exploitation—is a means through which the exploitative relation, as Miles conceptualizes it, can be overthrown. In capitalism, human relations are only partially human. The objective basis of his critique is the attainment of an ideal human subject. Racism is an ideology that structures human creativity to its detriment. Class fractionalism is therefore to be tackled. As Miles' study of the British labor movement exemplifies,[87] in the absence of a class-based politics for human emancipation against racism, racial politics even positively conceived does not reverse the political context (in which he wrote) where "black" *and* "white" agents, postcolonial or reformist, lived as diminished subjects within the Western capitalist metropolis. Only the absence of progressive anticapitalist vision could celebrate their diminished emancipatory status. Despite their differences, both Goldberg and Gilroy left this absence intact.

Transcendent idealism is the essence of a politics that takes History as its premise. The measure of "what is" by "what could be" is at stake. In critiquing what is referred to as Hegelian idealism, what permits the possibility of "what could be"? If there is no such possibility, what is the basis of present critique? The collapse of a transcendent ideal leaves only immanent critique, criticism that alters, not transforms, the present. Gilroy insisted that future "radical collective action" would emanate from "identities spoken through 'race.'"[88] Here, History is read through the construction of "tradition" to mean the "symbolic repertoire" of "black Britain," including "the languages of Ethiopianism and Pan-Africanism and the heritage of anti-colonial resistance"[89] that syncretically fuse with protest against "differential access to civil rights and national belonging."[90] But is this necessarily the case? The quotations from black urban protestors used by Gilroy to highlight History in the making clearly invoke a distinction between essence and appearance:

> There is close cooperation between black youths and we have discussed the issue of plastic bullets. We are prepared to tackle any such moves by the government and the police to suppress our grievances. It is not just unemployment. We're regarded as third class citizens and we're not prepared to be treated like that any longer.[91]

Police brutality and treatment as third-class citizens require an understanding on the part of protesters that a Historical universal right has been denied them: equality. They are essentially human and wish to disrupt the *exclusionary* force of appearance. As Suke Wolton stresses, theories that attempt to "make race good" can make a virtue out of exclusion:

> Although it is true that young blacks seek their own language of rap to hide their anger in a form inaccessible to their white teachers, the blacks in Stonebridge Park, White City or Broadwater Farm did not "erect boundaries"; they were corralled into ghettos and policed into seeing "differences" by the presence of riot vans and early morning "visits." To suppose that black people in Britain are responsible for their isolation and segregation is to turn reality upside down.[92]

Neither Gilroy nor Hall would deny that the state, through municipal antiracism and other more authoritarian measures, set out to dismantle or demobilize black resistance. But in denying the transcendent ideal of Hegel's master-slave, the cultural turn did not retain a theoretical intervention that could produce transcendent results—raising consciousness beyond the present in pursuit of a better future—beyond "race." By arguing that "'race' must be retained as an analytical category . . . because it refers investigation to the power that collective identities acquire by means of their roots in tradition,"[93] Gilroy's radical cultural sociology ascribed an inflated sense of power to identity politics that, like that of reformist industrial class politics before it, did not break the exploitative premise of capitalism. Superficially the Fanon-Sartre debate is replicated, but the incommensurable self/other categories emanating from Hegel dispirited find their full fruition in Gilroy's unending dialectical treatment of "race." Although, unlike Goldberg, Gilroy at least attempts to privilege the human subject, pursuit of a future noncapitalist world is diminished as a theoretical and political intervention, while immanent alterity is privileged. Gilroy does not move to nothingness. Incommensurability, once championed, undermines his more recent pursuit of planetary humanism against "the uneven effects of globalisation and planetary commerce in blackness":

> These groups will need to be persuaded very carefully that there is something worthwhile to be gained from a deliberate renunciation of "race" as the basis for belonging to one another and acting in concert.
>
> The prospect of losing one's identity reduces cultural traditions to the simple process of invariant repetition. It has helped to secure deeply conservative notions that supply real comfort in dismal times but do little justice either to the fortitude and the improvisational skills of the slaves and their embattled descendents or to the complexities of contemporary cultural life.[94]

Gilroy's recent seeming about-face on "race" in actual fact shares a strong continuity with his previous disavowal of the proletarian subject. While his essays in *Darker Than Blue* attempt to draw on the emancipatory vision of Fanon, this is somewhat curtailed by his adoption of Arendt and Foucault.[95] Where Marcuse and Adorno's earlier pessimism toward the failed working-class subject of History—a working class bought off by commodities and consumption—set the historical marker for Gilroy's earlier critique of class, it is now leveled at the once celebrated black subject. Pessimism has moved (and barely noticed) from critique to critique, a repetitive exercise in futility. Whether or not one agrees with Miles' position, the real distinction with Gilroy lay in the pursuit of a proletarian revolution and the barriers to such precipitated by the racialization of human beings. Miles' ideal was the proletarian overthrow of capitalism, Gilroy's critique of "class" condemned us to remain within capitalism's boundaries, thus reflecting the despondency of the times; the historical moment was Gilroy's, and Miles lost.

Gilroy was surely right when he argued that racism "must be understood as a process" and so antiracism must "bring . . . blacks into history outside the categories of problem and victim, and establish . . . the historical character of racism in opposition to the idea that it is an eternal or natural phenomenon, [which] depends on a capacity to comprehend political, ideological and economic change."[96] However, we are presented with two problems:

1. While blacks may come into History, the History entered is one in which human emancipation has been denigrated.
2. The current epoch being made is one which has been proclaimed as a final destination.

Of course, the latter point is open to contestation, but the common elements of "End of History" thought—a lack of belief in viable alternatives to capitalism and the decentering of the conscious human subject as an agent of emancipatory change—simultaneously allow for the emergence of explanations for inequality that place its origins beyond human hands. Ultimately, for all their talk of agency and desilencing, theorists of the "cultural turn" are unable to successfully challenge this fatalistic development. Immanent critique is all that remains available to us.

*Marxism Today*'s New Times post-Fordist thesis crowned the fatalistic moment. *Fordism*, an analytical term used by Gramsci to capture hegemonic industrial organization that constituted class formation under national rubrics of mass production and methods of scientific management, was no longer. Post-Fordism characterized:

A shift to the new "information technologies"; more flexible, decentralised forms of labour process and work organization; decline of the old manufacturing base and the growth of the "sunrise," computer-based industries; the hiving-off or contracting-out of functions and services; a greater emphasis on choice and product differentiation, on marketing, packaging and design, on the "targeting" of consumers by lifestyle, taste and culture rather than by the Registrar General's categories of social class; a decline in the proportion of the skilled, male, manual working class, the rise of the service and white-collar classes and the "feminisation" of the workforce; an economy dominated by the multinationals, with their new international division of labour and their greater autonomy from nation-state control; the "globalisation" of the new financial markets, linked by the communications revolution; and new forms of the spatial organization of social processes.[97]

The new other of difference, fragmentation, consumption, and fluid national boundaries decentered Fordism's "subject"—the mass unionized industrial actor—in "a time-zone marked by the march of capital simultaneously across the globe and through the Maginot Lines of our subjectivities,"[98] demanding a conceptual space for new social movements and subjectivities marked by extra-economic demands. Hall carefully and characteristically distances "the social" from "economy," remaining within that self/other dispirited "tradition" catalyzed by Kojève. In a sociology of unending self-other interplay, emancipation beyond the fetters of capitalism is no longer viable. Theory and politics merge.

It is no coincidence that Kojève was to exert a parallel—and this time acknowledged—influence on Francis Fukuyama. Heretical as it may be to pair champions and protagonists of "neoliberalism," the underlying logic of their respective positions—that there can be no transcendent subject of historical emancipation beyond capitalism—is their mutual legacy. Michael Hardt and Antonio Negri's treatment of contemporary "global capitalism" alerts us to this congruence:

> Empire establishes no territorial center of power. . . . It is a decentered and deterritorializing apparatus of rule. . . . Empire manages hybrid identities, flexible hierarchies, and plural exchanges through modulating networks of command.
>
> Empire presents its rule not as a transitory moment in the movement of history, but as a regime with no temporal boundaries and in this sense outside history or at the end of history.[99]

The Foucauldian turn seals the fate of critique that remains immanent to capitalism and reveals most clearly the anti-emancipatory credentials of End of History thought. The absence of any theoretical interplay between "race" and "class" is now somewhat banal in a pessimistic worldview that orders the immanent conceptualization of capitalism as empire without a subject. So what next?

CHAPTER SIX

# A PRELUDE TO CLASS

> The neoliberal utopia tends to embody itself in the reality of a kind of infernal machine, whose necessity imposes itself even upon the rulers. Like the Marxism of an earlier time, with which, in this regard, it has much in common, this utopia evokes powerful belief. . . .
>
> *Pierre Bourdieu*[1]

When the Berlin Wall fell in 1989, few could envisage what a post-bipolar world might look like. Then US president George H. W. Bush had already made a virtue out of not being "very good at the vision thing." This did not halt any early sense of triumphalism. With the collectivist project of socialism now firmly discredited, free-market individualism had won. "There Is No Alternative" (TINA) to the market, a slogan used to great effect by British prime minister Margaret Thatcher, haunted the British Left as the Labour Party failed for the fourth time to unseat the Conservatives and the new prime minister, John Major, had already taken the country into Middle East war. Those on the Left were not slow to respond to the proclaimed new order.[2] To this, István Mészáros added:

> If it is true that "*there is no alternative*" to the structural determinations of the capitalist system in the "real world," in that case the very idea of *causal interventions*—no matter how little or large—must be condemned as an absurdity. The only change admissible within such a vision of the world belongs to the type which concerns itself with some strictly limited *effects* but leaves their *causal foundation* . . . completely unaffected. . . .

Such wisdom continues to be uttered without any concern for how bleak it would be if this proposition were really true. It is much easier to resign oneself to the finality of the predicament asserted in this blindly deterministic political slogan of our times . . . than to devise the necessary challenge to it.[3]

Not surprisingly, many had already attempted to counter what they saw as a silencing of alternatives. At the level of critique, Perry Anderson mounted a considered appraisal of both Fukuyama's thesis and its critics,[4] while Alex Callinicos responded with a prognosis that placed the *radical* left, once held back by Soviet communism, on the ascendant. The end of Stalinism represented not history's end, argued Callinicos, but its revenge. The collective subject of socialism, the working class, was now unharnessed and ready to fulfill its historical mission, albeit in an epoch where they would have to contend not with the political and economic instability of national rivalries but with the inequities wrought by the global consolidation of capitalism.[5] Others have since attempted to situate the radical left,[6] but what many writers on the Left have in common is that they take their cue, directly or indirectly, from the "old New Left"—that is, those who had staked their claim as left-wing critics of both capitalism and Stalinist communism. Emerging steadfast from the 1968 student movements, New Leftists were already advocating a Third Way long before the Clinton and Blair administrations "redefined" its terms of reference.

Despite their many differences, with few exceptions, most who identify themselves with the Left accept that capitalism is now free to roam unchecked. This is particularly clear in one of the most well-known theoretical appraisals of the present: the critique of neoliberalism. Critics generally argue the following:

1. A process of hegemonic *neoliberalization* has occurred or is occurring.
2. This process is based, in part, on the development and political-economic application of neoliberal theory.
3. The application has variable effects according to the historical conditions in whichever part of the world the theory and concomitant policies/practices have been or are being implemented.

David Harvey[7] argues that a process of global neoliberalization has emerged gradually since the demise of the postwar socioeconomic order in the early 1970s, and is only now attaining prevalence. Harvey locates this process as a consequence of the implementation of policies based on neoliberal theory within the context of capitalist crisis. And he illustrates the variable effects of implementation strategies at different times and in different parts of the world. Four important cases are 1970s Chile, 1980s America and Britain, and present-day Iraq. In the West, the process of neoliberalization can be traced through political-economic transformations in the postwar period, which are characterized as a move from "embedded liberalism."[8] Briefly, embedded liberalism refers to the postwar capital-labor compromise, where free-market capitalism and the power of labor movements were subject to the regulative functions of the welfare state. Economic growth and welfare rights merged in the implementation of the Keynesian political-economic social contract. In short, the social democratic state ensured capital accumulation but insured against its negative social effect.

The theory of neoliberalization entails that a negative process, premised on the preeminence of individualism and the free market, characterizes the present as wholly different from the social democratic order. It is a concept used to denote that which comes *after* social democracy. In the words of Douglas Kellner, it is a movement "from Keynes to Schumpeter as the master ideologues of the current form of capitalism in which a relentless form of Schumpeter's 'creative destruction' and privileging of the vicissitudes of the market replace Keynes' form of a highly rationalized and organized state capitalism."[9]

In one sense liberalism is "neo" because it is a reaction against the historically specific political-economic order of the immediate postwar period. Neoliberalism began as a response to the postwar social democratic alignment. The turning point was its implementation and victory in the United Kingdom under Margaret Thatcher and in the United States under Ronald Reagan. However, against a collectivist social ethic, argues Harvey, "the current hegemony of neoliberal thinking" is but "utopianism" in that its promise to deliver a better life for all individuals is in effect a camouflage for the restoration of ruling-class power[10]; an "endless capital accumulation as the dominant process that shapes our lives," compelled by authoritarian neoconservatism, exacerbates global inequalities.[11] In short, a significant difference between neo- and classical liberalism is that despite its individualist and freedom discourses, anti-statism is now merely a rhetorical device in that neoliberals utilize the state, and increasingly so, to restructure the economy in favor of the ruling class.

Unchecked by the kind of social contract that gave the labor movement a share of state power in the social democratic era, capitalism is free from inhibition, and its freedom is guaranteed by the state.

This categorization of the present extends beyond the macro political-economy into the realm of everyday urban life. A compendium of essays published by Mike Davis and Daniel Monk in 2007 explicitly explores the question, "Toward what kind of future are we being led by savage, fanatical capitalism?" Or, to frame the same question in a different way, "What do contemporary 'dream-worlds' of consumption, property, and power tell us about the fate of human solidarity?"[12] For the authors in this collection, neoliberalism is synonymous with globalization, an epochal development in which capitalism unfettered by state regulation transforms the urban environment into its own image, with the new global cityscapes built "from Arizona to Afghanistan" segregated by the unbridled individualist consumption of the rich and a contemptible disdain for those subject to the underlying inequities and immiseration on which they are built. The gated communities of Los Angeles are exported globally as prototype, the exploited migrant labor power on which they are constructed locked out, patrolled and objectified by surveillance. These "evil paradises of neoliberalism" are the outcome and epitome of the "utopian greed" that pervades contemporary culture—a culture in which the collective bond of mutual responsibility has dissolved, capitalism has won, and many have lost.

Such critiques of the present are compelling in that they speak to a contemporary sense of hopelessness and a need to counter helplessness by making sense out of and finding meaning in the present. But theories of neoliberalization are unable to counter, and in an important respect reinforce, the fatalism of TINA alluded to by Mészáros. While neoliberalization critics intuit newness, the change of significance they pinpoint is the collapse of the postwar social contract. This is undoubtedly correct, but the critique suffers in that its force depends on the key reference points of modernity, of Left and Right. It is logical within these terms of reference to argue, as Harvey does, that countries lying outside the developed industrialized West are distinct in that neoliberal applications do not aim to uncover a buried liberalism but to impose it where it has never existed before. However, comparing 1970s Chile, a time when the political ideologies of Left and Right were locked global adversaries, with post–Left twenty-first-century Iraq is problematic. Such comparison assumes not only that the Right remained intact after the collapse of the Left but that the capitalist system can shift rightward from a Left adversary that no longer exists.

Our alternative reading of the present that has guided our thesis in the preceding chapters centralizes not the continuance but the *collapse* of the Left-Right ideological framework. Crucial to this framework was the antagonistic and mutually defining radical and conservative subjectives. Theories of neoliberalization do consider that social democracy emerged as a response to the inability of capitalism to deliver. And for those who identify themselves with the Left, capitalism's crisis tendency is central to the appraisal of neoliberalism as utopian. However, critics do not generally notice that capitalism took a social democratic character *because of* a locked *adversarial* position. This is problematic. Capitalism, if understood as a social form of organization and not merely as an economic system, cannot be understood as a thing external to human endeavor; it is not supernatural. Ideologically and politically, two sides mutually self-defined and reinforced the stance of the other. Free marketism makes little sense without the Left because the power of market-orientated critique has historically taken its force *against* the existence of its antimarket rival. Modern free marketism was an adversarial political identity that could not exist without its antithesis: socialism.

Thatcher's and Reagan's ideological allegiances to individualism and the free market were not derived from faith but were the demarcation of an antithetical worldview that shared the modern premise of its adversary: freedom of the individual via the unrestrained market as opposed to freedom of the individual via the collective suppression (social democracy) or abolition (communism) of the market. For this reason the collapse of the East could not, as was imagined by 1980s free marketers, usher in the hegemonic victory of Western capitalism. The argument misses the objective mutual reinforcement afforded by competing visions of Man and, more importantly, the extent to which liberalism owed its twentieth-century existence, its character and form, to the existence of its rival. In short, the end of the Cold War signified the end of the Enlightenment experiment, the decentralization of Man, the dislocation of meaning from power and a lowered horizon of expectation: the end of utopia.

It is perplexing, then, but telling nonetheless that critics identify neoliberalism with utopia. Anti-utopianism borrows its "logic" from a consensual critique of totalitarianism proffered by postwar liberal anticommunist theorists in defense of individualism. If utopian thought is deemed inherently bad, then branding an idea or political system as "utopian" allows it to be dismissed outright as negative. As Russell Jacoby notes, this standard reading of utopias is the legacy, at least intellectually, of Cold War liberals such as Hayek, Karl Popper, and Isaiah Berlin. In addition to denoting an unrealistic and unachievable goal, utopianism is generally used as a homologue of authoritarianism, since it presupposes a desired end-state that is *inevitably imposed* on all dissenters—thus its "usefulness" both as a characterization of communism's Stalinist incarnation and as a defense of liberalism's antiauthoritarian pluralism. On this reading, freedom entailed the absence of imposition on human will. Postwar liberal anti-utopianism defined utopia as "the other" of human freedom.

Anti-utopianism takes very different and specific forms in current critique. As Laïdi notes, the absence of an envisioned alternative world predicated on a positive belief in human potential—and, more specifically, the discrediting of such projects—leads to a calling into question of any project that is identified with modernity's future orientated utopias: projects that supplied meaning. Tony Blair's oft-quoted proclamation that "the Third Way is not a new way between progressive and conservative politics" but is "progressive politics distinguishing itself from conservatism of left or right" is usually misunderstood as a cynical mixture of policies from both the Left and the Right. This may be so, but in pairing the Third Way with progress, Blair attempted to impart a fresh meaning—to define a project for New Labour by distancing it from the sociopolitical matrix of the Left and the Right.

Modernity's emancipatory visions were considered conservative, outdated modes of thought, and this is why Blair could not in the end provide meaning. New Labour's policies fell victim to the inherent distrust of meaning, distrust that Blair himself galvanized. While the dislocation of power and meaning unleashes a profound need for meaning, the search is canceled out by a deep suspicion of "meaning-givers." Projects of meaning are associated with modernity's discredited past, to which there is no going back. Conversely, because we cannot trust, invest in, or contemplate any future orientated program, we remain trapped at the zero-hour of history with no way forward, stuck in the constant negotiation and criticism of the present. Here, Fukuyama's concept of "struggle" is revealing. The End of History, Liberalism's victory, did not usher in the conscious free individual as one would expect of a robust liberalism. For Fukuyama the central driving force was now that of a constant struggle for recognition. In the absence of an alternative future, all that remains is a miserable state of existence; the conceptual poverty of resigned struggle is contrived as a virtue only in an unchangeable present.

The Third Way attempted to make the present livable, but it is a present in which time waits for no "Man." Due to the need for meaning, the present can be no comfort zone; rather, it is inherently unstable. Any identified quest for meaning creates a feeling of insecurity—a subjective state of emergency that requires the elimination of the perpetrator, whether it be Osama Bin Laden, representative of Middle Eastern Muslim fundamentalism, or George W. Bush, representative of an ascendant US Christian Right. It is the subjective state of emergency that magnifies and is magnified by the war on terror.[13] In April 2009, the BBC reported from a US Department of Homeland Security study that supposedly demonstrated "the election of America's first black president and the economic slump helped racist groups recruit." Apart from the suggestion that the truth of the study was demonstrated by the volume of debate on the issue included in "right-wing blogs and talk shows," the idea that "America could be facing a surge in right-wing extremism" was considered credible.[14]

A closer look reveals that the Department of Homeland Security report[15] does not present evidence for a growth in membership of right-wing groups. In fact, the report states that no findings suggested an objective rise in right-wing recruitment following President Obama's election. Rather, the results are based primarily on what right-wing groups are saying and the effect of what it calls "right-wing extremist paranoia" on recruitment. Evidence of recruitment relates to a rise in membership in the early 1990s and a decline following the Oklahoma bombing. The report, however, makes two flawed assumptions. First, the idea that conditions today are similar to the early 1990s cannot be substantiated. The early 1990s saw an immediate rise of right-wing ideas based on the victory of the Right following the collapse of communism. But their celebrations quickly vanished as the Right fell into the vacuum created by an exiting Left. The Oklahoma bombing was a disturbing act of nihilism, but the decline of right-wing group membership following the bombing represented the bankruptcy and not the ascendency of the Right. Second, the redundancy of the Right does not halt people's quest for meaning, a need to make sense of the world. That people are drawn to explore debates on matters that are presented through the lens of emergency is not surprising, but it does not translate into right-wing recruitment in the way we would have once understood that political identity. Moreover, it is naive to expect that the disintegrating right-wing block would claim publicly that support for their ideas had *declined.*

By taking the claims of bloggers or talk show debates seriously as a rightward shift, both the HS study and BBC report raise alarm around the specter of meaning by giving credibility to these voices as serious organized political forms. The level of threat increases subjectively, but it also provides a basis for a possible *actual* rise in violence or acts of terrorism as unscrupulous protagonists attempt to capitalize on the validity given to them by public exposure. Both reports could be colluding in what Naomi Klein calls "the shock doctrine"—that is, populations are made malleable, their resistance to neoliberal free-market capitalism broken by fear. In this case, however, it is merely the threat and not the actuality of disaster that pacifies us.[16] Klein gives too much credence not only to conspiracy but to the power of Milton Friedman's disciples. The ruling elite cannot escape the crisis of meaning that besets the international and domestic arenas. The state of emergency is fed upon by ruling groups—not cynically or conspiratorially but genuinely in response to "What if?" A pessimistic consensus pursues a principle of precaution that simultaneously unites and fragments the desire for security.

When antineoliberalism combines with critical approaches to race, it becomes difficult if not impossible to ascertain the utility of neoliberalism as a concept. In *The End of Tolerance: Racism in 21st Century Britain*, Arun Kundnani argues that the current climate of neoliberalism is represented most clearly by the New Leviathan, "a state that fuses absolute power and absolute fear to create absolute conformity and absolute peace."[17] Kundnani makes the point, with which we are sympathetic, that a climate of fear has been established through a host of legal injunctions premised on the war on terror. But he goes on to add that such measures—police and intelligence actions—have been used historically against suspected members of the Irish Republican Army. Moreover, Kundnani acknowledges that police stop-and-search measures that now target Muslims have a long history in the United Kingdom, especially in relation to the African-Caribbean population. What is explicitly mentioned as novel is that "the British state created a new kind of court system in which men could face secret trials, be found 'guilty' of unspecified charges, according to unspecified evidence and then be detained indefinitely."[18] But why this *newness* should be taken as representative of neoliberalism is unclear. Under Tony Blair, we are told, there was a constant "sundering of the principles of liberalism—just as the previous decade had seen the party leadership abandon socialism."[19] How can we inhabit neoliberalism if liberalism has been jettisoned? One would expect a reinvigoration of liberalism to be emblematic of neoliberalism. Kundnani is right to characterize the state and recent antiterrorist measures as authoritarian in effect, but such measures are not explained with recourse to a neoliberal agenda.

A similar problem confronts us in David Theo Goldberg's characterization of the present as *racial neoliberalism*. Goldberg argues that "post-Katrina New Orleans has simply made bare for all to see what neoliberalizing America amounts to."[20] Increased privatization of services and eradication of welfare are emblematic of an emergent neoliberalism. According to Goldberg, "Since the Reagan administration, and exacerbated dramatically under George W. Bush, the state has been restructured in such a way that poor people generally, which means especially black and brown citizens, are not to be taken into consideration, cared for, or exhibited compassion by the institutional apparatuses representing the state."[21] The response to Katrina exhibited one approach toward the wealthy and another toward the urban poor, who were cajoled into stadiums, abused by authorities, starved, and rendered permanently homeless.

Goldberg makes the point that natural catastrophes are in effect politically induced in that they exhibit decisions not to act, not to put in place mechanisms that can counter the devastating effects. We do not disagree, but claiming that the current context is induced by neoliberalism misses the wider dynamic at play. Blacks, minorities, and the urban and rural poor have been the objects of "natural" catastrophes throughout the epoch we have discussed in this book. Lynching slaves was historically justified as a consequence of the laws of nature, of the racial struggle, and each slave life lost was in actuality a political act predicated on anti–"Big P" Politics. These were antihuman acts that the radically subjective sought to counter with varying degrees of success. Emancipatory logic was premised on the availability of possibility. On what basis can we advocate possibility today; more to the point, why should we? Where is the alternative? Neither Kundnani nor Goldberg has an answer. It is the impact of the absence of solution that pervades today's paradigms of pessimism and that ultimately needs to be explained.

The lowering of horizons presents us with a sense of foreboding that we subjectively project onto the actions of ruling groups. Critics call on us to find "meaning makers" where they do not exist so as to expose hidden agendas. Due to our own sense of powerlessness, any experience of power can only feel like an external force exerted upon us and over which we have no lasting control. By attributing the powers-that-be with purposeful meaning (which they do not actually have), we attempt to make sense of, and to give meaning to, power. In the end, our quest for meaning is extinguished by dread. Thus, for Davis and Monk, neoliberalism is a "terminal" utopia. It conjures up a "dreamworld" that brings only barbarism.[22]

Nor do the authors find anything in the current condition that could furnish an alternative utopia (positively conceived). In their description of the present, they consciously distance themselves from progressives who in the past celebrated capitalism as a stepping-stone to a better world. Where, for example, radicals have in the past held onto a universal ideal of social progress, the transcendent aspiration toward the creation of a world beyond capitalism, an alternative utopia cannot be derived from the present condition. Rather, today the self-attributed "radical" stance can only be that of anti-utopia, and it is anything but radical.

Jacoby argues that the irony of multiculturalism, our celebration of cultural difference, is that in actual fact we tend toward its antithesis: "sameness." Market forces carry us toward convergence while aggrandizing our incessant self-gratifying contemporary need to present ourselves as different. One could argue that in the absence of politics, we are presented with a myriad of choices that give us the impression that we all have unique cultural dispositions. We are sold difference as "cultural authenticity," which in actuality distracts us from our *real* similarity in the present sociohistorical context—that is, our banal ability to choose identities like new hats. The irony of "successful" assimilation is that we are assimilated to believe in our inherent difference. We make our difference meaningful. In one sense Jacoby is right: The politics of multiculturalism seemingly fits well with capitalism's ceaseless rebranding for short-term profits. But we are in some respects skeptical of this formulation. The move toward cosmopolitan capitalism or multicultural capitalism's discontents indicates an urgent demand to break up any rigid sense of belonging or belief. This is quite antithetical to the subjective logic of a robust neoliberal capitalism. Today capitalism is not driven by confident neoliberal elites, nor is it a process without a subject. Daniel Ben-Ami has suggested that we live under the rubric of "cowardly capitalism" driven by the fear of risk. Yes, accumulation still occurs, and yes, it is underwritten by an exploitative relation, but the elite classes who once championed the unbridled progress of capitalist expansion are imploding in on themselves.[23] This is a markedly more dangerous set of circumstances than neoliberalism.

One measure of capitalist confidence is the rate of economic growth. As Ben-Ami notes, a cursory glance at the figures reveals that over the past 100 years, the global rate of growth has, despite a few peaks when the working class has been disciplined by the market, continuously declined. We are moving toward the zero-limit of no growth. The move in the West toward finance capital indicates not a robust neoliberal capitalism that aims to grow new wealth but the absence of the will to "make things" through human engagement with the material world. In 1993, the elite industrialist Club of Rome pronounced that "in searching for a common enemy against whom we can unite, we came up with the idea that [all the identified dangers] were caused by *human* intervention in natural processes. . . . The real enemy then is humanity itself."[24]

The shift from production—not just to new global locations but away from the *production of things* to finance, credit, and banking—indicates that capitalism is increasingly orientated against the *source* of profit: human labor–material production. This "heresy" indicates two points for consideration. First, if the level of economic surplus in any given society is decreasing to dangerous levels, redistribution of wealth can only mean the redistribution of a dwindling surplus. This is hidden by what appears to us as vast and extravagant displays of wealth by the few. But the ever-dwindling surplus is represented in policy as a redefinition of equality that we have unpacked in our thesis as the equality of mind. The *mental economy* does not promise economic abundance and an equal share for all, nor does it deliver political rights; rather, it is a system of corporate management that seeks to make the present livable. Thus, whether or not we accept Ben-Ami's position, the equality of difference does not contradict the tenets of cowardly capitalism. It is the political failure of the promise of universal human equality that renders us in constant negotiation with an absent center; an unequal present that was once challenged by utopia is rebranded in utopia's absence as "equality." Equality is reduced, like economic growth, to invisible minutiae. This is an inherently antihuman formulation. Holding the center together entails managing the mental economy so any social or cultural form that resembles past ideologies of Left or Right can be policed even in their real empirical absence. It is the loss of belief in any future alternative that traverses the political spectrum and elevates the idiom of threat and, consequently, our demand for "safety." Where once we were "facta" but with wills, today the human will to determine is branded as dangerous. The various trends we have identified crystallize most profoundly in our fear of "postracial disorder."

We are aware of just how heretical all this might sound, especially to those readers who traditionally position themselves on the Left. But what we have tried to draw out in our thesis on the pessimism and politics of racial ordering is the centrality of radical subjectivity to the forward movement of human becoming and the limitation placed on that movement by conservative irrationalism—the limit point of capitalist equality. Today social limitation has increased exponentially with capitalist crisis. But this is a crisis that cannot be captured analytically as "economic"; rather, there is a deeper crisis of possibility. The word "possibility" may be considered unworthy of our attention, banal even. But the first step toward radical renewal entails that possibility be reinvigorated. It is crucial that the idiom of possibility is resurrected. In laying out a paradigm of possibility, we have taken on our nemesis: the paradigms and politics of pessimism. In this book we attempted to engage with the intellectual impediments to such a renewal by unpacking the role of pessimism as a conduit of racial doctrine. The conservative parties of order that promoted their own crisis through race invoked a deep and damaging attachment to a pessimistic worldview. The current absence of "Big P" Politics is their legacy, but there can be no premise for radicalism without first making a case for the *essential* capacity of the human subject—the ability to imagine that which does not and has never existed and the *nerve* to work toward its unpredictable realization. Make no mistake: This is a universal capacity shared by all humans, and it trumps all others. Ultimately a defense and reawakening of possibility is *the* prelude to class.

As we write this final paragraph overlooking the Eastern Mediterranean from the postcolonial island of Cyprus not far from the unraveling Cold War regimes of Middle East containment in Tunisia, Egypt, and Libya, we are profoundly reminded that nothing is permanent. There can be no greater testament to the human spirit, and it is in this spirit that we end our thesis on the radically subjective—always as hopeful subjects.

# NOTES

### CHAPTER ONE

1. Antonio Gramsci, Letter from Prison (December 19, 1929), cited in *Letters from Prison*, vol. 1, *Antonio Gramsci*, trans. Raymond Rosenthal, ed. Frank Rosengarten (New York: Columbia University Press, 1994), 299.

2. Adolf Hitler, cited in *Hitler's Table Talk 1941–1944: His Private Conversations*, Conversation no. 90, "The Quality of Optimism" (New York: Enigma Books, 2000), 169.

3. John Gray, *Black Mass: Apocalyptic Religion and the Death of Utopia* (London: Penguin, 2007), 186.

4. Russell Jacoby, *The End of Utopia: Politics and Culture in an Age of Apathy* (New York: Basic Books, 2000), 8.

5. Zaki Laïdi, *A World Without Meaning: The Crisis of Meaning in International Politics* (London: Routledge, 1998), 13.

6. Ibid., 1.

7. Tariq Ali, *The Obama Syndrome: Surrender at Home, War Abroad* (London: Verso, 2010).

8. Interview with Angela Davis in Gary Younge, "We Used to Think There Was a Black Community," *The Guardian*, November 8, 2007, http://www.guardian.co.uk/world/2007/nov/08/usa.gender.

9. UNESCO, *The Race Question, UNESCO and Its Programme*, vol. 3 (Paris: UNESCO, 1950), 1.

10. Ibid.

11. Ibid., 2.

12. Ibid.

13. Hannah Arendt, *Eichmann in Jerusalem: A Report on the Banality of Evil* (New York: Viking, 1963), 106.

14. Laïdi, *World Without Meaning*, 17.

15. Margaret Canovan, *Hannah Arendt: A Reinterpretation of Her Political Thought* (Cambridge: Cambridge University Press, 1994).

16. The distinction between Stalinism and the radically subjective is clarified by Slavoj Žižek. Stalinism shared Western sociology's positivist orientation, when it "reduced the class struggle to a struggle between 'classes' defined as social groups with a set of positive features (place in the mode of production, etc.)," but "from a truly radical Marxist perspective, although there is a link between 'working class' as a social group and 'proletariat' as the position of the militant fighting for universal Truth, this link is not a determining causal connection, and the two levels must be strictly distinguished: to be a 'proletarian' involves assuming a certain *subjective stance* . . . which, in principle, can be adopted by any individual. . . . The line that separates the two opposing sides in the class struggle, is therefore not 'objective,' it is not the line separating two positive social groups, but ultimately *radically subjective*. . . ." Slavoj Žižek, *The Ticklish Subject: The Absent Centre of Political Ontology* (London: Verso, 2000), 226–227.

17. Theodor W. Adorno, Else Frenkel-Brunswik, Daniel J. Levinson, and R. Nevitt Sanford, *The Authoritarian Personality* (New York: Harper and Row, 1950).

18. Ibid., 627.

19. Stanley Milgram, "Behavioral Study of Obedience," *Journal of Abnormal Social Psychology* 67 (1963): 371–378.

20. See Stanley Milgram, *Obedience to Authority: An Experimental View* (New York: Harper and Row, 1974).

21. See David Cesarani, *Becoming Eichmann: Rethinking the Life, Crimes, and Trials of a "Desk Murderer"* (Cambridge, MA: Da Capo, 2006).

22. Theodor W. Adorno, *Negative Dialectics* (London: Continuum, 1981), 320.

23. See Simon Jarvis, *Adorno: A Critical Introduction* (Cambridge: Polity, 1998).

24. Angela Davis, "Marcuse's Legacies," in *The New Left and the 1960s*, ed. Douglas Kellner (London: Routledge, 2005), xi.

25. See Kellner, *New Left and the 1960s*.

26. Davis, "Marcuse's Legacies," viii.

27. Paul Gilroy, "The End of Anti-Racism," *Journal of Ethnic and Migration Studies* 17, no. 1 (1990): 73.

28. Zygmunt Bauman, *Modernity and the Holocaust* (Ithaca, NY: Cornell University Press, 2001).

29. David Theo Goldberg, *Racist Culture* (Oxford: Blackwell, 2002).

30. Ibid., 2.

31. Zygmunt Bauman, *Socialism: The Active Utopia* (New York: Holmes and Meier, 1976).

32. Ibid., 18.

33. Ibid., 19.

34. Ibid., 19–20.

35. Ibid., 11.

36. Ernst Bloch, *The Principle of Hope* (Cambridge, MA: MIT Press, 1959).

37. Cornel West, "Prisoners of Hope," in *The Impossible Will Take a Little While: A Citizen's Guide to Hope in a Time of Fear*, ed. Paul Loeb (New York: Basic Books, 2004), 294, 297. For an in-depth discussion of Cornel West's use of the "tragic," see Robert Pirro, "Remedying Defective or Deficient Political Agency: Cornel West's Uses of the Tragic," *New Political Science* 26, no. 2 (2004): 147–170.

38. The other crucial aspect of Lukács' theory of reification, that the process of capitalist individualization, where workers assume the position of free-wage individuals cut off from the foundation of their own existence—labor—leading individuals to invest great power in objects over which they have no control, such as nature, was also left underdeveloped by Adorno, and we will return to this point later.

39. Bloch, *Principle of Hope*. We stress that it is the "outcome," not simply the defiance per se, that defines. Either domination is overcome or it remains intact while taking on a new form. In this

we differentiate our analytical field from that of "struggle," a concept that has been used too loosely of late, usually borrowed from Gramsci's conceptualization but divested of its radical content. Francis Fukuyama is a fan of the concept. For Fukuyama, constant "struggle" without outcome is what defines our condition of existence at History's End.

40. For a discussion, see Bauman, *Socialism*.

41. Richard Sennet, *The Fall of Public Man* (London: Faber and Faber, 1993).

42. Cornelius Castoriadis, in *Philosophy, Politics, Autonomy*, ed. D. A. Curtis (New York: Oxford University Press, 1991).

43. Cornelius Castoriadis, *The Imaginary Institution of Society*, trans. K. Blamey (Cambridge: Polity/Blackwell, 1987), 97.

44. Castoriadis, *Philosophy, Politics, Autonomy*, 162.

45. For a discussion of the relationship between autonomy and modern patriarchy or masculinism, see Linda Martin Alcoff, *Visible Identities: Race, Gender, and the Self* (New York: Oxford University Press, 2006).

46. Cornelius Castoriadis, "The First Institution of Society and Second-Order Institutions," *Free Associations* 12 (1988): 42–43.

47. Castoriadis, *Philosophy, Politics, Autonomy*, 144.

48. Ibid., 160.

49. See William F. Bynum, "The Great Chain of Being After Forty Years: An Appraisal," *History of Science* 13 (1975): 5.

50. Bauman, *Socialism*, 15.

51. Ibid., 17.

52. We are not here implying that hope is a creation of modernity and therefore a Western invention. There can be no beginning of modernity that situates "hope" in the West. Modernity is a human, and not a Western, phenomenon. Consequently, it is an error to locate the Hopeful Subject's emergence as a "white Western European construct." Martin Bernal has already demonstrated that what usually gets classified as "classical civilization" ignores its "Afroasiatic roots," while Marshall Hodgson has uncovered the force and impact of Islamic thought on human knowledge due primarily to the "Venture of Islam." There can be no unbroken unilinear line that delineates, either positively or negatively, a so-called Western civilization inherited from the ancient Greeks by Enlightenment philosophes and that substantiates or valorizes hope as a Western or modern discovery. "The West" has no demonstrable origin beyond an ideological construction as a specific historical and spatial seat of power from which the original global path of capitalist domination is dictated. To state otherwise is the logic of racial thinking adopted by theories of Orientalism without irony. One cannot simultaneously rebuke "the West" for thinking of "itself" as historically continuous while castigating it for actually being so. (See Benjamin Isaac and Raphael Lagier for conflicting accounts.) This was Said's error: Either "the West" is historically continuous or, as is evidently the case, it is not. The Hopeful Subject does not originate or belong to/in a closed historical demarcation: "the West." Moreover, any subaltern third space, as proposed by Homi Bhabha, could only be credible if we first accept that the displacement of authority requires an idealist positing of existence free from unwanted imposition. Hope is a universal condition that takes historically specific forms. Martin Bernal, *Black Athena: The Afroasiatic Roots of Classical Civilisation* (London: Free Association Books, 1987); Marshall G. S. Hodgson, *The Venture of Islam: Conscience and History in a World Civilisation* (Chicago: University of Chicago Press, 1974); Benjamin H. Isaac, *The Invention of Racism in Classical Antiquity* (Princeton, NJ: Princeton University Press, 2006); Raphael Lagier, *Les races humaines selon Kant* (Paris: Presses Universitaires de France, 2004); Edward Said, *Orientalism: Western Concepts of the Orient* (Harmondsworth, UK: Penguin, 1985); Homi Bhabha, *The Location of Culture* (New York: Routledge, 1994).

53. Bauman, *Socialism*, 33.

54. See David Theo Goldberg, *The Threat of Race: Reflections on Racial Neoliberalism* (Malden, MA: Wiley-Blackwell, 2009), 328.

55. Adorno et al., *Authoritarian Personality*, 620.

56. Bauman, *Socialism*, 33.

57. Erich Fromm, *Fear of Freedom* (London: Routledge, 1991).

58. Zygmunt Bauman, "Utopia with No Topos," *History of the Human Sciences* 16, no. 1 (2003): 11.

59. Cornel West and Kevin S. Sealey, *Restoring Hope: Conversations on the Future of Black America* (Boston: Beacon, 1997), xii.

60. Cornel West, *Prophetic Thought in Postmodern Times* (Monroe, ME: Common Courage Press, 1993), 32.

61. David Theo Goldberg, *The Racial State* (Oxford: Blackwell, 2002), 52–53.

62. Kenan Malik, *The Meaning of Race: Race, History and Culture in Western Society* (London: Macmillan, 1996), 41.

63. Georg Lukács, *The Destruction of Reason* (London: Merlin, 1980), 104. For a discussion of Lukács' *Destruction of Reason*, especially in relation to the utility of the concept of "pessimism," see János Kelemen, "In Defense of *The Destruction of Reason*," *Logos Online* 7, no. 1 (2008), http://www.logosjournal.com/issue_7.1/kelemen.htm. For an early critique of pessimism as used by Lukács, see Paul Gottfried, "Pessimism and the Revolutions of 1848," *Review of Politics* 35 (1973): 193–203.

64. Karl Marx and Frederick Engels, *The Economic and Philosophical Manuscripts of 1844* (New York: Prometheus Books, 1988), 1.

65. Karl Marx, *Capital: A Critique of Political Economy*, vol. 1, pt. 1, *The Process of Capitalist Production* (New York: Cosimo, [1867] 2007), 217.

66. We use "parties of movement" as a conceptualization of progressive liberal and socialist voices (the Left) and "parties of order" to delineate those of conservatives and reactionaries (the Right). This is partially derived from Arno J. Mayer, *Wilson vs. Lenin: Political Origins of the New Diplomacy, 1917–1918* (Cleveland, OH: World Publishing, 1964).

67. De Maistre, cited in Malik, *Meaning of Race*, 266.

68. See Karl E. Case and Ray C. Fair, *Principles of Economics*, 5th ed. (Upper Saddle River, NJ: Prentice Hall, 1999).

69. See John Avery, *Progress, Poverty and Population: Re-reading Condorcet, Godwin and Malthus* (London: Routledge, 1996).

70. In many respects our analytical framework is sympathetic to and shares some tenets in common with the racial orders framework developed by Desmond S. King and Rogers M. Smith. King and Smith analyze American political development through the contest and interplay between competing "white supremacist" and "egalitarian transformative" racial institutional orders. As they note, the method is especially useful in comparative analysis. Our approach differs, however, not only in that it is not orientated within a political science institutional framework, but also in that we find the conceptualization of "white supremacy" limited in its applicability to the historical development of "racial" antiegalitarianism on both sides of the Atlantic (which will become apparent in Chapter 2). See Desmond S. King and Rogers M. Smith, "Racial Orders in American Political Development," *American Political Science Review* 99, no. 1 (2005): 1–19.

71. Edward P. Thompson, *The Poverty of Theory: Or an Orrery of Errors* (London: Merlin, 1978), 275–276.

72. David Harvey, *The Condition of Postmodernity* (Cambridge: Blackwell, 1990).

73. Derek Sayer, *Marx's Method: Ideology, Science and Critique in "Capital"* (Hassocks, UK: Harvester, 1979); Derek Sayer, *The Violence of Abstraction: The Analytic Foundations of Historical Materialism* (Oxford: Blackwell, 1987).

CHAPTER TWO

1. Michael Banton, *Racial Theories* (Cambridge: Cambridge University Press, 1998), 6.

2. Banton's contention that Cuvier maintained the divine origin of humans has significant support. However, Stephen Jay Gould argues that the theory of catastrophe does not allow for a complete commitment to divine origin. According to Gould, the Old Testament was but one of many sources utilized by Cuvier, the Enlightenment Rationalist. See Stephen Jay Gould, *The Structure of Evolutionary Theory* (Cambridge, MA: Harvard University Press, 2002), 489. For a more detailed discussion of the relation between theories of race, religion, and Cuvier's theory of human origins, see H. F. Augstein, "From the Land of the Bible to the Caucasus and Beyond: The Shifting Ideas of the Geographical Origin of Humankind," in *Race, Science and Medicine, 1700–1960*, ed. Waltraud Ernst and Bernard Harris (London: Verso, 1999), 58–79.

3. Gould, *Structure of Evolutionary Theory*, 292.

4. Jeremy Jennings, "The Déclaration des droits de l'homme et du citoyen and Its Critics in France: Reaction and Idéologie," *Historical Journal* 35, no. 4 (1992): 849.

5. Shirley M. Gruner, "Political Historiography in Restoration France," *History and Theory* 8, no. 3 (1969): 346–365.

6. For a detailed analysis of patronage in relation to Cuvier's work, see Dorinda Outram, *Georges Cuvier: Vocation, Science, and Authority in Post-Revolutionary France* (Manchester: Manchester University Press, 1984).

7. Augstein, "From the Land of the Bible to the Caucasus and Beyond," 72.

8. Ibid., 73.

9. Cuvier cited in Augstein, ibid., 64.

10. Gobineau cited in Georg Lukács, *The Destruction of Reason* (London: Merlin, 1980), 679.

11. On this, see Cyril Lionel Robert James, *The Black Jacobins: Toussaint L'Ouverture and the San Domingo Revolution* (New York: Vintage, 1989).

12. Douglas R. Egerton, *Gabriel's Rebellion: The Virginia Slave Conspiracies of 1800 and 1802* (Chapel Hill: University of North Carolina Press, 1993), 17.

13. Thomas Jefferson, *The Works of Thomas Jefferson*, vol. 8, *Correspondence 1793–1798* (New York: Cosimo, 2009), 335–336.

14. We refer to "Prosser" here in scare quotes so as to indicate that this was his slave master's surname and has been applied to Gabriel through convention without any historical evidence that Gabriel's surname was "Prosser." We have therefore chosen to refer to the revolutionary by his parentally bequeathed singular first name and do not refer to "Prosser" in the remainder of the text.

15. For a detailed discussion of the various restrictions that were imposed, see Egerton, *Gabriel's Rebellion*, 163–178.

16. Cited in Banton, *Racial Theories*.

17. Cited in Peter Fryer, *Staying Power: The History of Black People in Britain* (London: Pluto, 1984), 68.

18. Ibid., 234.

19. Alastair Bonnett, "How the British Working Class Became White: The Symbolic (Re) formation of Racialized Capitalism," *Journal of Historical Sociology* 1, no. 3 (1998): 326.

20. David Cannadine, *Ornamentalism: How the British Saw Their Empire* (New York: Oxford University Press, 2001).

21. Robert Young, *Colonial Desire: Hybridity in Theory, Culture, and Race* (London: Routledge, 1995), 100.

22. Edward P. Thompson, *Making of the English Working Class* (New York: Vintage, 1966), 43.

23. Linda Colley, "Britishness and Otherness: An Argument," *Journal of British Studies* 31, no. 4 (1992): 316.

24. John Brewer, *The Sinews of Power: War, Money and the English State 1688–1783* (London: Unwin Hyman, 1989); Joanna Innes, "The Domestic Face of the Military-Fiscal State: Government and Society in 18th-Century Britain," in *An Imperial State at War: Britain from 1689 to 1815*, ed. Lawrence Stone (London: Routledge, 1994), 96–127.

25. See David Armitage, *The Ideological Origins of the British Empire* (Cambridge: Cambridge University Press, 2000); Roxann Wheeler, *The Complexion of Race: Categories of Difference in 18th-Century British Culture* (Philadelphia: Philadelphia University Press, 2000); Kathleen Wilson, *A New Imperial History: Culture, Identity, and Modernity in Britain and the Empire, 1660–1840* (Cambridge: Cambridge University Press, 2004).

26. Eric J. Hobsbawm, *Nations and Nationalism Since 1780* (Cambridge: Cambridge University Press, 1990), 18–19.

27. Details cited in Noel Ignatiev, *How the Irish Became White* (New York: Routledge, 1999), 74–75. Our interpretation of these events as antinationalist does not stem from Ignatiev.

28. For a discussion of the Black Chartists, see Fryer, *Staying Power*, 237–246 and 407–409.

29. See Eric J. Hobsbawm, *Industry and Empire: The Birth of the Industrial Revolution* (London: Penguin, 1999); Keith McClelland, "From Chartism to the Reform League," in *Defining the Victorian Nation: Class, Race, Gender and the British Reform Act of 1867*, ed. Catherine Hall, Keith McClelland, and Jane Rendall (Cambridge: Cambridge University Press, 2000); Gareth Steadman Jones, "Rethinking Chartism," in *Languages of Class: Studies in Working Class History 1832–1982* (Cambridge: Cambridge University Press, 1983), 133–139; Dorothy Thompson, *The Chartists: Popular Politics in the Industrial Revolution* (New York: Pantheon, 1984).

30. Miles Taylor, "The 1848 Revolutions and the British Empire," *Past and Present* 166 (2000): 159.

31. Ibid.

32. Henry Mayhew, *London Labour and the London Poor* (New York: Dover, 1968), 1–2.

33. Kenan Malik, *The Meaning of Race: Race, History and Culture in Western Society* (London: Macmillan, 1996), 91–100.

34. Catherine Hall, "Missionary Stories: Gender and Ethnicity in England in the 1830s and 1840s," in *Cultural Studies*, ed. Lawrence Grossberg, Cary Nelson, and Paula A. Treichler (London: Routledge, 1992), 246.

35. For an earlier discussion of racisms of the interior, see Robert Miles, *Racism After Race Relations* (London: Routledge, 1993), 80–104.

36. Young, *Colonial Desire*, 11.

37. See Martin O'Brien and Sue Penna, *Theorising Welfare: Enlightenment and Modern Society* (London: Sage, 1998).

38. See Jose Harris, "Between Civic Virtue and Social Darwinism: The Concept of the Residium," in *Retrieved Riches: Social Investigation in England 1840–1914*, ed. David Englander and Rosemary O'Day (Aldershot, UK: Scholar Press, 1995), 65–89; McClelland, "From Chartism to the Reform League," 77–89.

39. Karl Marx letter to Frederick Engels, November 2, 1867, http://www.marxists.org/archive/marx/works/1867/letters/67_11_02.htm.

40. Maurice Cowling, *1867 Disraeli, Gladstone and Revolution: The Passing of the Second Reform Bill* (Cambridge: Cambridge University Press, 1967).

41. Robert Knox, *The Races of Men* (London: Renshaw, 1850), 27.

42. Ibid., 253–254.

43. Quote cited from Lewis Perry Curtis, *Anglo-Saxons and Celts: A Study of Anti-Irish Prejudice in Victorian England, Studies in British History and Culture*, vol. 2 (Bridgeport, CT: University of Bridgeport Press, 1968), 63.

44. Dan Stone, *Breeding Superman: Nietzsche, Race and Eugenics in Edwardian and Interwar Britain* (Liverpool: Liverpool University Press, 2002), 95. For the class-not-race argument, see Nancy Stepan, *The Idea of Race in Science: Great Britain, 1800–1960* (London: Macmillan, 1982).

45. Galton quoted in Larry T. Reynolds and Leonard Lieberman, eds., *Race and Other Misadventures: Essays in Honor of Ashley Montagu in His Ninetieth Year* (Lanham, MD: Rowman and Littlefield, 1996), 56.

46. Stone, *Breeding Superman*, 102.

47. Ibid., 103.

48. Daniel Pick, *Faces of Degeneration: A European Disorder, c. 1848–1918* (Cambridge: Cambridge University Press, 1989).

49. Thomas Teo, *The Critique of Psychology: From Kant to Postcolonial Theory* (New York: Springer, 2005).

50. See Houston Stewart Chamberlain, *The Foundations of the Nineteenth Century* (Boston: Adamant Media Corporation, [1899] 2003).

51. Cited in Bernard Harris, "Pro-Alienism, Anti-Alienism and the Medical Profession in Late-Victorian and Edwardian Britain," in *Race, Science and Medicine, 1700–1960*, ed. Waltraud Ernst and Bernard Harris (London: Verso, 1999), 197.

52. David Powell, *Nationhood and Identity: The British State Since 1800* (New York: Tauris, 2002).

53. Lewis C. B. Seaman, *Victorian England: Aspects of English and Imperial History 1837–1901* (London: Routledge, 1973).

54. Jonathan P. Parry, "Disraeli and England," *Historical Journal* 43, no. 3 (2000): 699–728.

55. Freda Harcourt, "Disraeli's Imperialism, 1866–1868: A Question of Timing," *Historical Journal* 23, no. 1 (1980): 87–109.

56. Parry, "Disraeli and England," 707.

57. Ibid., 719.

58. See Edward J. Larson, *Sex, Race, and Science: Eugenics in the Deep South* (Baltimore: Johns Hopkins University Press, 1995).

59. Paul A. Lombardo, "Three Generations, No Imbeciles: New Light on *Buck v. Bell*," *New York University Law Review* 60, no. 1 (1985): 30–62 .

60. Matt Wray, *Not Quite White: White Trash and the Boundaries of Whiteness* (Durham, NC: Duke University Press, 2006), 92.

61. Ibid., 94.

62. Peter Quinn, "Looking for Jimmy," in *Making the Irish American: History and Heritage of the Irish in the United States*, ed. Joseph Lee and Marion R. Casey (New York: New York University Press, 2006), 674.

63. Ibid.

64. Michael P. Carroll, *American Catholics in the Protestant Imagination: Rethinking the Academic Study of Religion* (Baltimore: Johns Hopkins University Press, 2007).

65. Peter F. Stevens, *Rogue's March: John Riley and the St. Patrick's Battalion 1846–48* (Washington, DC: Brassey's, 1999).

66. Robert R. Miller, *Shamrock and Sword: The Saint Patrick's Battalion in the U.S.-Mexican War* (Norman: University of Oklahoma Press, 1989).

67. Michael Hogan, "The Irish Soldiers of Mexico," *Freedom Daily*, November 1, 2004, http://www.fff.org/freedom/fd0407f.asp.

68. See George W. Kendall and Lawrence Delbert Cress, *Dispatches from the Mexican War* (Norman: University of Oklahoma Press, 1999), 350.

69. Miller, *Shamrock and Sword*; James Callaghan, "The San Patricios," *American Heritage Magazine* 46, no. 7 (1995), http://www.americanheritage.com/content/san-patricios.

70. Etienne Balibar, "Racism and Nationalism," in *Race, Nation, Class: Ambiguous Identities*, ed. Etienne Balibar and Immanuel Wallerstein (London: Verso, 1991), 55.

71. Ibid., 57.

72. See Thomas G. Dyer, *Theodore Roosevelt and the Idea of Race* (Baton Rouge: Louisiana State University Press, 1992), 149.

73. See Theodore Roosevelt, *History as Literature*, chap. 8, "The Foundations of the Nineteenth Century" (New York: Scribner's, 1913; Bartleby.com, 1998).

74. Gilbert Gonzales and Raul Fernandez, *A Century of Chicano History: Empire, Nations and Migration* (New York: Routledge, 2003), 125.

75. Ibid., 135.

76. Ibid., 139.

77. Wallace Thompson, *The Mexican Mind: A Study of National Psychology* (Boston: Little, Brown, 1922), 1.

78. Ibid., 3–4.

79. Ibid., 3.

80. Ibid., 7.

81. Mae M. Ngai, *Impossible Subjects: Illegal Aliens and the Making of Modern America* (Princeton, NJ: Princeton University Press, 2004), 59.

82. Kitty Calavita, "The Paradoxes of Race, Class, Identity, and 'Passing': Enforcing the Chinese Exclusion Acts, 1882–1910," *Law and Social Inquiry* 25, no. 1 (2004): 4.

83. John Higham, *Strangers in the Land: Patterns of American Nativism, 1860–1925* (New Brunswick, NJ: Rutgers University Press, 2002), 202.

84. Cited in Paul Gordon Lauren, *Power and Prejudice: The Politics and Diplomacy of Racial Discrimination* (Boulder, CO: Westview, 1996), 67.

85. See Arno J. Mayer, *Wilson vs. Lenin: Political Origins of the New Diplomacy, 1917–1918* (Cleveland, OH: World Publishing, 1964).

86. Jan Voogd, *Race Riots and Resistance: The Red Summer of 1919* (New York: Peter Lange, 2008).

87. Jacqueline Jenkinson, "The 1919 Riots," in *Racial Violence in Britain in the Nineteenth and Twentieth Centuries*, ed. P. Panayi (Leicester, UK: Leicester University Press, 1996).

88. Frank Furedi, *The Silent War: Imperialism and the Changing Perception of Race* (New Brunswick, NJ: Rutgers University Press, 1998), 119.

## CHAPTER THREE

1. Herbert A. Miller, "The Oppression Psychosis and the Immigrant," *Annals of the American Academy of Political and Social Science* 93 (1921): 142.

2. Herbert A. Miller, "The Menace of Minorities," *Annals of the American Academy of Political and Social Science* 175 (1934): 64.

3. Fred Siegel, "Taking Communism Away from the Communists: The Origins of Modern American Liberalism," *Telos*, April 4, 2009.

4. Joseph Stalin and H. G. Wells, *Marxism vs. Liberalism: An Interview* (New York: New Century, 1937), 298.

5. Ellen Herman, *The Romance of American Psychology: Political Culture in the Age of Experts* (Berkeley: University of California Press, 1995), 174.

6. Ibid., 179.

7. Max Horkheimer, "Preface," in *The Authoritarian Personality*, ed. Theodor W. Adorno, Else Frenkel-Brunswik, Daniel J. Levinson, and R. Nevitt Sanford (New York: Harper and Row, 1950), ix.

8. Mary L. Dudziak, *Cold War Civil Rights: Race and the Image of American Democracy* (Princeton, NJ: Princeton University Press).

9. Columbia University, "The Media vs. the Nation of Islam," *The Malcolm X Project*, 2005, http://www.columbia.edu/cu/ccbh/mxp/blog.html.

10. *The Hate That Hate Produced* can be viewed on YouTube at http://www.youtube.com/watch?v=Z-odALf_1zs.

11. Ibid.

12. Ibid.

13. Peter L. Hahn, *Caught in the Middle East: U.S. Policy Toward the Arab-Israeli Conflict, 1945–1961* (Chapel Hill: University of North Carolina Press, 2004), 290.

14. John F. Kennedy, *Profiles in Courage* (New York: Black Dog/Leventhal, 1998).

15. John Solomos, *Race and Racism in Britain* (London: Palgrave Macmillan, 2003).

16. For an earlier discussion, see Lewis M. Killian, "Two Decades of Anti-Discrimination Laws in US and Britain: Policies and Results," *Journal of Ethnic and Migration Studies* 14, no. 1 (1987): 40–44.

17. Sheila Patterson, *Immigration and Race Relations in Britain 1960–1967* (London: Institute of Race Relations/Oxford University Press, 1969).

18. Nadine Peppard, "The Age of Innocence: Race Relations Before 1965," *Journal of Ethnic and Migration Studies* 14, no. 1 (1987): 45–55.

19. Findings from the survey were reported in Michael Banton, "The Influence of Colonial Status on Black-White Relations in England 1948–58," *Sociology* 17 (1983): 546–559.

20. Kenan Malik, *The Meaning of Race: Race, History and Culture in Western Society* (London: Macmillan, 1996), 19–25.

21. Richmond cited in Banton, "Influence of Colonial Status," 551.

22. Richmond, perhaps in response to Banton's criticism, seemed to draw out the situational and group factors that accounted for prejudice in Britain. See Anthony H. Richmond, "Economic Insecurity and Stereotypes as Factors in Colour Prejudice," *Sociological Review* 42 (1950): 147–167. See also Anthony H. Richmond, "Sociological and Psychological Explanations of Racial Prejudice: Some Light on the Controversy from Recent Researches in Britain," *Pacific Sociological Review* 4, no. 2 (1961): 63–68.

23. Labour Party Election Manifesto, *Let Us Win Through Together: A Declaration of Labour Policy for the Consideration of the Nation*, 1950, http://www.labour-party.org.uk/manifestos/1950/1950-labour-manifesto.shtml.

24. Harold Macmillan, speech delivered at the Bedford Conservative Party rally, July 1957.

25. Robert Miles, "The Riots of 1958: Notes on the Ideological Construction of 'Race Relations' as a Political Issue in Britain," *Immigrants and Minorities* 3, no. 3 (1984): 252–275.

26. We use the term "nonwhite" deliberately in order to indicate that the identity of British whiteness was being reproduced against these colonial migrants who were differentiated from white colonial migrants. Their identity as migrants was reproduced by what they were not. They were "not white."

27. Sir William Beveridge, *Why I Am a Liberal* (London: Herbert Jenkins, 1945), 9.

28. Bob Carter, Clive Harris, and Shirley Joshi, "The 1951–55 Conservative Government and the Racialisation of Black Immigration," *Immigrants and Minorities* 6, no. 3 (1987): 335–347. See Shirley Joshi and Bob Carter, "The Role of Labour in the Creation of a Racist Britain," *Race and Class* 25 (1984): 53–71.

29. See Robert Miles and Annie Phizacklea, *The TUC, Black Workers and New Commonwealth Immigration, 1954–1973* (Bristol, UK: SSRC Research Unit on Ethnic Relations, 1977).

30. Mark Bonham Carter, "The Liberal Hour and Race Relations Law," *Journal of Ethnic and Migration Studies* 14, no. 1 (1987): 3.

31. Anthony F. Dickey, "English Law and Incitement to Racial Hatred," *Race and Class* 9 (1968): 311.

32. In total, 12 bills on racial discrimination had been introduced unsuccessfully prior to 1965.

33. Fenner Brockway, "Racial Discrimination," House of Commons Debate, *Hansard* 554 (1956): 247–250, http://hansard.millbanksystems.com/commons/1956/jun/12/racial-discrimination.

34. Ibid.

35. John D. Skrentny, *The Ironies of Affirmative Action* (Chicago: University of Chicago Press, 1996).

36. Kevin L. Yuill, *Richard Nixon and the Rise of Affirmative Action: The Pursuit of Racial Equality in an Era of Limits* (Lanham, MD: Rowman and Littlefield, 2005).

37. Brockway, "Racial Discrimination," 247–250.

38. Ibid.

39. Ibid.

40. Cited in Jennie Bourne, "The Life and Times of Institutional Racism," *Race and Class* 43, no. 2 (2001): 6–22.

41. George Jackson, "Field Marshal George Jackson Analyzes the Correct Method in Combating American Fascism," *The Black Panther*, September 4, 1971.

42. Stokely Carmichael and Charles V. Hamilton, *Black Power: The Politics of Liberation* (New York: Vintage, 1992), 5.

43. Ibid.

44. Yuill, *Richard Nixon and the Rise of Affirmative Action*, 169.

45. From an interview with Sivanandan conducted by Raj Pal, *Birmingham Black History*, 2000, http://birminghamblackhistory.com/index2.php?option=com_content&do_pdf=1&id=47.

46. In comparison with Scotland, where antiracist activity did not mobilize under a black political umbrella; see Christopher Kyriakides, "The Anti-Racist State: An Investigation Into the Relationship Between Representations of 'Racism,' Anti-Racist Typification and the State: A 'Scottish' Case Study" (Glasgow: University of Glasgow, 2005).

47. Margaret Thatcher, TV interview for Granada *World in Action*, January 27, 1978, http://www.margaretthatcher.org/document/103485.

48. Margaret Thatcher, Conservative Party Conference, Blackpool, October 10, 1975.

49. Sir Keith Joseph quoted from the *New Statesman*, April 18, 502, cited in David Yaffe, *The State and the Capitalist Crisis*, 1978 abridged version of speech given to VESVU Conference, Amsterdam, October 1975, http://www.rcgfrfi.easynet.co.uk/marxism/articles/crisis.htm.

50. Ralph Fevre, *Cheap Labour and Racial Discrimination* (London: Avebury, 1984).

51. Labour MP Bob Mellish, cited in Keith Thompson, *Under Siege: Racial Violence in Britain Today* (London: Penguin, 1988).

52. From *The Times*, February 16, 1978, cited in Thompson, ibid.

53. Stuart Hall, Chas Critcher, Tony Jefferson, John N. Clarke, and Brian Roberts, *Policing the Crisis: Mugging, the State and Law and Order* (London: Palgrave Macmillan, 1978).

54. Paul Gilroy, *There Ain't No Black in the Union Jack* (London: Routledge, 1993), 57.

55. In 1979, Labour Home Secretary Merlyn Rees "humiliated Asians by sanctioning the compulsory medical testing, in cubicles at Heathrow Airport, of young Asian brides for 'proof' of their virginity," cited in Thompson, *Under Siege*, 70.

56. Margaret Thatcher, TV interview for Granada.

57. George Young quoted from *Sunday Times*, October 10, 1982, cited in Workers Against Racism, *The Roots of Racism* (London: Junius, 1985), 52.

58. Anthony Rampton, *West Indian Children in Our Schools: Interim Report of the Committee of Inquiry Into the Education of Children from Ethnic Minority Groups* (London: HMSO, 1981); Leslie George Scarman, *The Brixton Disorders 10–12 April: Report of an Enquiry* (London: HMSO, 1981).

59. Thompson, *Under Siege*, 115–122.

60. Ibid., 93–97.

61. Paul Gilroy, "The End of Anti-Racism," *Journal of Ethnic and Migration Studies* 17, no. 1 (1990): 81.

62. Ibid., 81–82.

63. Ibid., 83.

64. Ibid.

65. Martin Barker, *The New Racism* (London: Junction Books, 1981).

66. Ronald Reagan, "Evil Empire," speech given to the National Association of Evangelicals, March 8, 1983, http://www.americanrhetoric.com/speeches/ronaldreaganevilempire.htm.

67. John Miller, "Ronald Reagan's Legacy: His Destructive Economic Policies Do Not Deserve the Press's Praise," *Dollars and Sense Magazine*, July–August 2004, http://www.dollarsandsense.org/archives/2004/0704miller.html.

68. Lawrence B. Goodheart and Richard Orr Curry, "A Confusion of Voices: The Crisis of Individualism in Twentieth-Century America," in *American Chameleon: Individualism in Trans-National Context*, ed. Richard Orr Curry and Lawrence B. Goodheart (Kent, OH: Kent State University Press, 1991), 188–205.

69. John W. Sloan, "The Reagan Presidency, Growing Inequality and the American Dream," *Policy Studies* 25, no. 3 (1997): 371.

70. Cited in James Heartfield, *Green Capitalism: Manufacturing Scarcity in an Age of Abundance* (London: OpenMute, 2008), 28.

71. Daniel Horowitz, *Jimmy Carter and the Energy Crisis of the 1970s: The "Crisis of Confidence" Speech of July 15, 1979* (Boston: Bedford/St. Martin's, 2004).

72. Sean Wilentz, *The Age of Reagan: A History, 1974–2008* (New York: HarperCollins, 2008).

73. Ronald Reagan, acceptance speech at the Republican National Convention, July 17, 1980, http://usa.usembassy.de/etexts/speeches/rhetoric/rraccept.htm.

74. Cornel West, *Toward a Socialist Theory of Racism* (New York: Institute for Democratic Socialism, 1985), 9.

75. T. L. Traynor and R. H. Fichtenbaum, "The Impact of Post-Patco Labor Relations on U.S. Union Wages," *Eastern Economic Journal* 23, no 1 (1997): 61–72.

76. Frances Fox Piven and Richard A. Cloward, *The Breaking of the American Social Compact* (New York: New Press, 1997), 21.

77. Robert R. Detlefsen, *Civil Rights Under Reagan* (San Francisco: Institute for Contemporary Studies, 1991), 3.

78. Hugh Davis Graham, "The Politics of Clientele Capture: Civil Rights Policy in the Reagan Administration," in *Redefining Equality*, ed. Neal Devins and Davison Douglas (New York: Oxford University Press, 1997), 105.

79. Hugh Davis Graham, "Unintended Consequences: The Convergence of Affirmative Action and Immigration Policy," *American Behavioral Scientist* 41, no. 7 (1998): 898–912.

80. Ibid.

81. Robert R. Detlefsen, "Affirmative Action and Business Deregulation: On the Reagan Administration's Failure to Revise Executive Order No. 11246," *Policy Studies Journal* 21, no. 3 (1993): 556.

82. Frank R. Dobbin, Lauren Edelman, John W. Meyer, W. Richard Scott, and Ann Swidler, "The Expansion of Due Process in Organizations," in *Institutional Patterns and Organizations: Culture and Environment*, ed. Lynne G. Zucker (Cambridge, MA: Ballinger, 1988), 71–98; Lauren Edelman, "Legal Environments and Organizational Governance: The Expansion of Due Process in the American Workplace," *American Journal of Sociology* 95 (1990): 1401–1440.

83. Erin Kelly and Frank Dobbin, "How Affirmative Action Became Diversity Management: Employer Response to Antidiscrimination Law, 1961 to 1996," *American Behavioral Scientist* 41, no. 7 (1998): 960–984.

84. R. Roosevelt Thomas Jr., "From Affirmative Action to Affirming Diversity," *Harvard Business Review* (March–April, 1990): 114.

85. Ibid., 113.

86. James B. Jacobs and Kimberly Potter, *Hate Crimes: Criminal Law and Identity Politics* (New York: Oxford University Press, 1998).

87. Ibid., 67–68.

88. Ronald Reagan, *A Tribute to President Ronald W. Reagan*, launch of Victims' Rights Week, 2010, https://www.ncjrs.gov/ovc_archives/ncvrw/2005/pg4e.html.

## CHAPTER FOUR

Portions of this chapter appeared in Christopher Kyriakides, "Post-Racial Pessimism: Therapolitics and the Anti-Utopian Present," *Dark Matter* (June 2012); and Christopher Kyriakides, "Third Way Anti-Racism: A Contextual Constructionist Approach," *Journal of Ethnic and Racial Studies* 31, no. 3 (2008): 592–610.

1. Eyewitness report, "He Looked Like a Cornered Fox," CNN, July 22, 2005, http://www.cnn.com/2005/WORLD/europe/07/22/london.eyewitness/index.html.

2. See Robert Gooding-Williams, ed., *Reading Rodney King/Reading Urban Uprising* (New York: Routledge, 1993); Edward J. Escobar, *Race, Police, and the Making of a Political Identity: Mexican Americans and the Los Angeles Police Department, 1900–1945* (Berkeley: University of California Press, 1999); Jill Nelson, *Police Brutality: An Anthology* (New York: Norton, 2001); Ronald Weitzer and Steven A. Tuch, *Race and Policing in America: Conflict and Reform* (New York: Cambridge University Press, 2006); Leonard Nathaniel Moore, *Black Rage in New Orleans: Police Brutality and African American Activism from World War II to Hurricane Katrina* (Baton Rouge: Louisiana State University Press, 2010).

3. Amnesty International USA, *Threat and Humiliation: Racial Profiling, Domestic Security, and Human Rights in the United States* (New York: Amnesty International, 2004).

4. Leo R. Chavez, *The Latino Threat: Constructing Immigrants, Citizens, and the Nation* (Stanford, CA: Stanford University Press, 2008), 133.

5. Border Protection, Anti-Terrorism, and Illegal Immigration Control Act of 2005, 95.

6. David Theo Goldberg, "Devastating Disasters: Race in the Shadows of New Orleans," in *Race and State*, ed. Alana Lentin and Robert Lentin (Newcastle, UK: Cambridge Scholars Publishing, 2006), 22.

7. US Congress, Senate Select Committee on Intelligence, *National Security Threats to the United States*, 109th Cong., 1st sess., February 16, 2005.

8. Congressional Research Service, *Border Security: Apprehensions of "Other Than Mexican" Aliens* (Washington, DC: CRS, 2005).

9. "No Charges for Menezes Officers," BBC News Online, July 17, 2006, http://news.bbc.co.uk/2/hi/uk/5186050.stm.

10. Philippe Naughton, "Scotland Yard Guilty Over De Menezes Death," *The Times*, November 1, 2007, http://www.timesonline.co.uk/tol/news/uk/crime/article2786380.ece.

11. Rachel Sylvester and Alice Thomson, "Brian Paddick: 'Why I Want to Be Mayor,'" *The Telegraph*, November 17, 2007, http://www.telegraph.co.uk/news/politics/1569631/Brian-Paddick-Why-I-want-to-be-mayor.html.

12. Statement by Governor Jan Brewer, April 24, 2010, http://ktar.com/?nid=6&sid=1287687.

13. "Arizona Immigration Law Threatens Civil Rights and Public Safety, Says ACLU/Law Will Poison Community Policing Efforts," April 23, 2010, http://www.aclu.org/immigrants-rights/arizona-immigration-law-threatens-civil-rights-and-public-safety-says-aclu.

14. Randal C. Archibold, "Arizona Enacts Stringent Law on Immigration," *New York Times*, April 23, 2010, http://www.nytimes.com.

15. Darlene Superville and Suzanne Gamboa, "Arizona Gov. Jan Brewer Meets with Obama, Presses for Completion of Border Fence," Associated Press, June 4, 2010, http://www.cnsnews.com.

16. Earl Ofari Hutchinson, "Playing the Obama Bolshevik Card," *New America Media*, February 2, 2010, http://news.newamericamedia.org.

17. Amitai Etzioni, *The Third Way to a Good Society* (London: Demos, 2000), 30.

18. Michelle Mittelstadt, "GOP Pushes Bush for Commitment to Border Security/Some of the Senators Call for Emergency Bill to Spend Billions on Enforcement," *Houston Chronicle*, June 13, 2007, http://www.chron.com.

19. "George W. Bush in His Own Words: Immigration Reform," *Houston Chronicle*, January 13, 2009, http://blogs.chron.com/txpotomac/2009/01/george_w_bush_in_his_own_words_3.html.

20. Home Office, *Secure Borders, Safe Haven: Integration with Diversity in Modern Britain* (London: HMSO, 2002), 3.

21. Ibid.

22. Christopher Kyriakides, "Third Way Anti-Racism: A Contextual Constructionist Approach," *Ethnic and Racial Studies* 31, no. 3 (2008): 592–610.

23. Bhikhu Parekh, "Three Theories of Migration," in *Strangers and Citizens: A Positive Approach to Migrants and Refugees*, ed. Sarah Spencer (London: Institute for Public Policy Research/Rivers Oram Press, 1994), 92.

24. Anthony Giddens, *The Third Way: The Renewal of Social Democracy* (Cambridge: Polity, 1998); Tony Blair, *The Third Way: New Politics for the New Century* (London: Fabian Society, 1998).

25. Frank Furedi, *Culture of Fear: Risk-Taking and the Morality of Low Expectation* (London: Cassell, 1997), 109.

26. James Heartfield, *The "Death of the Subject" Explained* (Sheffield, UK: Sheffield Hallam University Press, 2002), 174–201.

27. James Nolan, *The Therapeutic State: Justifying Government at Century's End* (New York: New York University Press, 1998); Frank Furedi, *Therapy Culture: Cultivating Vulnerability in an Uncertain Age* (London: Routledge, 2004).

28. Nolan, *Therapeutic State*, 22.

29. William J. Clinton, First Inaugural Address, Washington, DC, January 20, 1993, http://www.theusgov.com/billclinton%20first%20inaugural%20speech.htm.

30. Robert Pear, "Riots in Los Angeles: Challenger; Nation Needs Healing, Clinton Says," New York Times.com, May 4, 1992, http://www.nytimes.com/1992/05/04/us/riots-in-los-angeles-challenger-nation-needs-healing-clinton-says.html.

31. Sam Fulwood III, "Clinton Praises Judgment of Jury, Urges Healing, Harmony Across U.S.: Administration: President Speaks Before Giving Address on Economy. His New Attorney General, Janet Reno, Says, 'Justice Was Done,'" Los Angeles Times.com, April 18, 1993, http://articles.latimes.com/1993-04-18/news/mn-24495_1_janet-reno.

32. President Clinton's Second Inaugural Address, January 20, 1997, http://www.let.rug.nl/usa/P/bc42/speeches/clinton2.htm.

33. Etzioni, *Third Way to a Good Society*, 17.

34. Claire Jean Kim, "Clinton's Race Initiative: Recasting the American Dilemma," *Polity* 33, no. 2 (2000): 175–197.

35. Etzioni, *Third Way to a Good Society*, 53.

36. Anthony Giddens, "The Third Way Can Beat the Far Right," *The Guardian*, May 3, 2002, http://www.guardian.co.uk.

37. Anthony Giddens, *The Third Way: The Renewal of Social Democracy* (Cambridge: Polity, 1998), 117.

38. Anthony Giddens, *Beyond Left and Right: The Future of Radical Politics* (Cambridge: Polity, 1995), 129.

39. Giddens, *Third Way*, 135.

40. Ibid., 136.

41. Giddens, *Beyond Left and Right*, 243.

42. Ibid., 244.

43. Ibid., 245.

44. Ibid.

45. Anthony Giddens, *Modernity and Self-Identity: Self and Society in the Late Modern Age* (Cambridge: Polity, 2001), 196.

46. Ibid.

47. Ibid.

48. Home Office, "Faith Groups in the Community," 2004, http://www.homeoffice.gov.uk/comrace/faith/community/#5.

49. Giddens, *Modernity and Self-Identity*, 43–45.

50. Home Office, "Faith Groups in the Community."

51. Giddens interviewed by Guy Lodge, n.d., http://www.geocities.com/Athens/Bridge/8651/Giddens.htm.

52. Alex Hailey, interview with Malcolm X, *Playboy Magazine*, May 1963.

53. "Bush's Reaction, Airline Terror Plot," *Orlando Sentinel*, August 11, 2006, http://articles.orlandosentinel.com/2006-08-11/news/A20RAIL11_1_terrorist-plot-thwarted-terrorist-united-kingdom.

54. Jack G. Shaheen, "Reel Bad Arabs: How Hollywood Vilifies a People," *Annals of the American Academy of Political and Social Science* 588 (July 2003): 171–193.

55. Tom Raum, "Republicans Target 'Islamic Fascism,'" *Washington Post*, August 30, 2006, http://www.washingtonpost.com/wp-dyn/content/article/2006/08/30/AR2006083000490.html.

56. Ibid.

57. "U.S. Muslims Bristle at Bush Term 'Islamic Fascists,'" Reuters, August 10, 2006, http://www.jihadwatch.org/archives/012631.php.

58. Ibid.

59. Katha Pollitt, "Wrong War, Wrong Word," *The Nation*, August 24, 2006, http://www.thenation.com/doc/20060911/pollitt.

60. Frank Furedi, *Culture of Fear*, 13.

61. Bruce Bartlett quoted by Ron Suskind in "Faith, Certainty and the Presidency of George W. Bush," *New York Times*, October 17, 2004, http://www.nytimes.com.

62. This quote is from psychologist Oliver James, whom Burbach and Tarbell cite from an article in the United Kingdom's *Guardian* newspaper. See Roger Burbach and Jim Tarbell, *Imperial Overstretch: George W. Bush and the Hubris of Empire* (London: Zed Books, 2004), 114–117. See also Marcus Raskin and Robert Spero, *The Four Freedoms Under Siege: The Clear and Present Danger from Our National Security State* (Westport, CT: Praeger, 2007).

63. A good example was Clinton's speech at the annual White House prayer breakfast on Friday, September 11, 1998, to an audience that consisted of ministers, priests, other religious leaders, and Hillary Clinton. The speech preceded publication of the first report to Congress by Independent Counsel Ken Starr that laid out the grounds for President Clinton's impeachment, accusing Clinton of perjury, obstruction of justice, and other offenses related to his concealment of his relationship with former White House intern Monica Lewinsky. His public apology included Lewinsky and an admission that his much-criticized previous TV apology of August 17, 1998, was not sufficiently repentant. See "I Have Sinned" at http://www.historyplace.com/speeches/clinton-sin.htm.

64. Martin Luther King speaking on the topic of social justice at Western Michigan University as part of a series called "Conscience of America," December 18, 1963, http://www.wmich.edu/library/archives/mlk/transcription.html.

65. Alex Hailey, interview with Martin Luther King, *Playboy Magazine*, January 1965, http://www.alex-haley.com/alex_haley_martin_luther_king_interview.htm.

66. Martin Luther King, "Remaining Awake Through a Great Revolution," speech delivered at the National Cathedral, Washington, DC, March 31, 1968.

67. Furedi, *Culture of Fear*, 13.

68. Eric Boehlert, "Islamism Is Fascism—An Interview with Daniel Pipes," November 9, 2001, http://www.danielpipes.org/article/81.

69. George W. Bush, speaking before the National Endowment for Democracy, "President Discusses War on Terror at National Endowment for Democracy." Press release from Ronald Reagan Building and International Trade Center, Washington, DC, October 6, 2005, http://www.whitehouse.gov/news/releases/2005/10/20051006-3.html.

70. Burbach and Tarbell, *Imperial Overstretch*, 117.

71. Ibid., 173.

72. Francis Fukuyama, "The End of History," *National Interest* 16 (1989): 3–18; Francis Fukuyama, *The End of History and the Last Man* (London: Penguin, 1992).

73. Samuel P. Huntington, "The Clash of Civilizations?" *Foreign Affairs* 72, no. 3 (1993): 22–49.

74. Noam Chomsky, "Militarism, Democracy and People's Right to Information," lecture at the National Campaign for the People's Right to Information, November 5, 2001, http://www.india-seminar.com/2002/509/509%20noam%20chomsky.htm. See also Edward W. Said, "The Clash of Ignorance," *The Nation*, October 22, 2001.

75. Hishaam Aidi, "Jihadis in the Hood: Race, Urban Islam and the War on Terror," *Middle East Report* 224 (Fall 2002), http://www.merip.org/mer/issues?page=3.

76. George Bush speaking at the American Legion National Convention in Salt Lake City, Utah, August 31, 2006.

77. David Horowitz, "What We Did Last Week," FrontPageMagazine.com, October 29, 2007, http://www.terrorismawareness.org/news/127/what-we-did-last-week.

78. Norman Fairclough, *Language and Power* (Harlow, UK: Longman, 2001). Fairclough makes this distinction in reference to New Labour's "social inclusion/exclusion" rhetoric.

79. Paul Iganski, "Legislating Against Hate: Outlawing Racism and Anti-Semitism in Britain," *Critical Social Policy* 19, no. 1 (1999): 129–141; Paul Iganski, "Why Make 'Hate' a Crime," *Critical Social Policy* 19, no. 3 (1999): 365–395.

80. House of Commons, 1993–4 HC 71-I para. 477, cited in Home Office, *The Crime and Disorder Bill, Bill 167 of 1997–98: Anti-Social Neighbours, Sex Offenders, Racially Motivated Offences and Sentencing Drug-Dependent Offenders* (London: HMSO, 1998), 44.

81. Iganski, "Legislating Against Hate," 133.

82. The 1986 Public Order Act defined racial hatred as "hatred against a group of persons in Great Britain defined by reference to colour, race, nationality (including citizenship), or ethnic or national origins."

83. Giddens, "Third Way Can Beat Far Right."

84. Home Office, *Secure Borders, Safe Haven*, 12.

85. Stanley Cohen, *Folk Devils and Moral Panics* (London: Routledge, 2002), xxv.

86. Sir William Macpherson, *The Stephen Lawrence Inquiry* (London: HMSO, 1999). The Commission for Racial Equality (CRE) called the report's publication "a defining moment for race relations in Britain." See CRE, "A Time for Change," *Connections* (Spring 1999): 3.

87. Ibid., chap. 6, para. 35.

88. Leslie George Scarman, *The Brixton Disorders 10–12 April: Report of an Enquiry* (London: HMSO, 1981). See also Stuart Hall, "From Scarman to Macpherson," *Society* 3 (2000): 8–9.

89. Macpherson, *Lawrence Inquiry*, chap. 6, para. 46.

90. Ibid.

91. Ibid., para. 47.

92. Ibid., para. 34.

93. Frank Furedi, *Therapy Culture*, 26.

94. See Home Office, *Community Cohesion: A Report of the Independent Review Team* (London: HMSO, 2001); Home Office, *A Report of the Ministerial Group on Public Order and Community Cohesion* (London: HMSO; 2001); David Ritchie, "Oldham Independent Review: One Oldham One Future" (London: Government Office for the North West, 2001); Burnley Task Force, "Burnley Speaks, Who Listens?" Burnley Task Force Report, 2001.

95. See "Force the Races to Mix, Says CRE Chief," *The Guardian*, March 18, 2002, http://www.guardian.co.uk; "Race Riot Report Author Dismisses Integration Plan," *The Guardian*, March 18, 2002, http://www.guardian.co.uk; "Behind the Gloom, Hope for a Better Future," *The Guardian*, March 18, 2002, http://www.guardian.co.uk.

96. CRE/CAB, *Community Cohesion: Our Responsibility* (London: Commission for Racial Equality, 2002); CRE, *A Place for Us All: Learning from Bradford, Oldham and Burnley* (London: Commission for Racial Equality, 2002).

97. Ibid., 5.

98. The controversy that erupted in 2005 following University of Colorado professor of ethnic studies Ward Churchill's reference to the victims of 9/11 as "Little Eichmanns" and therefore as "legitimate targets" reveals two salient points. First, there is a basic Left misunderstanding of how the contemporary political process orientates itself around victimization and fear, not particularly in relation to 9/11, but around the more salient need to legitimize itself through safety and trust. Churchill's anachronistic "antifascist" comment placed him in the position of the victimizer. Second, it revealed how Arendt's original analysis of Nazi atrocity has been taken out of its historical context and rendered banal but dangerous either as a feature of Left or of Right critique, neither of which retain political currency in the contemporary context.

## CHAPTER FIVE

An extended version of this chapter appeared in Christopher Kyriakides and Rodolfo D. Torres, "The Allure of Race: From New Left to New Times," *New Political Science* 34, no. 1 (2012): 55–80.

1. Robin D. G. Kelley, *Freedom Dreams: The Black Radical Imagination* (Boston: Beacon, 2002), 51.

2. The televised Chomsky-Foucault debate of 1971 can be watched on YouTube at http://www.youtube.com/watch?v=WveI_vgmPz8. See also Noam Chomsky and Michel Foucault with foreword by John Rajchman, *The Chomsky-Foucault Debate: On Human Nature* (New York: New Press, 2006).

3. Louis Althusser, *Lenin and Philosophy and Other Essays* (New York: Monthly Review Press, 2001), 123.

4. See Edward P. Thompson, *The Poverty of Theory: Or an Orrery of Errors* (London: Merlin, 1978).

5. Christopher Arthur, "Stalinism and Dialectics," *Critique* 20, no. 1 (1993): 114.

6. Louis Althusser, *For Marx* (London: Allen Lane/Penguin, 1969), 200n41.

7. Michel Foucault, *Discipline and Punish: The Birth of the Prison* (London: Allen Lane, 1977), 167.

8. Jean-Paul Sartre, *Black Orpheus* (New York: French and European Publications, 1948).

9. Frantz Fanon, *Black Skin, White Masks* (New York: Grove, 1967). Reprint of *Peau noire, masques blancs* (Paris: Seuil, 1952).

10. Azzedine Haddour, "Sartre and Fanon: On Negritude and Political Participation," *Sartre Studies International* 11, no. 1–2 (2005): 286–301.

11. Fanon, *Black Skin, White Masks*, 14.

12. Ibid., 8.

13. Jean-Paul Sartre, preface to Frantz Fanon, *The Wretched of the Earth* (New York: Grove, 1963), 24–25.

14. Moulard-Leonard Valentine, "Revolutionary Becomings: Negritude's Anti-Humanist Humanism," *Human Studies* 28, no. 3 (2005): 231–249.

15. James Heartfield, *The "Death of the Subject" Explained* (Sheffield, UK: Sheffield Hallam University Press, 2002).

16. Slavoj Žižek, "What Can Lenin Tell Us About Freedom Today?" *Rethinking Marxism* 13, no. 2 (2001): 7.

17. Cyril Lionel Robert James, *Black Power*, talk given in London, 1967, http://www.marxists.org.

18. Stokely Carmichael, speech given at OLAS Conference 1967, cited in James, *Black Power*, ibid.

19. Kevin L. Yuill, *Richard Nixon and the Rise of Affirmative Action: The Pursuit of Racial Equality in an Era of Limits* (Lanham, MD: Rowman and Littlefield, 2006).

20. Ward Churchill and Jim Vander Wall, *Agents of Repression: The FBI's Secret Wars Against the Black Panther Party and the American Indian Movement* (Boston: South End Press, 1988), 61.

21. Brady Thomas Heiner, "Foucault and the Black Panthers," *City* 11, no. 3 (2007): 313–356.

22. Ibid., 314.

23. Ibid., 322.

24. Michel Foucault, "What Is Enlightenment?" in *The Foucault Reader*, ed. Paul Rabinow (New York: Pantheon, 1983), 44. While Foucault himself credited a debt to Kant, a charge of antiuniversalism is, we believe, correct, even if an antimodernist tag has been challenged as unworthy in part. See Nancy Fraser, "Michel Foucault: A 'Young Conservative'?" *Ethics* 96, no. 1 (1985): 165–184. In this respect, Richard Bernstein has countered Foucauldian counteraccusation of "Enlightenment blackmail": "Foucault's rhetoric, even the attraction of a distinctive type of sceptical freedom he adumbrates, the appeal of 'the possibility of no longer being, doing, or thinking what we are, do, think' is itself dependent or parasitic upon an ethical-political valorisation. What does it even mean to say that some possibilities are desirable? Without thematising this question it is difficult to discern what precisely is critical about his genre of critique. It is *not* Foucault's critics that have imposed this problem on him—it emerges from Foucault's own insistence that there are changes that are desirable, and that critique enables us 'to determine the precise form this change should take.' A sceptical freedom that limits itself to talk of new possibilities for thinking and acting but heroically or ironically refuses to provide any evaluative orientation as to which possibilities and changes are desirable is in danger of becoming merely empty—or even worse, it withholds judgement from the catastrophic possibilities which *have* erupted or *can* erupt." See Richard Bernstein, *The New Constellation: The Ethical-Political Horizons of Modernity/Postmodernity* (Cambridge: Polity, 1991), 162–163.

25. Heiner, "Foucault and the Black Panthers," 337.

26. Michel Foucault, "The Subject and Power," *Critical Inquiry* 8, no. 4 (1982): 777–795.

27. Ibid., 781.

28. Michel Foucault, *Power and Knowledge* (Brighton, UK: Harvester, 1980), 93.

29. Michel Foucault, *The History of Sexuality*, vol. 1, *An Introduction* (London: Allen Lane, 1979), 94.

30. Ibid., 94–95.

31. Foucault, *Power and Knowledge*, 104.

32. Mark Philp, "Foucault on Power: A Problem in Radical Translation?" *Political Theory* 11, no. 1 (1983): 29–52.

33. Michel Foucault, in *Power/Knowledge, Selected Interviews and Other Writings 1972–1977*, ed. C. Gordon (Hertfordshire, UK: Harvester Wheatsheaf, 1980), 188.

34. Philp, "Foucault on Power," 45.

35. David Theo Goldberg, *Racist Culture* (Oxford: Blackwell, 2002), 7.

36. Ibid., 90.

37. David Theo Goldberg, *The Racial State* (Oxford: Blackwell, 2002), 106.

38. Goldberg, *Racist Culture*, 53.

39. Ibid.

40. Ibid., 52.

41. Ibid., 57.

42. Ibid., 68.

43. Ibid., 52.

44. Ibid., 98.

45. Cornelius Castoriadis, *Philosophy, Politics, Autonomy* (New York: Oxford University Press, 1991), 136.

46. David Theo Goldberg, "Multicultural Conditions," in *Multiculturalism: A Critical Reader*, ed. D. T. Goldberg (Oxford: Blackwell, 1997), 2. The adoption of the Althusserian concept of interpellation is highly problematic. By this theory one can never think outside of the interpellated ideology, unless, of course, an alternative ideology is available. The shift from ideology to discourse, from Althusser to Foucault, does not remedy the passivity assigned to the subject in this regard, for force is not choice but merely an affect of the ideology/discourse. In both positions consciousness is decidedly absent. The theory does, however, make a space for the "critical intellectual" who no longer centralizes a universal subject of historical transformation. The Althusser/Foucault shift was elaborated by Heartfield in *"Death of the Subject" Explained*, and subsequently developed to a comparison between Stuart Hall and D. T. Goldberg in Christopher Kyriakides, "The Anti-Racist State: An Investigation Into the Relationship Between Representations of 'Racism,' Anti-Racist Typification and the State: A 'Scottish' Case Study" (Glasgow: University of Glasgow, 2005). It is on each of the latter two studies that we build our argument in this chapter.

47. Slavoj Žižek, *The Ticklish Subject: The Absent Centre of Political Ontology* (London: Verso, 2000), 264.

48. Linda Martin Alcoff, *Visible Identities: Race, Gender, and the Self* (New York: Oxford University Press, 2006), 6.

49. Goldberg, *Racist Culture*, 212.

50. Ibid.

51. Alcoff, *Visible Identities*, 114.

52. Ibid., 126.

53. Goldberg, *Racial State*, 264. See also David Theo Goldberg, "In/Visibility and Super/Vision: Fanon on Race, Veils, and Discourses of Resistance," in *Fanon: A Critical Reader*, ed. L. R. Gordon, T. Denean Sharpley-Whiting, and R. T. White (Oxford: Blackwell, 1996).

54. Frantz Fanon, *The Wretched of the Earth* (London: Penguin, 1976), 245.

55. Franz Neumann, *The Democratic and the Authoritarian State: Essays in Political and Legal Theory* (New York: Free Press, 1957), 4.

56. Michael Omi and Howard Winant, *Racial Formation in the United States* (London: Routledge, 1994), 83.

57. Ibid., 86–87.

58. Stuart Hall, "Who Needs 'Identity'?" in *Question of Cultural Identity*, ed. S. Hall and P. du Gay (London: Sage, 1996), 3.

59. Stuart Hall, "Cultural Identity and Diaspora," in *Identity: Community, Culture, Difference*, ed. Jonathan Rutherford (London: Lawrence and Wishart, 1990), 225.

60. Ibid., 222.

61. Stuart Hall, "Negotiating Caribbean Identities," *New Left Review* 209 (1995): 8.

62. Paul Gilroy, *There Ain't No Black in the Union Jack* (London: Routledge, 1987), 17.

63. Ibid., 23.

64. Ibid., 25.

65. Ibid., 233.

66. "Outflank" quote cited in Gilroy, *Ain't No Black*, 22. For an example of Milesian outflanking, see Robert Miles, "Marxism Versus the Sociology of 'Race Relations'?" *Ethnic and Racial Studies* 7, no. 2 (1984): 217–237.

67. See Michael Banton and Robert Miles, "Racism," in *Dictionary of Race and Ethnic Relations*, ed. E. Cashmore (London: Routledge, 1996), 308–312.

68. See Simon Clarke, "Marxism, Sociology and Poulantzas's Theory of the State," *Capital and Class* 2 (1977).

69. For an earlier analysis that discusses Miles, see John Solomos and Les Back, "Conceptualizing Racisms: Social Theory, Politics and Research," in *Racism: Essential Readings*, ed. E. Cashmore and J. Jennings (London: Sage, 2001), and more recently, Bob Carter and Satnam Virdee, "Racism and the Sociological Imagination," *British Journal of Sociology* 59, no. 4 (2008): 661–679.

70. Stuart Hall, "The Whites of Their Eyes: Racist Ideologies and the Media," in *Silver Linings*, ed. G. Bridges and R. Brunt (London: Lawrence and Wishart, 1981), 31.

71. Robert Miles, *Racism and Migrant Labour* (London: Routledge/Kegan Paul, 1982), 96.

72. Ibid., 176.

73. Robert Miles, *Racism* (London: Routledge, 1989), 87.

74. Ibid.

75. See Miles, *Racism and Migrant Labour*, 103; and Miles, *Racism*, 80.

76. Miles, *Racism and Migrant Labour*, 96.

77. Robert Miles, *Capitalism and Unfree Labour: Anomaly or Necessity?* (London: Tavistock, 1987), 221.

78. Ibid., 23.

79. Ibid., 195, 221.

80. Gilroy, *Ain't No Black*, 24–25.

81. Ibid., 27.

82. Ibid., 23.

83. Paul Gilroy, "The End of Anti-Racism," *Journal of Ethnic and Migration Studies* 17, no. 1 (1990): 71–83.

84. Goldberg, *Racist Culture*, 93.

85. David Theo Goldberg, "The Semantics of Race," *Ethnic and Racial Studies* 15, no. 4 (1992): 563.

86. Robert Miles, "Exploitation," in *Dictionary of Race and Ethnic Relations*, ed. E. Cashmore (London: Routledge, 1996), 129–131.

87. Robert Miles and Annie Phizacklea, *The TUC, Black Workers and New Commonwealth Immigration, 1954–1973* (Bristol, UK: SSRC Research Unit on Ethnic Relations, 1977).

88. Gilroy, *Ain't No Black*, 246–247.

89. Ibid., 236.

90. Ibid., 238.

91. Ibid.

92. Suke Wolton, "Racial Identities: The Degradation of Human Constructions," in *Marxism, Mysticism and Modern Social Theory*, ed. S. Wolton (London: Macmillan, in association with St. Martin's Press, 1996), 71.

93. Gilroy, *Ain't No Black*, 247.

94. Paul Gilroy, *Against Race: Imagining Political Culture Beyond the Color Line* (Cambridge, MA: Harvard University Press, 2000), 12–13.

95. Paul Gilroy, *Darker Than Blue: On the Moral Economies of Black Atlantic Culture* (Cambridge, MA: Belknap/Harvard University Press, 2010).

96. Gilroy, *Ain't No Black*, 27.

97. Stuart Hall, "Brave New World," *Marxism Today* (October 1988): 24.

98. Ibid., 27.

99. Michael Hardt and Antonio Negri, *Empire* (Cambridge, MA: Harvard University Press, 2001), xii–xv.

CHAPTER SIX

1. Pierre Bourdieu, "The Essence of Neoliberalism," *Le Monde diplomatique*, December 1998, http://mondediplo.com/1998/12/08bourdieu.

2. Robin Blackburn, ed., *After the Fall: The Failure of Communism and the Future of Socialism* (London: Verso, 1991).

3. István Mészáros, *Beyond Capital: Toward a Theory of Transition* (London: Merlin, 1995), xiii–xv.

4. Perry Anderson, "The Ends of History," in *A Zone of Engagement* (London: Verso, 1992).

5. Alex Callinicos, *The Revenge of History: Marxism and the East European Revolutions* (Cambridge: Polity, 1991).

6. Serenella Sferza, "What Is Left of the Left? More Than One Would Think," *Daedalus* 128 (1999): 101–126; Luke March and Cas Mudde, "What's Left of the Radical Left? The European Radical Left Since 1989: Decline and Mutation," *Comparative European Politics* 3, no. 1 (2005): 23–49.

7. David Harvey, *A Brief History of Neoliberalism* (Oxford: Oxford University Press, 2009).

8. Ibid., 11.

9. Douglas Kellner, "Theorizing the Present Moment: Debates Between Modern and Postmodern Theory," *Theory and Society* 28, no. 4 (1999): 651.

10. Harvey, *Brief History of Neoliberalism*, 36–37.

11. Ibid., 204.

12. Mike Davis and Daniel Bertrand Monk, eds., *Evil Paradises: Dreamworlds of Neoliberalism* (New York: New Press, 2007), ix.

13. Bill Durodié, "Communicating the War on Terror, An Open Public Debate Is Key to Striking the Right Note in the War on Terror," *Spiked Online*, May 22, 2003, http://www.spiked-online.com/Articles/00000006DDB7.htm.

14. Jon Donnison, "Far Right Groups 'Growing' in US," BBC News Online, April 15, 2009, http://news.bbc.co.uk/go/pr/fr/-/2/hi/americas/8000763.stm.

15. US Department of Homeland Security, *Rightwing Extremism: Current Economic and Political Climate Fueling Resurgence in Radicalization and Recruitment*, DHS Extremism and Radicalization Branch, April 7, 2009, http://www.fas.org/irp/eprint/rightwing.pdf.

16. Naomi Klein, *The Shock Doctrine: The Rise of Disaster Capitalism* (Toronto: Knopf Canada, 2008).

17. Arun Kundnani, *The End of Tolerance: Racism in 21st-Century Britain* (London: Pluto, 2007), 168.

18. Ibid., 174.

19. Ibid., 168.

20. David Theo Goldberg, *The Threat of Race: Reflections on Racial Neoliberalism* (Malden, MA: Wiley-Blackwell, 2009), 90.

21. Ibid., 91.

22. Davis and Monk, *Evil Paradises*, xvi.

23. Daniel Ben-Ami, *Cowardly Capitalism: The Myth of the Global Financial Casino* (New York: Wiley, 2001).

24. Alexander King and Bertrand Schneider, *The First Global Revolution: A Report by the Council of the Club of Rome* (Hyderabad: Orient Longman, 1993), 75.

# INDEX

The authorized representative in the EU for product safety and compliance is:
Mare Nostrum Group
B.V Doelen 72
4831 GR Breda
The Netherlands

www.ingramcontent.com/pod-product-compliance
Lightning Source LLC
Chambersburg PA
CBHW030400270326
41926CB00009B/1199

* 9 7 8 0 8 0 4 7 6 3 3 5 6 *